JavaFX 1.2 App Development Cookbook

Over 80 recipes to create rich Internet applications with many exciting features

Vladimir Vivien

BIRMINGHAM - MUMBAI

JavaFX 1.2 Application Development Cookbook

First published: August 2010

Production Reference: 1170810

Published by Packt Publishing Ltd.
32 Lincoln Road
Olton
Birmingham, B27 6PA, UK.

ISBN 978-1-847198-94-5

www.packtpub.com

Cover Image by Karl Moore (karl.moore@ukonline.co.uk)

Credits

Author
Vladimir Vivien

Reviewers
Anghel Leonard
Luca Masini
Meenakshi Verma

Acquisition Editor
Sarah Cullington

Development Editor
Dhwani Devater
Reshma Sundaresan

Technical Editors
Aaron Rosario
Mohd. Sahil

Indexer
Hemangini Bari
Tejal Daruwale

Editorial Team Leader
Akshara Aware

Project Team Leader
Priya Mukherji

Project Coordinator
Leena Purkait

Proofreader
Clyde Jenkins

Production Coordinator
Melwyn D'sa

Cover Work
Melwyn D'sa

About the Author

Vladimir Vivien is a software engineer living in the United States. Past and current experience include development in Java and .Net for industries including publishing, financial, and healthcare. He has worked with a varied number of technologies including user-facing GUI frontends and backend middleware. Vladimir enjoys taking part in open source projects. He is the author of JmxBuilder a Groovy DSL for instrumentation and management that is now part of the core Groovy project. Vladimir has presented some of his ideas at JavaOne, NFJS Software Symposium, and local Java user groups.

Besides JavaFX, he has a wide range of technology interests including Java, OSGi, Scala, BugLabs, Arduino, SunSPOT, and any other interesting projects running on the JVM. You can follow Vladimir through his blog: `http://blog.vladimirvivien.com/`, Twitter: `http://twitter.com/vladimirvivien`, and LinkedIn: `http://www.linkedin.com/in/vvivien`.

Firstly, I want to thank my wife for her support, especially during the crunch period when I would lock myself in my office for hours to finish a chapter. I also want to thank everyone who offered kind and encouraging words that kept me going when I wanted to literally walk away from the project.

A special shout out goes to Sarah Cullington, my editor, who is the reason that this book exists. Thank you, Sarah, for not giving up on the project despite its many setbacks. Thanks to the entire Packt Publishing team for taking the risk in a new author like myself, and in a nascent technology like JavaFX.

Finally, I must give a shout out to to the Sun team, who saw the need for a declarative language for rich client development on the VM, and seized the opportunity to bring JavaFX to life. Although JavaFX is new in this space, thanks to the hard work of these dedicated engineers, JavaFX is a complete platform with a complete toolset for developing rich and engaging visual applications on the JVM.

About the Reviewers

Anghel Leonard is a senior Java developer with more than 12 years of experience in Java SE, Java EE, and the related frameworks. He wrote and published more than 20 articles about Java technologies, and more than 100 tips and tricks. He also wrote two books about XML and Java (one for beginners and one for advanced readers), and one about JBoss Tools 3.0, with Packt Publishing. During this time, he developed web applications using the latest technologies on the market. In the past two years, he has been focused on developing RIA projects for GIS fields. He is interested in bringing as much desktop as possible to the Web; therefore, GIS applications represents a real challenge for him.

Luca Masini is a Senior Software Engineer and Architect, who started as a game developer for Commodore 64 (Football Manager) and Commodore Amiga (Ken il guerriero). He soon turned to object-oriented programming, and for that, he was always attracted by the Java language, right from its beginning in 1995.

After having found his passion, he worked as a consultant for major Italian banks, developing and integrating the main software projects for which he often took technical leadership. He was able to adopt Java Enterprise in an environment where COBOL was the flagship platform, converting it from mainframe-centric to distributed.

He then set his eyes upon open source technologies, starting from Linux and then with enterprise frameworks, with which he was able to introduce some low-impact concepts, such as IoC, ORM, MVC, and so on. For the the same reason, he was also an early adopter of Spring, Hibernate, Struts, and a whole host of other technologies that, in the long run, have given his customers a technological advantage, and therefore a development cost-cut.

Lately, however, his attention has been completely directed towards the simplification and standardization of development with Java EE, and for this reason, he is working at the ICT of a large Italian company to introduce advanced build tools (Maven and Continuous Integration), archetypes of project, and *Agile Development* with plain standards.

He has worked on the following books (from Packt):

- *Google Web Toolkit*
- *Spring Web Flow 2*
- *Spring Persistence with Hibernate*

Gaga tu sei qui. Ah tu non fuggi. Tu mi risponderai fino all'ulitmo grido.

Meenakshi Verma has been a part of the IT industry since 1998. She is experienced in putting up solutions across multiple industry segments using SAP BI, SAP Business Objects, and Java/J2EE technologies. She is currently based in Toronto, Canada, and is working with Enbridge Gas Distribution.

Meenakshi has been helping with technical reviews for books published by Packt publishing across varied enterprise solutions. Her earlier works include JasperReports for Java Developers, Java EE 5 Development using GlassFish Application Server, Practical Data Analysis and Reporting with BIRT', and EJB 3 Developer's Guide, Learning DOJO.

I'd like to thank my father (Mr. Bhopal Singh) and mother (Mrs. Raj Bala) for laying a strong foundation in me and giving me their unconditional love and support. I also owe thanks and gratitude to my husband (Atul Verma) for his encouragement and support throughout the review of this book, and many others: my four year old son (Prieyaansh Verma) for giving me the warmth of his love despite my hectic schedules, and my brother (Sachin Singh) for always being there for me.

This book is dedicated to my son MJV: his smile is my daily inspiration.

Table of Contents

Preface   1

Chapter 1: Getting Started with JavaFX   7
Introduction   7
Installing the JavaFX SDK   9
Setting up JavaFX for the NetBeans IDE   11
Setting up JavaFX for the Eclipse IDE   16
Using javafxc to compile JavaFX code   19
Creating and using JavaFX classes   22
Creating and using variables in JavaFX   25
Using binding and triggers to update variables   28
Creating and using JavaFX functions   32
Integrating your JavaFX code with Java   35
Creating and using JavaFX sequences   37
Working with JavaFX String   41

Chapter 2: Creating JavaFX Applications   45
Introduction   45
Building a JavaFX application   46
Drawing simple shapes   50
Creating complex shapes using Path   55
Creating shapes with constructive area geometry   57
Drawing letter shapes using the Text class   60
Handling user input   64
Arranging your nodes on stage   67
Making your scripts modular   70
Creating your own custom node   73
Controlling your application's window style   76
Going full-screen   79

Chapter 3: Transformations, Animations, and Effects   81

Introduction   82
Modifying shapes with the Transformation API   82
Creating simple animation with the Transition API   85
Composing animation with the Transition API   89
Building animation with the KeyFrame API   93
Creating custom interpolators for animation   100
Morphing shapes with the DelegateShape class   102
Using data binding to drive animation sequences   104
Applying cool paint effects with gradients   107
Creating your own customized Paint   109
Adding depth with lighting and shadow effects   111
Creating your own Text effect   114
Adding visual appeal with the Reflection effect   116

Chapter 4: Components and Skinning   119

Introduction   119
Creating a form with JavaFX controls   120
Displaying data with the ListView control   125
Using the Slider control to input numeric values   128
Showing progress with the progress controls   131
Creating a custom JavaFX control   134
Embedding Swing components in JavaFX   139
Styling your applications with CSS   143
Using CSS files to apply styles   148
Skinning applications with multiple CSS files   152

Chapter 5: JavaFX Media   157

Introduction   157
Accessing media assets   158
Loading and displaying images with ImageView   159
Applying effects and transformations to images   163
Creating image effects with blending   167
Playing audio with MediaPlayer   172
Playing video with MediaView   175
Creating a media playback component   179

Chapter 6: Working with Data   185

Introduction   185
Saving data locally with the Storage API   186
Accessing remote data with HttpRequest   189
Downloading images with HttpRequest   192
Posting data to remote servers with HttpRequest   196

Uploading files to servers with HttpRequest   200
Building RESTful clients with the PullParser API   204
Using the Feed API to create RSS/Atom clients   213
Visualizing data with the JavaFX chart API   220

Chapter 7: Deployment and Integration   **225**
Introduction   225
Building and packaging your app with an IDE   227
Building and packaging your app with javafxpackager   229
Packaging your app to be Web Start(ed)   232
Packaging your app as an applet   237
Passing arguments to JavaFX applications   242
Making your applets drag-to-install   245
Controlling JavaFX applets from JavaScript   250

Chapter 8: The JavaFX Production Suite   **259**
Introduction   259
Loading multiple images dynamically   260
Exporting Adobe Photoshop graphics to JavaFX   265
Exporting Adobe Illustrator graphics to JavaFX   269
Exporting Scalable Vector Graphics (SVG) to JavaFX   274
Using objects loaded from FXZ files   277

Appendin A: Mobile JavaFX   **285**

Appendin B: JavaFX Composer   **287**

Appendin C: JavaFX Products and Frameworks   **289**

Appendin D: Best Practices for Development   **291**

Appendin E: Best Practices for Deployment   **295**

Index   **299**

Preface

This book is a collection of code recipes, examples, and informative discourses designed to enable the reader to get started with creating JavaFX application quickly. The book is arranged as a series of loosely related code recipes that a reader can easily select to fit his or her needs. It exposes readers to a great variety of topics designed to satisfy different skill levels. Readers will learn about the language, animation techniques, paints, effects, JavaFX controls, integration of Swing components, styling with CSS, audio/video, deployment practices, and JavaFX integration with Adobe design tools.

What this book covers

Chapter 1, Getting Started with JavaFX... This is the "getting started" chapter of the book. It provides introductory materials to the platform, including installation instructions to get your environment set up. It also covers language basics such as classes, data types, function usage, variable declaration, data binding, triggers, Java and JavaFX integration.

Chapter 2, Creating JavaFX Applications... This chapter covers the essential building blocks of the JavaFX application framework, including primitive shapes, path, text, constructive area geometry, mouse/keyboard input, custom node, and window styling.

Chapter 3, Transformations, Animations, and Effects... This chapter explores the animation capabilities supported in JavaFX. You start with the Transition API to quickly build simple animations. The material continues to cover the KeyFrame API for more advanced animation sequences. You will learn about colors, effects, and how to create your own custom paint and effects.

Chapter 4, Components and Skinning... This chapter is divided into two sections. The first section shows readers how to use the set of standard JavaFX controls. The chapter also shows how to embed Swing components in your JavaFX scene graph. You will also learn how to create your own custom visual controls. The second section of the chapter introduces the reader to JavaFX's support for CSS. The reader will learn how to style controls using inline and externalized CSS to create skins.

Chapter 5, JavaFX Media... One of the exciting features of JavaFX is its inherent support for multimedia. JavaFX includes support for rendering of images in multiple formats and support for playback of audio and video on all platforms where JavaFX is supported. In this chapter, readers learn how to display and manipulate images using the Image API. They will also learn how to playback both audio and video using the Media API. The chapter shows also how to create practical custom playback controls.

Chapter 6, Working with Data... JavaFX provides superb support for accessing and manipulating data both locally and remotely. In this chapter, readers are introduced to the Storage API for local data storage. It provides extensive coverage of JavaFX's HttpRequest API for accessing data on remote web servers. Readers will learn how to use JavaFX's XML and JSON parsers to build RESTful client mashups using popular services such as Google Map, Yahoo Weather, and Zillow Listing. Finally, the chapter explores JavaFX's built-in Chart API for data visualization.

Chapter 7, Deployment and Integration... This chapter provides coverage of the deployment mechanism supported by JavaFX. Readers will learn how to properly build and package their applications to target the different runtimes supported by JavaFX, including the web browser and the desktop. Readers learn how to create Java Web Start-ready applications using the build tools included in the SDK. The chapter shows how to write JavaScript that communicates with your JavaFX applet while running within the browser.

Chapter 8, The JavaFX Production Suite... This chapter covers JavaFX's integral support for designer tools from Adobe, including Illustrator and Photoshop. Readers are walked through the process of exporting creative assets using the JavaFX Production Suite plugins available for these tools. The chapters also shows how to integrate exported objects from Photoshop and Illustrator into JavaFX.

Appendix A, Mobile JavaFX... In this appendix, readers learn about JavaFX's support for mobile development. You will learn about development techniques to target mobile devices and tool support available to get your JavaFX app in the mobile space.

Appendix B, JavaFX Composer... By the time you get your hands on this book, JavaFX Composer will be available as part of NetBeans. This appendix introduces the reader to the tool and its features.

Appendix C, JavaFX Products and Frameworks... This appendix introduces the user to the community support that is developing around JavaFX. Readers learn about several open source projects and commercial tools available for JavaFX.

Appendix D, Best Practices for Development... As the tile of this appendix indicates, readers will learn about key practices to use when creating JavaFX development.

Appendix E, Best Practices for Deployment... This appendix is a continuation of chapter 7. It discusses practices that should be applied when building and deploying JavaFX applications.

What you need for this book

▶ JavaFX SDK 1.2

▶ Java Development Kit (JDK)

▶ NetBeans or Eclipse

▶ JDK 6 update 14 (or later)

Who this book is for

This book is for Java developers, RIA content developers, and graphic designers who want to build RIAs featuring animations, videos and other feature-rich content. If you have knowledge of Java, JavaScript, JavaFX components, you can exploit this book to your advantage.

Conventions

In this book, you will find a number of styles of text that distinguish between different kinds of information. Here are some examples of these styles, and an explanation of their meaning.

Code words in text are shown as follows: "We can include other contexts through the use of the `include` directive."

A block of code is set as follows:

```
<jnlp>
...
    <resources>
        <j2se version="1.5+" java-vm-args="-Xmx256M"/>
            ...
    </resources>
...
</jnlp>
```

When we wish to draw your attention to a particular part of a code block, the relevant lines or items are set in bold:

```
<jnlp>
...
  <application-desc
    main-class="com.sun.javafx.runtime.main.Main">
      <argument>MainJavaFXScript=param.demo.Main</argument>
      <argument>name=World</argument>
    </application-desc>
...
</jnlp>
```

Any command-line input or output is written as follows:

```
javafxpackager -src src -appClass params.RuntimeArgsApplet
               -appName args-demo
               -appVendor "Vladimir Vivien" -appVersion 1.0
               -appCodebase "http://my.server/path/to/app/"
               -appWidth 640 -appHeight 75
```

New terms and important words are shown in bold. Words that you see on the screen, in menus or dialog boxes for example, appear in the text like this: "clicking on the Next button moves you to the next screen".

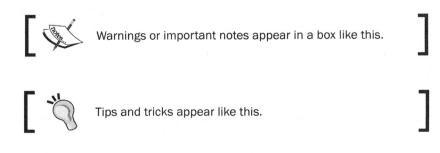

Warnings or important notes appear in a box like this.

Tips and tricks appear like this.

Reader feedback

Feedback from our readers is always welcome. Let us know what you think about this book—what you liked or may have disliked. Reader feedback is important for us to develop titles that you really would like to see.

To send us general feedback, simply send an e-mail to feedback@packtpub.com, and mention the book title via the subject of your message.

If there is a book that you need and would like to see us publish, please send us a note in the SUGGEST A TITLE form on www.packtpub.com or e-mail suggest@packtpub.com.

If there is a topic that you have expertise in and you are interested in either writing or contributing to a book, see our author guide on www.packtpub.com/authors.

Customer support

Now that you are the proud owner of a Packt book, we have a number of things to help you to get the most from your purchase.

[
Downloading the example code for this book

You can download the example code files for all Packt books you have purchased from your account at `http://www.PacktPub.com`. If you purchased this book elsewhere, you can visit `http://www.PacktPub.com/support` and register to have the files e-mailed directly to you.
]

Errata

Although we have taken every care to ensure the accuracy of our content, mistakes do happen. If you find a mistake in one of our books—maybe a mistake in the text or the code—we would be grateful if you would report this to us. By doing so, you can save other readers from would like to see. frustration and help us improve subsequent versions of this book. If you find any errata, please report them by visiting `http://www.packtpub.com/support`, selecting your book, clicking on the let us know link, and entering the details of your errata. Once your errata are verified, your submission will be accepted and the errata will be uploaded on our website, or added to any list of existing errata, under the Errata section of that title. Any existing errata can be viewed by selecting your title from `http://www.packtpub.com/support`.

Piracy

Piracy of copyright material on the Internet is an ongoing problem across all media. At Packt, we take the protection of our copyright and licenses very seriously. If you come across any illegal copies of our works, in any form, on the Internet, please provide us with the location address or website name immediately, so that we can pursue a remedy.

Please contact us at `copyright@packtpub.com` with a link to the suspected pirated material.

We appreciate your help in protecting our authors, and our ability to bring you valuable content.

Questions

You can contact us at `questions@packtpub.com` if you are having a problem with any aspect of the book, and we will do our best to address it.

1

Getting Started with JavaFX

In this chapter, we will cover the following topics:

- ▶ Installing the JavaFX SDK
- ▶ Setting up JavaFX for the NetBeans IDE
- ▶ Setting up JavaFX for the Eclipse IDE
- ▶ Using javafxc to compile JavaFX Code
- ▶ Creating and using JavaFX classes
- ▶ Creating and using variables in JavaFX
- ▶ Using binding and triggers to update variables
- ▶ Creating and using JavaFX functions
- ▶ Integrating your JavaFX code with Java
- ▶ Creating and using JavaFX sequences
- ▶ Working with JavaFX string

Introduction

Today, in the age of Web 2.0, AJAX, and the iPhone, users have come to expect their applications to provide a dynamic and engaging user interface that delivers rich graphical content, audio, and video, all wrapped in GUI controls with animated cinematic-like interactions. They want their applications to be connected to the web of information and social networks available on the Internet.

Developers, on the other hand, have become accustomed to tools such as AJAX/HTML5 toolkits, Flex/Flash, Google Web Toolkit, Eclipse/NetBeans RCP, and others that allow them to build and deploy rich and web-connected client applications quickly. They expect their development languages to be expressive (either through syntax or specialized APIs) with features that liberate them from the tyranny of verbosity and empower them with the ability to express their intents declaratively.

The Java proposition

During the early days of the Web, the Java platform was the first to introduce rich content and interactivity in the browser using the applet technology (predating JavaScript and even Flash). Not too long after applets appeared, Swing was introduced as the unifying framework to create feature-rich applications for the desktop and the browser. Over the years, Swing matured into an amazingly robust GUI technology used to create rich desktop applications. However powerful Swing is, its massive API stack lacks the lightweight higher abstractions that application and content developers have been using in other development environments. Furthermore, the applet's plugin technology was (as admitted by Sun) neglected and failed in the browser-hosted rich applications against similar technologies such as Flash.

Enter JavaFX

The JavaFX is Sun's (now part of Oracle) answer to the next generation of rich, web-enabled, deeply interactive applications. JavaFX is a complete platform that includes a new language, development tools, build tools, deployment tools, and new runtimes to target desktop, browser, mobile, and entertainment devices such as televisions. While JavaFX is itself built on the Java platform, that is where the commonalities end. The new JavaFX scripting language is designed as a lightweight, expressive, and a dynamic language to create web-connected, engaging, visually appealing, and content-rich applications.

The JavaFX platform will appeal to both technical designers and developers alike. Designers will find JavaFX Script to be a simple, yet expressive language, perfectly suited for the integration of graphical assets when creating visually-rich client applications. Application developers, on the other hand, will find its lightweight, dynamic type inference system, and script-like feel a productivity booster, allowing them to express GUI layout, object relationship, and powerful two-way data bindings all using a declarative and easy syntax. Since JavaFX runs on the Java Platform, developers are able to reuse existing Java libraries directly from within JavaFX, tapping into the vast community of existing Java developers, vendors, and libraries.

This is an introductory chapter to JavaFX. Use its recipes to get started with the platform. You will find instructions on how to install the SDK and directions on how to set up your IDE. The chapter also provides a high-level introduction to the main features of the JavaFX scripting language such as class creation, variable declaration, data types, JavaFX functional programming support, sequences, and loops.

Installing the JavaFX SDK

The JavaFX software development kit (SDK) is a set of core tools needed to compile, run, and deploy JavaFX applications. If you feel at home at the command line, then you can start writing code with your favorite text editor and interact with the SDK tools directly. However, if you want to see code-completion hints after each dot you type, then you can always use an IDE such as NetBeans or Eclipse to get you started with JavaFX (see other recipes on IDEs). This section outlines the necessary steps to set up the JavaFX SDK successfully on your computer. These instructions apply to JavaFX SDK version 1.2.x; future versions may vary slightly.

Getting ready

Before you can start building JavaFX applications, you must ensure that your development environment meets the minimum requirements. As of this writing, the following are the minimum requirements to run the current released version of JavaFX runtime 1.2.

Minimum system requirements

Windows	Mac OS X	Linux/OpenSolaris
▶ Windows XP (SP3) or Windows Vista 32-bit (all editions) ▶ Java Development Kit (JDK) 6 Update 13 ▶ Internet Explorer 6, Firefox 3.0	▶ Mac OS X version 10.4.1 ▶ Java Development Kit (JDK) 5 Update 16 ▶ Safari 3, Firefox 3	▶ Ubuntu 8.04 ▶ OpenSolaris 2009.06 ▶ Java Development Kit (JDK) 6 Update 13 ▶ Firefox 3.0 ▶ GStreamer Media Library

How to do it...

The first step for installing the SDK on you machine is to download it from `http://javafx.com/downloads/`. Select the appropriate SDK version as shown in the next screenshot.

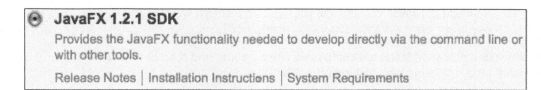

⊙ **JavaFX 1.2.1 SDK**

Provides the JavaFX functionality needed to develop directly via the command line or with other tools.

Release Notes | Installation Instructions | System Requirements

Once you have downloaded the SDK for your corresponding system, follow these instructions for installation on Windows, Mac, Ubuntu, or OpenSolaris.

Installation on Windows

1. Find and double-click on the newly downloaded installation package (.exe file) to start.
2. Follow the directions from the installer wizard to continue with your installation.

 Make sure to select the location for your installation. The installer will run a series of validations on your system before installation starts. If the installer finds no previously installed SDK (or the incorrect version), it will download a SDK that meets the minimum requirements (which lengthens your installation).

Installation on Mac OS

1. Prior to installation, ensure that your Mac OS meets the minimum requirements.
2. Find and double-click on the newly downloaded installation package (.dmg file) to start.
3. Follow the directions from the installer wizard to continue your installation.
4. The Mac OS installer will place the installed files at the following location: `/Library/Frameworks/JavaFX.framework/Versions/1.2`.

Installation on Ubuntu Linux and OpenSolaris

1. Prior to installation, ensure that your Ubuntu or OpenSolaris environment meets the minimum requirements.
2. Locate the newly downloaded installation package to start installation. For Linux, the file will end with `*-linux-i586.sh`. For OpenSolaris, the installation file will end with `*-solaris-i586.sh`.
3. Move the file to the directory where you want to install the content of the SDK.
4. Make the file executable (`chmod 755`) and run it. This will extract the content of the SDK in the current directory.
5. The installation will create a new directory, `javafx-sdk1.2`, which is your JavaFX home location (`$JAVAFX_HOME`).
6. Now add the JavaFX binaries to your system's `$PATH` variable, (`export PATH=$PATH:$JAVAFX_HOME/bin`).

When your installation steps are completed, open a command prompt and validate your installation by checking the version of the SDK.

```
$> javafx -version
$> javafx 1.2.3_b36
```

You should get the current version number for your installed JavaFX SDK displayed.

How it works...

Version 1.2.x of the SDK comes with several tools and other resources to help developers get started with JavaFX development right away

The major (and more interesting) directories in the SDK include:

Directory	Description
bin	This directory contains tools for compiling, packaging, documenting, and running JavaFX scripts. They include javafx, javafxc, javafxdoc, and javafxpackager.
docs	This directory contains documentation for various JavaFX tools and the JavaFX APIs.
emulator	This directory contains tools for JavaFX mobile emulator , which is useful for doing mobile development with JavaFX. As of version 1.2 of the SDK, mobile development is only available on the Windows platform.
lib	This directory contains .jar files necessary to build and run JavaFX applications for both desktop and mobile environments.
profiles	This directory contains configuration files for the SDK tools.
samples	This directory provides sample applications to help you get started.

Setting up JavaFX for the NetBeans IDE

The previous recipe shows you how to get started with JavaFX using the SDK directly. However if you are more of a syntax-highlight, code-completion, click-to-build person, you will be delighted to know that the NetBeans IDE fully supports JavaFX development. JavaFX has first-class support within NetBeans, with functionalities similar to those found in Java development including:

- ► Syntax highlighting
- ► Code completion
- ► Error detection
- ► Code block formatting and folding
- ► In-editor API documentation
- ► Visual preview panel
- ► Debugging
- ► Application profiling
- ► Continuous background build
- ► And more...

This recipe shows how to set up the NetBeans IDE for JavaFX development. You will learn how to configure NetBeans to create, build, and deploy your JavaFX projects.

Getting ready

Before you can start building JavaFX applications in the NetBeans IDE, you must ensure that your development environment meets the minimum requirements for JavaFX and NetBeans (see previous recipe *Installing the JavaFX SDK* for minimum requirements). Version 1.2 of the JavaFX SDK requires NetBeans version 6.5.1 (or higher) to work properly.

How to do it...

As a new NetBeans user (or first-time installer), you can download NetBeans and JavaFX bundled and ready to use. The bundle contains the NetBeans IDE and all other required JavaFX SDK dependencies to start development immediately. No additional downloads are required with this option.

To get started with the bundled NetBeans, go to `http://javafx.com/downloads/` and download the NetBeans + JavaFX bundle as shown in the next screenshot (versions will vary slightly as newer software become available).

> ### ⊙ NetBeans IDE 6.8 for JavaFX 1.2
> Start developing with the integrated development environment for building, previewing, and debugging JavaFX applications. Includes code samples and building blocks. JavaFX NB plugin is a multi-language release, including both Japanese and Simplified Chinese.
>
> Release Notes | Installation Instructions | System Requirements

NetBeans installation on Windows

1. Prior to installation, ensure that your Windows environment meets the minimum requirements (see recipe *Installing the JavaFX SDK*).

2. Find and double-click on the newly downloaded installation package (`.exe` file) to start.

3. Follow the instructions from the installer to install NetBeans (default install location `C:\Program Files\NetBeans {version-number}`).

Installation on Mac OS

1. Prior to installation, ensure that your Mac OS meets the minimum requirements (see the recipe *Installing the JavaFX SDK*).

2. Find and double-click on the newly downloaded installation package (.dmg file) to start.

3. Follow the directions from the insta ler to install NetBeans (default install location: `Macintosh HD/Applications/NetBeans/NetBeans {version-number}`).

Installation on Ubuntu Linux and OpenSolaris

Prior to installation, ensure that your Ubuntu or OpenSolaris installation meets the minimum requirements (see recipe *Installing the JavaFX SDK*).

1. Find the newly downloaded installation package: for Linux, the file will end in `*-linux-i586.sh`; for OpenSolaris, the file will end in `*-solaris-i586.sh`.

2. Make the file executable, and run it.

3. Follow the directions from the insta ler to install NetBeans (default location: `$HOME /netbeans-{version-number}`)

Now that NetBeans is ready, lets create a quick "Hello World" so you can test your JavaFX NetBeans installation. To get started, select **New Project** from the **File** menu.

When the **New Project** wizard opens, select **JavaFX** from the **Categories** list and click on the **Next** button. Enter the location where the project will be saved, and click on the **Next** button. You will end up with a shell of a JavaFX application ready to run. Update the `title` and `content` properties as highlighted in the next code snippet. You can see the full code listing at `ch01/source-code/src/hello/HelloJavaFX.fx`.

```
import javafx.stage.Stage;
import javafx.scene.Scene;
import javafx.scene.text.Text;
import javafx.scene.text.Font;
```

```
Stage {
  title: "Hello JavaFX"
  width: 250
  height: 80
  scene: Scene {
      content: [
          Text {
                font : Font {size : 16}
                x: 10
                y: 30
                content: "Hello World!"
                }
      ]
  }
}
```

When you run the code (right-click on the project and select **Run Project**), NetBeans automatically handles the compilation, packaging, and execution of the code in the JavaFX runtime for you, as shown in the next screenshot.

How it works...

When you download the bundled NetBeans + JavaFX SDK, it comes with everything needed to start developing JavaFX. The bundle will install the NetBeans IDE and will also automatically download and install the NetBeans plugins required for JavaFX development including the latest SDK. Be aware that if you have downloaded the SDK separately (as explained in the recipe *Installing the JavaFX SDK*), you will end up with two copies of the SDK on your local machine.

There's more...

If you already use NetBeans, you can make your IDE JavaFX-ready by downloading the necessary plugins. The plugins contain the JavaFX SDK and all required dependencies to start your JavaFX development immediately, no other download is required. Note that your NetBeans must meet the minimum requirements for JavaFX to work properly (see previous recipe).

Download JavaFX NetBeans plugin

Updates   Available Plugins (3/123)   Downloaded   Installed (0/25)   Settings

(Reload Catalog)   Search: javafx

Install	Name ▼	Category	Source
☑	JavaFX Kit	JavaFX	
☑	JavaFX SDK for Mac OS X	JavaFX	
☐	JavaFX Weather Sample	JavaFX	

JavaFX Kit

http://javafx.netbeans.org/

Plugin Description

The JavaFX Script Plugin for Netbeans provides JavaFX Script language support in the Netbeans IDE. The plugin provides JavaFX project type, editing capabilities such as code formatting, syntax highlighting, error detection, preview panel, etc.

(Install)   2 plugins selected, 31MB

1. Open the **Plugins** management window (**Tools | Plugins**) in NetBeans and click on the **Available Plugins** tab.

2. Do a search for `javafx` to filter the available plugins list as shown in the previous screenshot.

3. Select the **JavaFX Kit** and the **JavaFX SDK for {Your OS name}** bundles as shown in the previous screenshot, and then click on the **Install** button.

4. Follow the instructions from the NetBeans installer to install the selected plugins.

5. Make sure to select **Restart IDE Now** to complete the installation.

See also

▶ *Installing the JavaFX SDK*

▶ *Setting up JavaFX for the Eclipse IDE*

Setting up JavaFX for the Eclipse IDE

As of JavaFX version 1.2, Sun Microsystems the name (will be Oracle by the time you read this) officially released a fully functional plugin to support development in the Eclipse IDE. While the Eclipse plugin came after NetBean's, it still packs an invaluable set of functionalities for developers who feel more comfortable working in Eclipse, including:

- ▶ Project creation wizard and templates
- ▶ Syntax highlighting
- ▶ Code completion
- ▶ Error detection
- ▶ Code block formatting and folding
- ▶ In-editor API documentation
- ▶ Debugging
- ▶ Continuous background build
- ▶ And more...

This recipe shows how to set up the Eclipse IDE for JavaFX development. You will learn how to configure Eclipse and the JavaFX 1.2 plugin.

Getting ready

Before you can start building JavaFX applications in the Eclipse IDE, you must ensure that your development environment meets the minimum requirements for JavaFX 1.2, which requires Eclipse 3.4 (Ganamede) for Java EE developers (or higher). To get the Eclipse plugin to work properly, ensure that you have downloaded and configured the Java JDK and the JavaFX SDK (see the recipe *Installing the JavaFX SDK* for details).

How to do it...

As with anything else in Eclipse, JavaFX support comes in the form of a plugin. You have to download and configure the plugin to work with your previously installed local JavaFX SDK prior to building your applications. To get started, do the following:

1. Select **Software Updates** from the **Help** menu to open the **Plugins** management window.
2. Click on the **Available Software** tab.
3. Add the site `http://javafx.com/downloads/eclipse-plugin/` as the plugin site.

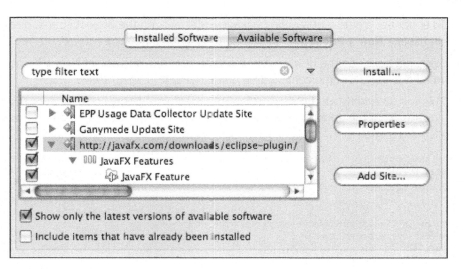

4. Select the JavaFX site, as shown in the previous screenshot, then click on **Install** to continue.

5. Follow the instructions of the plugin wizard.

6. Accept the terms of the license, and make sure to restart the Eclipse IDE when prompted.

Now that you have Eclipse setup with JavaFX, it makes sense to create a quick **Hello World** application in Eclipse to test the installation.

To get started, select **New** from the **File** menu (you may have to select **Other** if JavaFX is not listed as a project type).

 You must have the SDK installed and configured prior to creating your first application (see recipe *Installing the JavaFX SDK*).

7. When presented with the new project wizard, select **JavaFX Project** and click on the **Next** button.

8. Then, provide the project's name (HelloWorld), location, JRE version, and type (default is Desktop) to continue with the project's creation.

9. Click on the **Next** button and select a project template (which is a based on pre-existing sample code). Select the **Empty Project** template and click on the **Finish** button.

10. The wizard will complete the project creation, and you should have a project shell ready for you to start coding.

11. To continue, create a new code package (right-click on the project source directory, and select **New | Package**), and name the package `hello`.

12. Next, right-click on the newly created source package and select **New | Empty JavaFX Script** from the context menu, and name it `HelloJavaFX.fx`.

13. This will do exactly what it says, which is to create an empty code window. Notice, however, that the editor comes with several code snippets that you can reuse in your own code.

14. In the **Snippets** window, shown in the previous screenshot, click on **Applications** and double-click on **Stage**. This will bring up a template editor. Accept the default values and continue.

Edit the sample code by adding the highlighted portion. You can see the full code listing at `ch01/source-code/src/hello/HelloJavaFX.fx`.

```
import javafx.stage.Stage;
import javafx.scene.Scene;
import javafx.scene.text.Text;
import javafx.scene.text.Font;

Stage {
  title: "Hello JavaFX"
  scene: Scene {
  width: 250
  height: 200
  content: [
        Text {
```

```
            font : Font {size : 16}
            x: 10
            y: 30
            content: "Hello World!"
        }
    ]
}
```

Once you have updated the code, right-click on the project and select **Run As | JavaFX Application**. If you are running the application for the first time, you will be prompted to select the application's targeted profile and the main class.

How it works...

Support for JavaFX in Eclipse comes as separate plugin download. When you install the plugin, it adds the capabilities of JavaFX development to your IDE. Unlike the NetBeans plugin, as of version 1.2, the SDK is not available as part of the plugin download. You must download and have the SDK installed on your workstation. When the plugin is installed, it will look for the SDK on your machine.

See also

- ▶ *Installing the JavaFX SDK*
- ▶ *Setting up JavaFX for the NetBeans IDE*

Using javafxc to compile JavaFX code

While it certainly makes it easier to build JavaFX with the support of an IDE (see the NetBeans and Eclipse recipes), it is not a requirement. In some situations, having direct access to the SDK tools is preferred (automated build for instance). This recipe explores the build tools that are shipped with the JavaFX SDK and provides steps to show you how to manually compile your applications.

Getting ready

To use the SDK tools, you will need to download and install the JavaFX SDK. See the recipe *Installing the JavaFX SDK* for instructions on how to do it.

How to do it...

Open your favorite text/code editor and type the following code. The full code is available from `ch01/source-code/src/hello/HelloJavaFX.fx`.

```
package hello;

import javafx.stage.Stage;
import javafx.scene.Scene
import javafx.scene.text.Text;
import javafx.scene.text.Font;

Stage {
    title: "Hello JavaFX"
    width: 250
    height: 80
    scene: Scene {
        content: [
            Text {
                    font : Font {size : 16}
                    x: 10
                    y: 30
                    content: "Hello World!"
                    }
        ]
    }
}
```

Save the file at location `hello/Main.fx`.

To compile the file, invoke the JavaFX compiler from the command line from a directory up from the where the file is stored (for this example, it would be executed from the `src` directory):

```
javafxc hello/Main.fx
```

If your compilation command works properly, you will not get any messages back from the compiler. You will, however, see the file `HelloJavaFX.class` created by the compiler in the `hello` directory.

If, however, you get a `"file not found"` error during compilation, ensure that you have properly specified the path to the `HelloJavaFX.fx` file.

How it works...

The javafxc compiler works in similar ways as your regular Java compiler. It parses and compiles the JavaFX script into Java byte code with the `.class` extension.

javafxc accepts numerous command-line arguments to control how and what sources get compiled, as shown in the following command:

```
javafxc [options] [sourcefiles] [@argfiles]
```

where `options` are your command-line options, followed by one or more source files, which can be followed by list of argument files. Below are some of the more commonly javafxc arguments:

- **classpath (-cp)**—the classpath option specifies the locations (separated by a path separator character) where the compiler can find class files and/or library jar files that are required for building the application.

  ```
  javafxc -cp .:lib/mylibrary.jar MyClass.fx
  ```

- **sourcepath**—in more complicated project structure, you can use this option to specify one or more locations where the compiler should search for source file and satisfy source dependencies.

  ```
  javafxc -cp . -sourcepath .:src:src1:src2 MyClass.fx
  ```

- **-d**—with this option, you can set the target directory where compiled class files are to be stored. The compiler will create the package structure of the class under this directory and place the compiled JavaFX classes accordingly.

  ```
  javafxc -cp . -d build MyClass.fx
  ```

  When specifying the source files, you can use the wild card characters to indicate multiple source files to be compiled as follows:

  ```
  javafxc -d build src/*.fx
  ```

- The **@argfiles** option lets you specify a file which can contain `javafxc` command-line arguments. When the compiler is invoked and a `@argfile` is found, it uses the content of the file as an argument for javafxc. This can help shorten tediously long arguments into short, succinct commands.

  Assume file `cmdargs` has the following content

  ```
  -d build
  -cp .:lib/api1.jar:lib/api2.jar:lib/api3.jar
  -sourcepath core/src:components/src:tools/src
  ```

  Then you can invoke javafxc as:

  ```
  $> javafxc @cmdargs
  ```

See also

- *Installing the JavaFX SDK*

Creating and using JavaFX classes

JavaFX is an object-oriented scripting language. As such, object types, represented as classes, are part of the basic constructs of the language. This section shows how to declare, initialize, and use JavaFX classes.

Getting ready

If you have used other scripting languages such as ActionScript, JavaScript, Python, or PHP, the concepts presented in this section should be familiar. If you have no idea what a class is or what it should be, just remember this: a class is code that represents a logical entity (tree, person, organization, and so on) that you can manipulate programmatically or while using your application. A class usually exposes *properties* and *operations* to access the state or behavior of the class.

How to do it...

Let's assume we are building an application for a dealership. You may have a class called `Vehicle` to represent cars and other type of vehicles processed in the application. The next code example creates the `Vehicle` class. Refer to `ch01/source-code/src/javafx/Vehicle.fx` for full listing of the code presented here.

1. Open your favorite text editor (or fire up your favorite IDE).
2. Type the following class declaration.

```
class Vehicle {
    var make;
    var model;
    var color;
    var year;

    function drive () : Void {
        println("You are driving a "
                "{year} {color} {make} {model}!")
    }
}
```

3. Once your class is properly declared, it is now ready to be used. To use the class, add the following (highlighted code) to the file:

```
class Vehicle {
    . . .
}
```

```
var vehicle = Vehicle {
    year:2010
    color: "Grey"
    make:"Mini"
    model:"Cooper"
};

vehicle.drive();
```

4. Save the file as `Vehicle.fx`. Now, from the command-line, compile it with

```
$> javafxc Vehicle.fx
```

 If you are using an IDE, you can simply right, click on the file to run it.

When the code executes, you should see:

```
$> You are driving a 2010 Grey Mini Cooper!
```

How it works...

The previous snippet shows how to declare a class in JavaFX. Albeit a simple class, it shows the basic structure of a JavaFX class. It has properties represented by variables declarations:

```
var make;
var model;
var color;
var year;
```

and it has a function:

```
function drive () : Void {
    println("You are driving a "
            "{year} {color} {make} {model}!")
}
```

which can update the properties and/or modify the behavior (for details on JavaFX functions, see the recipe *Creating and Using JavaFX functions*). In this example, when the function is invoked on a `vehicle` object, it causes the object to display information about the vehicle on the console prompt.

Object literal initialization

Another aspect of JavaFX class usage is object declaration. JavaFX supports **object literal declaration** to initialize a new instance of the class. This format lets developers declaratively create a new instance of a class using the class's literal representation and pass in property literal values directly into the initialization block to the object's named public properties.

```
var vehicle = Vehicle {
    year:2010
    color: "Grey"
    make:"Mini"
    model:"Cooper"
};
```

The previous snippet declares variable `vehicle` and assigns to it a new instance of the Vehicle class with `year = 2010`, `color = Grey`, `make = Mini`, and `model = Cooper`. The values that are passed in the literal block overwrite the default values of the named public properties.

There's more...

JavaFX class definition mechanism does not support a constructor as in languages such as Java and C#. However, to allow developers to hook into the life cycle of the object's instance creation phase, JavaFX exposes a specialized code block called `init{}` to let developers provide custom code which is executed during object initialization.

Initialization block

Code in the `init` block is executed as one of the final steps of object creation after properties declared in the object literal are initialized. Developers can use this facility to initialize values and initialize resources that the new object will need. To illustrate how this works, the previous code snippet has been modified with an `init` block. You can get the full listing of the code at `ch01/source-code/src/javafx/Vehicle2.fx`.

```
class Vehicle {
...

    init {
        color = "Black";
    }

    function drive () : Void {
        println("You are driving a "
                "{year} {color} {make} {model}!");
    }
}

var vehicle = Vehicle {
    year:2010
```

```
        make:"Mini"
        model:"Cooper"
    };

    vehicle.drive();
```

Notice that the object literal declaration of object `vehicle` no longer includes the color declaration. Nevertheless, the value of property `color` will be initialized to `Black` in the `init{ }` code block during the object's initialization.

When you run the application, it should display:

```
    You are driving a 2010 Black Mini Cooper!
```

See also

- ▶ *Declaring and using variables in JavaFX*
- ▶ *Creating and using JavaFX functions*

Creating and using variables in JavaFX

JavaFX is a statically type-safe and type-strict scripting language. Therefore, variables (and anything which can be assigned to a variable, including functions and expressions) in JavaFX, must be associated with a type, which indicates the expected behavior and representation of the variable. This sections explores how to create, initialize, and update JavaFX variables.

Getting ready

Before we look at creating and using variables, it is beneficial to have an understanding of what is meant by data type and be familiar with some common data types such as `String`, `Integer`, `Float`, and `Boolean`. If you have written code in other scripting languages such as ActionScript, Python, and Ruby, you will find the concepts in this recipe easy to understand.

How to do it...

JavaFX provides two ways of declaring variables including the `def` and the `var` keywords.

```
    def X_STEP = 50;
    prntln (X_STEP);
    X_STEP++; // causes error
    var x : Number;
    x = 100;
    ...
    x = x + X_LOC;
```

How it works...

In JavaFX, there are two ways of declaring a variable:

▶ `def`—The `def` keyword is used to declare and assign constant values. Once a variable is declared with the `def` keyword and assigned a value, it is not allowed be reassigned a new value.

▶ `var`—The `var` keyword declares variables which are able to be updated at any point after their declaration.

There's more...

All variables must have an associated type. The type can be declared explicitly or be automatically coerced by the compiler. Unlike Java (similar to ActionScript and Scala), the type of the variable follows the variable's name separated by a colon.

```
var location:String;
```

Explicit type declaration

The following code specifies the type (class) that the variable will receive at runtime:

```
var location:String;
location = "New York";
```

The compiler also supports a short-hand notation that combines declaration and initialization.

```
var location:String = "New York";
```

Implicit coercion

In this format, the type is left out of the declaration. The compiler automatically converts the variable to the proper type based on the assignment.

```
var location;
location = "New York";
```

Variable location will automatically receive a type of String during compilation because the first assignment is a string literal.

Or, the short-hand version:

```
var location = "New York";
```

JavaFX types

Similar to other languages, JavaFX supports a complete set of primitive types as listed:

`:String`—this type represents a collection of characters contained within within quotes (double or single, see following). Unlike Java, the default value for String is empty ("").

```
"The quick brown fox jumps over the lazy dog" or
'The quick brown fox jumps over the lazy dog'
```

`:Number`—this is a numeric type that represents all numbers with decimal points. It is backed by the 64-bit double precision floating point Java type. The default value of Number is `0.0`.

```
0.01234
100.0
1.24e12
```

`:Integer`—this is a numeric type that represents all integral numbers. It is backed by the 32-bit integer Java type. The default value of an Integer is `0`.

```
-44
7
0
0xFF
```

`:Boolean`—as the name implies, this type represents the binary value of either `true` or `false`.

`:Duration`—this type represent a unit of time. You will encounter its use heavily in animation and other instances where temporal values are needed. The supported units include `ms`, `s`, `m`, and `h` for millisecond, second, minute, and hour respectively.

```
12ms
4s
12h
0.5m
```

`:Void`—this type indicates that an expression or a function returns no value. Literal representation of `Void` is `null`.

Variable scope

Variables can have three distinct scopes, which implicitly indicates the access level of the variable when it is being used.

Script level

Script variables are defined at any point within the JavaFX script file outside of any code block (including class definition). When a script-level variable is declared, by default it is globally visible within the script and is not accessible from outside the script (without additional access modifiers).

Instance level

A variable that is defined at the top-level of a class is referred to as an instance variable. An instance level is visible within the class by the class members and can be accessed by creating an instance of the class.

Local level

The least visible scope are local variables. They are declared within code blocks such as functions. They are visible only to members within the block.

See also

▸ *Creating and using JavaFX classes*

▸ *Creating and using JavaFX functions*

Using binding and triggers to update variables

Languages, such as JavaFX, which target a visual domain have to be event-based in order to handle the non-linearity of GUI interactions. Traditionally, in a visual programming paradigm, events are generated by components when their internal states are updated. This can require an elaborate notification-handler syntax to properly express the relationship between event broadcasters and handlers.

This section explores the easy and intuitive declarative syntax of JavaFX's event-based programming. It looks at how variable values can remain synchronized using a mechanism called binding.

Getting ready

This section discusses concepts that require familiarity with variable bindings as found in other scripting languages. **Binding** usually refers to the ability to automatically react and handle events caused by resources (or other events) to which handlers are bound.

How to do it...

JavaFX facilitates variable binding using the `bind` keyword. Let us look at a simple example that shows the ease with which you can bind variables. Note that you can find listings for binding examples at `ch01/source-code/src/binding/`.

```
var step = 100;
def locX = bind step;

println ("locX = {locX}");
```

```
step = 110;
println ("locX = {locX}");

step = 150;
println ("locX = {locX}");
```

When you run the application, you will get the following output:

```
locX = 100
locX = 110
locX = 150
```

Notice that the value of variable `locX` is synchronized with the value of variable `step`. Whenever `step` is updated, `locX` changes in value automatically.

How it works...

The general syntax for binding looks like the following:

```
def variableX = bind expression
```

The idea behind binding is to keep `variableX`, on the left-hand side of the assignment, updated whenever there is a change in the bound `expression` on the right-hand side. JavaFX supports several forms of `expressions` which can be used to update the variable on the left-hand side.

Binding to variables

This is the simplest form of the binding syntax where the variable on the left is bound to other variables.

```
var x = 100;
def y = bind x + 10;
```

When the value of variable `x` changes, `y` is updated with the new value of `x + 10`.

Binding to a conditional

JavaFX also supports conditional binding expressions, which update the left-hand side of the assignment based on a predefined condition.

```
var x = 2;
def row = bind if((x mod 2) == 0) "even" else "odd";

for(n in [0..5]){
  x = n;
  println ("Row {n} is {row}");
}
```

The value of variable `row` is updated depending on the evaluation of the bound conditional expression.

```
Row 0 is even
Row 1 is odd
Row 2 is even
Row 3 is odd
```

In the example, when the `if` statement evaluates to true, `row` is assigned "even", else it receives "odd".

Binding to a code block

The code block binding lets developers create compound expressions to logically control how the declared variable is updated.

```
var x = 2;
def xDoubled = bind {
  var y = 2;
  y * x;
}
x = 3;
println ( "X = 3, doubled = {xDoubled}");
x = 27;
println ( "x = 27, doubled = {xDoubled}");
```

When `x` is updated, the code block is re-evaluated, and `xDoubled` is updated with the new value of the last expression in the block.

 Be aware that assigning a code block to a variable without the `bind` keyword is legal in JavaFX. So, make sure not to leave the `bind` keyword out, as omitting it changes the meaning of the assignment, and it will behave differently.

Binding to a function

JavaFX can bind a variable to a function call as well.

```
function squareIt(x):Number {
  x*x;
}
var param = 0;
def squared = bind squareIt(param);
param = 96;
println ("Param = {param}, squared = {squared}");
```

When the parameter of the function (value assigned to `param`) call is updated, the function is automatically re-invoked and the variable `squared` receives the newly calculated value.

Bind to an object literal

A variable can bind to an object literal declaration. When the values of the bound object properties change, the expression is updated with a new object.

```
class Location {
   var x:Integer;
   var y:Integer;
}

var xLoc = 0;
var yLoc = 0;
def loc = bind Location {
   x: xLoc;
   y: yLoc;
}
xLoc = 12;
yLoc = 234;
println ("loc.x = {loc.x}, loc.y = {loc.y}");
```

> To avoid creating a new object every time a bound property value is updated, bind each literal property in the object declaration separately as shown.

```
var xLoc = 0;
var yLoc = 0;
def loc = Location {
   x: bind xLoc;
   y: bind yLoc;
}
```

There's more...

JavaFX offers another event-based mechanism called a trigger. A **trigger** is a code block that gets executed when the variable it is assigned to is updated. At its simplest form, a trigger is declared as follows

```
def variable = value on replace [oldValueVarName]{
    // code to execute
}
```

Here, the code block is executed when the `variable` on the left-hand side of the assignment is updated. The `oldValueVarName` variable name is optional and holds the value of variable before the update.

Using triggers

The following is a simple trigger example. You can see the full code listing for this code at `ch01/source-code/src/binding/TriggerDemo.fx`.

```
def X_BOUND = 10;
var locX = 7 on replace oldX {
  if(locX <= X_BOUND) {
     println ("{oldX} ==> {locX}, in bound");
  }else{
     println ("{oldX} ==> {locX}, Out of bound!");
  }
}
locX = 12;
locX = 4;
```

Whenever the value of variable `locX` is updated (including the initial assignment), the `on replace` trigger is executed as well.

```
0 ==> 7, in bound
7 ==> 12, out of bound!
12 ==> 4, in bound
```

See also

▶   *Declaring and using variables in JavaFX*

Creating and using JavaFX functions

One of the types supported by JavaFX is named a **function type**. To be clear, this is not the type of the returned value of the function, but rather an actual data type that represents a function. This versatility throws JavaFX squarely in the realm of functional programming, where functions are regarded as first-order data types and can be manipulated just like any other supported data types. This section shows you how to create functions in JavaFX and use them as expressions in your code.

Getting ready

The concepts presented here discuss functions as an executable code unit that can be assigned and reused. You are expected to know the general purpose of a function and how to use it. If you have written any code before, you most likely know how to create and use a function.

How to do it...

In JavaFX, A function is a specialized code block preceded by the `function` keyword. It can accept zero or more typed parameters and always returns a typed value. Here is the declaration of a function type assigned to variable called `squareIt`, which returns the squared value of the number passed in as parameter. Complete code listing can be found at `ch01/source-code/src/javafx/SimpleFunction.fx`.

```
var squareIt : function(:Number):Number;
squareIt = function (x) {
    x * x;
}
var square3 = squareIt(3);
println ("3 squared = {square3}");
```

How it works...

In JavaFX, a function has a distinct, definable type (similar to String, Number, and Integer). A function type is defined by its parameter signature and its return type. Variables (and parameters) can be assigned a function type. For instance, in the previous snippet, variable `squareIt` is declared as being a function type. This means that the variable `squareIt` can be assigned a function that takes one parameter of type `Number` and returns a value of type `Number`. `squareIt` can be used anywhere a function call can be used, as shown in the call `var square3 = squareIt(3)`.

Note that the declaration and definition of the function can be combined in one step, as show next:

```
function squareIt(x:Number):Number{
    x * x;
}
```

The JavaFX compiler can infer the types associated with a function's parameter signature and return value. Therefore, the function definition can be reduced to:

```
function squareIt(x) {
    x*x;
}
```

The type inference engine in JavaFX will determine the proper type of the parameter based on value of the parameter at runtime. The return type of the function is based on the type of the last statement in the function or the type of the value used in the `return` statement.

There's more...

There are couple more features about functions in which you may be interested.

Bound functions

Since a function is a considered to be an expression in JavaFX, it can be bound to a variable (similar to a code block binding, see *Using Binding and Triggers to Update Variables*).

```
var f = 10;
bound function increaseIt(a:Number):Number {
  a + f;
}
var x = 5;
def y = bind increaseIt(x);
```

When a function is defined as being bound, any change to values inside the function block (including its parameters) will cause an update to the binding variable. Here, whenever variable `f` or `x` changes, the value of `y` is updated automatically.

The run() function

JavaFX offers a way to define a script file's **main entry point** using the special script-level function `run()`. If you place the following in a script file:

```
function run() {
    println ("I am always called!");
}
```

When you execute the script, the `run()` function will be executed as the starting point of the script by the JavaFX runtime. This similar to having the `public static void main(String[] args)` method in Java.

When you create a script file with script-level code without `run()`, the compiler creates one for you and places your script's code inside of it. As such, your script seems to execute top to bottom. However, when you provide your own `run()`, that is no longer the case. The JavaFX runtime will only call whatever code is inside of the `run()` function.

See also

- ▶ *Creating and using JavaFX classes*
- ▶ *Declaring and using variables in JavaFX*
- ▶ *Using binding and triggers to update variables*

Integrating your JavaFX code with Java

JavaFX is built directly on top of the **Java Virtual Machine** (**JVM**). Therefore, your JavaFX code has access to the entire Java ecosystem including all of the standard Java libraries such as IO, JDBC, XML, Swing, and so on. Any compiled Java code accessible on the class path can be called from within a JavaFX script. This recipe covers the techniques required to integrate JavaFX and Java code together.

Getting ready

This section explore integration techniques between JavaFX and Java. You should have familiarity with the Java language, its libraries, or have the ability to create your own classes or libraries to be called from JavaFX.

How to do it...

The easiest way to see Java and JavaFX interoperate is to create an instance of a Java object and invoke a method on the instance from within JavaFX. Let's go through an example. You can see the full code listing in package `ch01/source-code/src/java`.

First create and compile this simple class:

```
public class JavaObject {
  private String name;
  public JavaObject(String n){
    name = n;
  }
  public void printReverse() {
    for(int i = name.length()-1; i >= 0; i--){
      System.out.print (name.charAt(i));
    }
    System.out.println();
  }
}
```

Now create a JavaFX script which creates an instance of `JavaObject` and invoke the the `printReverse()` method on the class.

```
var javaObject = new JavaObject("Hello World!");
javaObject.printReverse();
```

How it works...

Java classes and JavaFX classes are binary-compatible. When you compile your JavaFX classes, the JavaFX compiler creates a Java class file (a.class extension file). There are three points that should be made regarding the code snippet in this recipe:

1. Similar to Java, JavaFX script supports the `new` operator when creating a new object instance. This makes it easy to instantiate objects written in Java from within JavaFX.

> While JavaFX objects can be instantiated using Object Literal Notation and the `new` operator, Java objects can only be instantiated with the new operator.

2. The type inference engine will automatically determine the type of the assignment using the Java object's type.
3. Once you have access to the Java object instance, you may invoke any public members on that object.

There is more...

In JavaFX, not only can you instantiate pure Java classes, you can also implement Java interfaces directly. Using this mechanism, you can achieve two-way integration between Java and JavaFX. Again, the full listing of the code presented here can be found in package `ch01/source-code/src/java`.

Implementing a Java interface in JavaFX

The steps required to implement a Java interface in JavaFX are simple. You first create a JavaFX class which extends the interface. Then, you provide JavaFX functions which implement methods defined in the interface, as given the following Java interface:

```
interface JavaInterface {
   int add(int num1, int num2);
}
```

You can create JavaFX script with the following implementation:

```
public class JavaInterfaceImpl extends JavaInterface {
    override function add(num1, num2) {
        num1 + num2;
    }
}
public function run() {
    var adder = JavaInterfaceImpl { }
    println(adder.add(1, 2));
}
```

Note that in JavaFX, the `extends` keyword is used to implement the interface instead of `implements` as in Java.

Note that there are other ways to achieve integration between Java and JavaFX. The rules vary depending on the level of integration you are seeking:

1. **Type integration**—using Java types from JavaFX, as shown in this recipe.
2. **Framework integration**—for example, calling Swing components from JavaFX.
3. **API integration**—wrapping native Java libraries within JavaFX classes to expose them as JavaFX components

See also

▸ *Creating and using JavaFX classes*
▸ *Declaring and using variables in JavaFX*

Creating and using JavaFX sequences

JavaFX sequences can be described as being analogous to arrays in other languages. Imagine that you want to keep track of a group of items of the same type (say a list of numbers, for instance). You can use a sequence to store that list of items and manipulate the list with operations such as **insert**, **query**, and item **removal**. This section looks at how to create and work with JavaFX sequences.

Getting ready

You should be familiar with the concepts of array, list, and map data types. These are common types found in all popular languages. They are designed to function as a container of other values of arbitrary types.

How to do it...

A sequence type is declared using a non-sequence type followed the square brackets "[ ]". Below are some literal declarations of sequences. You can get full listing of the code from `ch01/source-code/src/javafx/SequenceType.fx` and `Sequence.fx`.

```
var numbers:Number[] = [10.0,5.6,12.3,0.44];
var numbers2 = [0,2,3,4,5,6,7,8];
var notes:String[] = ["Avion","Airplane"];
var timespans = [5s,3m,100s,5m];
var misc = [2,4.0,"messages", 5m];
```

How it works...

Sequence types represent a collection of other types in JavaFX. Sequences provide a flat (depth of one) container where you store references to other objects. A sequence is a first-class type in JavaFX. Therefore, it has a return type and can participate in expressions.

JavaFX supports a initialization of sequence types using literal declaration which provides a more natural way of representing the sequence. The literal expression for the sequence shows each item in the sequence separated by a comma as shown below:

```
var numbers:Number[] = [10.0,5.6,12.3,0.44];
```

The type inference engine will attempt to determine the type of the sequence variable based on the types of the items within the square brackets.

If all items within the bracket of the literal declaration are of the same type, the variable is coerced into a sequence of that type. For instance, the following example, variable `numbers2` is of type `Integer[]`:

```
var numbers2 = [0,2,3,4,5,6,7,8];
```

If items within the brackets are of different types, the inference engine will coerce the variable to be of type `Object[]`. In the following code snippet, variable `misc` will be of type `Object[]` and can receive member of any type:

```
var misc = [2,4.0,"messages", 5m];
```

Similar to Java arrays, items in a sequence are referenced using a zero-based positional index. Sequence items are stored in order they are added (or declared) as shown in the snippet below from `ch01/source-code/src/javafx/Sequence.fx`.

```
var q1 = ["Jan", "Feb", "Mar"];
println (q1[0]);
println (q1[1]);
println (q1[2]);
```

There is more...

Sequences come with several other important features worth mentioning here. Although the literal representations of sequences looks like an array, that is where the similarity ends. Sequences support several data management operations such as insert, union, query, and delete. As you will see below, sequence expressions can also be used as generators in JavaFX loops. The code samples are from script file `ch01/source-code/src/javafx/Sequence.fx`.

Sequence operators

JavaFX sequences support several operators:

sizeof—operators return the size when applied to a sequence.

```
sizeof [1,2,3,4];
```

Comparison—JavaFX sequences can be tested for deep equality. This means that two sequences are the same if they are of the same size and contain the same items. The statement below will print `true`

```
println([1,2,3,4] == [4,3,2,1])
```

Reverse—this operator automatically reverses the order in which items are referenced in a sequence.

```
println(reverse ["Jan", "Feb", "Mar", "Apr");
```

Sequence operations

JavaFX sequences also support operations to manipulate sequences and sequence items directly.

Insert Operation—as the name implies, this operation inserts item(s) into a given sequence. The following example shows all of the supported form of `insert`.

```
var months = ["Jan"];
insert "May" into months;
insert ["Mar","Apr"] before months[1];
insert "Feb" after months[0];
```

Besides the `into` directive, note that the insert operation support a `before` and `after` clause which specifies the location (index) where the item is to be inserted.

Union—sequences can be nested using literal declaration to create new lists:

```
var q1 = ["Jan", "Feb", "Mar"];
var h1 = [q1, ["Apr", "May", "Jun"]];
```

Delete Operation—the `delete` operation removes items from a given sequence. The following example shows the supported forms of delete.

```
var months = ["Jan", "Feb", "Mar", "Apr", "May"];
delete "May" from months;
delete months[3];
```

It is critical to understand that sequences are immutable, meaning that the values in a sequence do not change. Rather, any modification to a sequence (insert, delete, and so on) generates a new sequence object to reflect the modification desired.

When deleting by value (that is, `delete "May" from months`), all items of same value will be removed from the sequence.

Sequence slices

Sequence slice notations are used to generate subsets of larger sequences. Given this sequence

```
var months = ["Jan", "Feb", "Mar", "Apr", "May", "Jun"];
```

Here are some slice operations supported by JavaFX:

- `months[1..4]`—returns a sequence `["Feb", "Mar", "Apr", "May"]`
- `months[0..<3]`—returns sequence `[ "Jan", "Feb", "Mar"]`
- `months[3..]`—returns sequence `["Apr", "May", "Jun"]`
- `months[0..<]`—returns sequence `["Jan", "Feb", "Mar", "Apr", "May"]`

Sequence Projection—you can use constraint expressions to project sub-sequences on a given sequence using format `sequence[x | {Boolean expression}]`. This notation reads as "select all element x where the Boolean expression is true".

```
:
months[m|m.startsWith("M")]
```

The above code returns sequence `["Mar", "May"]` from `var months` declared previously. This expression creates slices based on given arbitrary Boolean condition. It reads as "for all item m in months where m starts with M."

Sequence loop query

The loop structure is used to query elements in sequences to create subsets based on conditional expressions. The general format is:

```
for (x0 in seq0 [where {Boolean expression}][, queryn]){}
```

The loop expression can use a `where` clause along with a Boolean expression to filter down to specific elements to build the subset. A simple example is:

```
var points = [1,2,3,4,5,6,7,8,9,10,11,12,13,14];
var evenPoints = for(n in points where n mod 2 == 0) {n}
println (evenPoints);
```

In the previous code, the loop generates a new sequence with only even members from the original sequence, [2, 4, 6, 8, 10, 12, 14], using the where clause to specify a selection expression.

Also notice you can add more than one query in the loop expression where the result is a Cartesian product of all subsets expressed in each query. For instance, the following will produce 14 elements

```
var doublePoints = for(n in points where n mod 2 == 0,
      i in [2,4]){
  n * i
}
println (doublePoints);
```

This code loops over two sequences; the first sequence contains all even members of the original points variable declared previously; the other is a two-member sequence containing 2 and 4, the loop generates new sequence [4, 8, 8, 16, 12, 24, 16, 32, 20, 40, 24, 48, 28, 56].

Working with JavaFX String

String is a fundamental value type in JavaFX. Similar to Java and other languages on the JVM, the String type is used to represent text literals within a single or double quotes. Unlike Java, however, JavaFX strings have additional capabilities which will be explored in this section.

Getting ready

You should be familiar with the notion of string literals and expressions.

How to do it...

We have already seen how to use String types in other recipes. When creating a String, you simply create a literal or expression to represent the string's content, and use the curly braces to embed expressions as shown below. The full listing for this code can be found in ch01/source-code/src/javafx/StringDemo.fx.

```
var str1:String = "Hello World.";
var str2 = "Goodbye forever";
var title = "King";
println ("The {title} has arrived!");

var evens = [0, 2, 4, 6, 8];
println("What are the odds {for(d in evens) "{d + 1} "}");

var amount = 445234.66;
println ("Your house is worth ${%,.2f amount}");
```

How it works...

Similar to other types, a string can be declared with a literal representation, participate in expressions, and hold a value. The previous snippet shows the literal declaration of a string. Variable `str2` is coerced by the type-inference engine into a String type implicitly.

One of the interesting features of the String type in JavaFX is its ability to have embedded expressions (similar to other templating languages) enclosed in curly braces. In the previous code snippet, `println ("The {title} has arrived!")` will print the string with the value of the variable `title` embedded in it.

You can also have complex expressions embedded in the string, as is shown from the code snippet `println("What are the odds {for(d in evens) "{d + 1} "}")` from the recipe. The embedded expression contains a loop that traverses elements from variable `evens` and outputs the result from the nested string `"{d + 1} "` with each pass, producing new string `What are the odds 1 3 5 7 9`.

The JavaFX Sting type has the ability to process string formatting expressions based on Java's `java.util.Formatter` class. In the previous code snippet, we used format expression `%,.2f` to format the variable `amount` which displays `Your house is worth $445,234.66`. You can find information about supported format expressions at `http://java.sun.com/javase/6/docs/api/java/util/Formatter.html`.

There is more...

Before we leave the discussion on String, it's worth taking a look at localization. In JavaFX, the localization mechanism is an extension of the string expression.

Using JavaFX localization

To mark a String literal as a localized string, simply prefix the string with double hashes. This causes JavaFX to substitute the string with a localized string, if one is found, from a locale properties file.

To illustrate, let's look at an example. The code for this example is found in package `ch01/source-code/src/locale`.

Create a JavaFX script file with the following content:

```
var msg1 = ##"Lift the cover";
var msg2 = ##[red button]"Press the red button to destroy";
println (msg1);
println (msg2);
```

Save the file as `Localization.fx` and compile. Now, create a text file named `Localization_fr.fxproperties` and type in the following:

```
"Lift the cover"="Soulevez le couvercle"
"red button"="Appuyez sur le bouton rouge pour détruire"
```

Notice that JavaFX can use either the actual string or a string key (`red button`) to do the substitution for the localized string. When the code is compiled and executed, the output is:

```
Soulevez le couvercle
Appuyez sur le bouton rouge pour détruire
```

The strings are substituted automatically by the JavaFX runtime with their French translation. If no properties file is found for the locale, JavaFX defaults to the actual String assigned to the variable.

2
Creating JavaFX Applications

In this chapter, we will cover the following topics:

- ▶ Building a JavaFX application
- ▶ Drawing simple shapes
- ▶ Creating complex shapes using Path
- ▶ Creating shapes with constructive area geometry
- ▶ Drawing letter shapes using the Text class
- ▶ Handling user input
- ▶ Arranging your nodes on stage
- ▶ Making your scripts modular
- ▶ Creating your own custom node
- ▶ Controlling your application's window style
- ▶ Going full-screen

Introduction

JavaFX Script was designed with the sole intent of being a language to create graphically-rich user interfaces. Instead of the traditional imperative and dense boilerplate code (as found in Java and other general purpose languages), JavaFX adopted an intuitive and declarative scripting-style that lets developers quickly create complex graphical components with simplified constructs.

JavaFX benefited from years of experience that engineers at Sun Microsystems (now Oracle) gained creating desktop platforms such as Swing. Therefore, the JavaFX framework comes loaded with features and functionalities that make it ready for production-grade deployment.

In this chapter, we are going to explore how to use fundamental building blocks to create functional JavaFX applications. This chapter covers the following topics:

- ▶ **Shapes**—the most basic representation of a visual element is the geometric shape. You will learn how to create simple and complex shapes using `Shape` classes.

- ▶ **Text**—besides geometric shapes, JavaFX facilitates the rendition of text as graphical nodes as well. You will learn how to render text on the stage using the `Text` class.

- ▶ **User input events**—all visual components can receive user input through the mouse and keyboard. You will see how to handle input events using event handler functions.

- ▶ **Application organization**—as your application grows in complexity, it is imperative that you modularize your code into logical components. We will look at code organization using packages, member access modifiers, and other modularization techniques.

Building a JavaFX application

The first chapter of the book introduced you to the fundamentals of the JavaFX language. Now, you are ready to start building your own JavaFX desktop application. In this recipe, we will look at the minimal requirements to build a runnable / JavaFX application.

Getting ready

In order to write your application, you will need to use an IDE or your favorite text editor. Refer to *Chapter 1, Getting Started with JavaFX*, to find out how to download and get started with JavaFX with the NetBeans or Eclipse IDE.

How to do it...

The listing below shows how to create a simple, yet functional JavaFX application that uses several components of the JavaFX application framework. The full listing of the code is available at `ch02/source-code/src/application/SimpleApplication.fx`.

```
import javafx.stage.Stage;
import javafx.scene.Scene;
import javafx.scene.paint.Color;
import javafx.scene.text.Font;
import javafx.scene.shape.Rectangle;
import javafx.scene.text.Text;
```

```
Stage {
  title : "JavaFX App"
  width: 300
  height: 200
   visible: true
   scene: Scene {
      fill:Color.SILVER
      width:320
      height:220
        content: [
          Rectangle {
            x: 100 y: 50
            width: 100 height: 100
            arcWidth: 10
            arcHeight : 10
            fill: Color.RED
          },
          Text {
                content: "JavaFX"
                x:110 y:60
                fill: Color.WHITE
                font:Font {size: 16}
          }
        ]
    }
}
```

When you run this code, you should see a window similar to what is shown in the next screenshot:

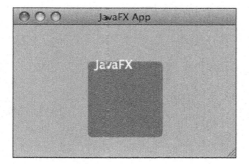

How it works...

Before you can get your application to run, you must import the correct packages into your script. To display visual objects on the screen, you must, at a minimum, have the following two packages:

- ► `javafx.stage.Stage`
- ► `javafx.scene.Scene`

These packages contain the base classes `Stage` and `Scene` that are required to create a windowed area to display visual content of a JavaFX application. Other packages used in this recipe include the following:

- ► `javafx.scene.paint.Color`—the `Color` class is used to apply color to visual components when rendered. The paint package also contains effects such as linear and radial gradients (see *Chapter 3, Transformation, Animations, and Effects*).

- ► `javafx.scene.text.Font`—this class specifies a font and its attributes used for the `Text` component (see next bullet). The text package contains all other supporting text-related classes used for rendering textual shapes.

- ► `javafx.scene.text.Text`—the `Text` class is used to render text as shapes on the screen. The text package contains all other supporting text-related classes used for rendering textual shapes.

- ► `javafx.scene.shape.Rectangle`—this class is part of the larger collection of shapes offered by the Shape API. It represents a rectangular shape.

Decomposing the application

The JavaFX framework expects application content to be organized as a hierarchical stack of Stage → Scene → Node (Tree), with Stage being the outer-most container. The next image shows how these high-level components are organized on the desktop.

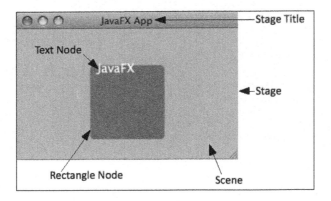

Let's explore each of these high-level items shown in the previous image:

- **Stage**—this component represents the outer-most visible window in a JavaFX desktop application. It defines the application's main physical window and serves as a container for all other graphical components that make up the application. The Stage exposes several useful properties that are used in the previous code sample:

  - `title:String`—this is the title of the stage. In a windowed-application, this is the title displayed in the title bar of the top-level window.

  - `width:Number`—this property specifies the initial width of the application's window.

  - `height:Number`—this property specifies the initial height of the application's window.

  - `visible:Boolean`—this property indicates whether the window is visible. The default is visible.

  - `x:Number` and `y:Number`—by default the the JavaFX application framework will center the application window on the device screen. You can however, specify the location of the window.

  - `scene:Scene`—this property is used to plug in an instance of the Scene class to the stage. The scene is where all visible content to be rendered is placed (see description of `Scene` next).

- **Scene**—this class represents the canvas where visible content will be drawn. Content to be rendered on the scene is logically grouped in a tree-like structure called the **Scene Graph** (see *Nodes* next) and is attached to the Scene's `content` property. The `Scene` class exposes several useful properties when building the application including:

  - `fill:Color`—this property specifies a `Color` instance used for the scene. As of version 1.2 of the SDK, the default color for the stage is white.

  - `height:Number, width:Number`—by default, the scene inherits the stage's dimension. However, you can use these properties to override the dimensions of the stage.

  - `content:Node[]`—this property is of type `Sequence` where one or more scene graphs containing visual objects to be rendered are attached (see *Nodes* next).

- **Nodes** (or **Node Tree**)—these are the visual objects that are added to the scene to be rendered. Nodes are logically grouped in tree-like structures, named scene graphs, where nodes can be either leaf nodes (visual components) with at most one parent, or branch nodes (containers) with many leaf nodes attached.

In the code, we are using two leaf nodes: a **Text Node** and a **Rectangle Node**. JavaFX offers class `Group` which functions as a branch node containing leaf nodes for more complex scene graphs. You can see how to use the `Group` class in the recipe *Creating your own custom node*.

See also

- *Setting up JavaFX for NetBeans*
- *Setting up JavaFX for Eclipse*
- *Declaring and using JavaFX classes*
- *Creating and using JavaFX sequences*

Drawing simple shapes

The JavaFX application framework was designed from the ground up to handle graphical elements. JavaFX provides inherent support for basic geometrical shapes as a first-class API. This recipe shows how to programmatically draw lines, rectangles, circles, and ellipses using the `Shape` APIs found in the `javafx.scene.shape` package.

Getting ready

Before you can draw your shapes using JavaFX, you must know how to create a basic JavaFX application and know how to add content to the application's scene. To refresh your memory, see the first recipe of this chapter, *Building a JavaFX application*.

How to do it...

The following code snippet shows how to draw a line, a rectangle, a circle, and an ellipse on the screen. You can get the full listing of the code from `ch002/source-code/src/shapes/SimpleShapes.fx`.

```
def spacer = 100;
Stage {
    title: "Simple Shapes!"
    width: 500
    height: 300
    x: 100;
    y: 200
    scene: Scene {
        content: [
            Line {
                startX: 10
                startY: 10
```

```
                endX: 10 + spacer
                endY: 10 + spacer
                strokeWidth: 5.0
                stroke: Color.BLUE
                strokeLineCap: StrokeLineCap.BUTT
            },
            Rectangle {
                x: spacer + 50
                y: spacer + 20
                width: spacer + 20
                height: spacer
                arcWidth: 20
                arcHeight: 20
                fill: Color.RED
                strokeWidth: 5.0
                stroke: Color.BLUE
            },
            Circle {
                centerX: spacer + 300
                centerY: 50
                radius: 50
                fill: Color.GREEN
                strokeWidth: 1.0
                stroke: Color.BLACK
            },
            Ellipse {
                centerX: spacer + 300
                centerY: 150
                radiusX: 100
                radiusY: 20
                fill: Color.RED
                strokeWidth: 5.0
                stroke: Color.BLUE
            }
        ]
    }
}
```

The code draws a line, rectangle, circle, and ellipse at different locations on the application's window as shown in the following screenshot:

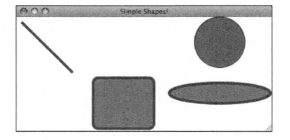

How it works...

Creating shapes using the `Shape` API is a straightforward process. You simply declare an instance of the `shape` class that you want to draw, specify its properties, and then place it as a node inside the stage's scene so that it can be rendered. Let's see how the shapes presented in this recipe work:

- ► Line—when drawing a line, you declare an instance of the `Line` class specifying, at minimum, the line's starting coordinates with properties `startX` and `startY` and the ending coordinates using properties `endX` and `endY`.

  ```
  Line {
      startX:10 startY: 10
      endX: 10 endY: 10
  }
  ```

- ► Rectangle—for drawing a rectangle, you use the `Rectangle` class from the `Shape` API. At a minimum, you must specify the coordinates of the upper-left corner using properties `x` and `y`, and the size of the rectangle using properties `width` and `height`:

  ```
  Rectangle {
      x: 50 y: 20
      width: 300 height: 200
      arcWidth: 20 arcHeight : 20
  }
  ```

  `arcWidth` and `arcHeight`—optionally, you can use these properties to specify vertical and horizontal diameters for rounded corners of the rectangle.

- ► Circle—to draw a circle in JavaFX, you declare an instance of the `Circle` class. You must, at a minimum, specify the circle's center coordinates using `centerX` and `centerY` properties and the circle's radius using the `radius` property. When placing a circle on stage, keep in mind that the circle's center is used as its point of reference. Be sure to adjust your coordinates to avoid drawing circles partially off-screen.

  ```
  Circle {
      centerX: 50 centerY: 50
      radius: 50
  }
  ```

- ► Ellipse—both ellipse and circle work similarly. To draw the ellipse, you declare an instance of the `Ellipse` class specifying the x and y coordinates of the center using properties `centerX` and `centerY`. Additionally, you must specify the horizontal and vertical length of the radius for the ellipse using properties `radiusX` and `radiusY`:

  ```
  Ellipse {
      centerX: 100 centerY: 150
      radiusX: 100 radiusY: 20
  }
  ```

There's more...

There are other basic, though irregular, geometric shapes available from the JavaFX Shape toolbox. `Polyline` and `Polygon` classes can be used to create shapes by connecting line segments together. The `Arc` class creates circular shapes by specifying points on angular path. Let's take a closer look at them.

Polyline and Polygon

The `Polyline` (and the `Polygon`) class creates shapes by specifying a collection of coordinates to create line segments that are automatically connected. The `Polygon` class works the same way. However, the `Polygon` class will also close the shape after the last segment is drawn and fill it with a color (default is black). The `Polygon` code segment given next draws a triangle, as shown in the figure alongside. The full listing of the code can be found in `ch002/source-code/src/shapes/PolygonShape.fx`.

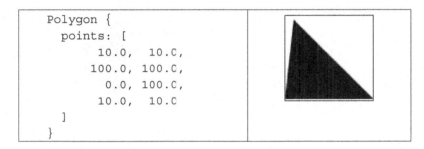

```
Polygon {
    points: [
          10.0,   10.0,
         100.0,  100.0,
           0.0,  100.0,
          10.0,   10.0
    ]
}
```

Arc

The `Arc` shape class draws an arc by specifying the center coordinates, vertical/horizontal radii, the start angle (in degrees), and the angular length (in degrees) of the arc. The arc shape is automatically closed and filled in with a specified color (the default is black). The next code segment draws the arc shown in the figure alongside (Pacman anyone?). The full listing of the code can be found in `ch002/source-code/src/shapes/ArcShape.fx`.

```
Arc {
    centerX: 300   centerY: 50
    radiusX: 50 radiusY: 50
    startAngle: 45
    length: 270
    type: ArcType.ROUND
}
```

You can control how the arc is closed using the property `type:ArcType`. Supported arc types include:

- ► `ArcType.OPEN`—this is the default type where no segments connect the arc ends
- ► `ArcType.ROUND`—this type draws a line segment from the start to the center and from the center to the end of the arc (see previous image)
- ► `ArcType.CHORD`—a straight line connects the start and end of the arc

Bézier curves

Finally, the Shape API offers two Bézier curve classes: **QuadCurve** and **CubicCurve**. The `QuadCurve` class represents a quadratic Bézier curve with control points specified by properties `controlX` and `controlY`; the curve's endpoints are specified by properties `startX`, `startY`, `endX`, and `endY` (see the figure alongside). The full listing of the code can be found in `ch02/source-code/src/shapes/QuadCurveShape.fx`.

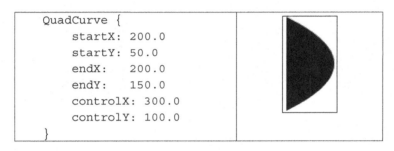

The `CubicCurve` class represents a cubic Bézier curve with the two control points represented by properties `controlX1`, `controlY1`, `controlX2`, `controlY2`; the curve's endpoints are specified by properties `startX`, `startY`, `endX`, and `endY` (see next figure). The full source can be found in `ch02/source-code/src/shapes/CubicCurveShape.fx`.

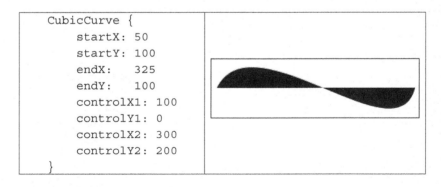

See also

- ► *Creating complex shapes using Path*

Creating complex shapes using Path

The simple geometrical shapes offered by the Shape API may not adequately meet your requirements. JavaFX also offers the **Path API** to simplify the creation of complex and irregular shapes using a step-wise approach of drawing shape segments. In this recipe, you will learn how to use the Path API and its associated classes to create a complex shape.

Getting ready

Before you can draw complex shapes using JavaFX, you must know how to create a basic JavaFX application and how to add content to the application's scene. To refresh your memory, see recipe *Building a JavaFX application* from this chapter. It will also be helpful to review the recipe *Drawing simple shapes* to get an idea of how the Shape API works. To use the Path API, you will need to import classes found in the `javafx.scene.shape` package.

How to do it...

The next code snippet is an example of how to use the Path API to create irregular shapes. You can find the complete listing of this code in `ch002/source-code/src/shapes/PathDrawing.fx`.

```
Stage {
    title: "Path Drawing"
    width: 500
    height: 300
    x:100;
    y:200
    scene: Scene {
      content: [
        Path {
          elements: [
            MoveTo { x: 150  y: 75 },
            ArcTo {x: 200  y: 50
                radiusX:25 radiusY:25 sweepFlag: true}
            MoveTo { x: 200  y: 50 },
            ArcTo {x: 250  y: 50
                radiusX:25 radiusY:25 sweepFlag: true }
            MoveTo { x: 250  y: 50 },
            ArcTo { x: 300  y: 75
                radiusX:25 radiusY:25 sweepFlag: true }
            MoveTo { x: 25  y: 75 },
            HLineTo {x: 425},
            MoveTo { x: 160  y: 85 },
            HLineTo {x: 290},
```

```
        MoveTo { x: 170   y: 95},
        HLineTo {x: 280},
        MoveTo { x: 180   y: 105},
        HLineTo {x: 280},
    ]
  }
]
}
}
```

The previous code segment will draw the image shown in the next screenshot:

<h2>How it works...</h2>

The `Path` class and its associated element classes provide a small domain-specific language (DSL) to express complex shapes programatically. Each path element is represented by a class with name pattern *xxxTo*. The Path element provides an idiom with which to express a drawing action. An action can either move an imaginary pointer to a location on the screen, or it draws a shape that corresponds to a primitive geometrical shape discussed in the recipe *Drawing simple shapes*. The `Path` class serves as a container providing a property called `elements` where path elements are added to the scene graph for rendering.

- `MoveTo`—this path element causes the path context to be set to a coordinate from which all subsequent drawing actions will be taken

- `ArcTo`—this path element creates an arc from the last coordinate to the specified x and y location

- `LineTo`—this path element draws a line from the last coordinate (specified with `MoveTo`) to an x and y location

- `HLineTo`—this path element draws an horizontal line from the last specified x location to the specified location

- `VLineTo`—this path element draws a vertical line from the last specified y position to a newly specified y value

<h2>See also</h2>

- *Building a JavaFX application*
- *Drawing simple shapes*

Creating shapes with constructive area geometry

JavaFX offers a rich set of tools for creating basic and complex shapes. Sometimes, though, those drawing tools alone are not enough to express intricate and delicate shapes. In this recipe, we will show you how to use the notion of constructive geometry to create new shapes from the combination of existing shapes.

Getting ready

The approach covered in this recipe is known as **Constructive Area Geometry (CAG)**. It uses Boolean operations to create new shapes from existing sets of shapes. Given shapes (or sets of shapes) represented by circles A and B, JavaFX supports the following CAG Boolean operations:

Operation	Description	Shape
A OR B (A union B)	Returns the shaded area formed by both shapes A and B.	
A NOT B (A subtract B)	Returns the shaded area calculated by subtracting shape A from B.	
A AND B (A intersect B)	Returns the shaded area created by the intersection of shapes A and B.	

These operations are implemented in JavaFX by classes `ShapeIntersect` and `ShapeSubtract`, found in the package `javafx.scene.shape`. These two classes are container nodes with sequence properties `a:Shape[]` and `b:Shape[]` that represent shape set A and set B used as operands in the geometric operations.

How to do it...

The next code snippet uses `ShapeSubtract` to create a new shape using constructive area geometry to form the dome (see the next figure). You can find the full code in `ch02/source-code/src/shapes/ShapeIntersection.fx`.

1. First, let's define the shapes that will make up the tip of the dome:

```
def c1 = Circle {centerX: 175, centerY:28 radius:25}
def c2 = Circle {centerX: 225, centerY:28 radius:25}
def r1 = Rectangle {x:175 y :25 width:50  height:25}
```

2. Then we define an arc for the bottom of the dome as follows:

```
def a1 = Arc {
    centerX:200
    centerY:149
    radiusX:100
    radiusY:100
    startAngle:0 length:180
    fill:Color.BISQUE
}
```

3. Next, we apply the shape operations using the `ShapeSubtract`.

```
Scene {
    width: w height: h
    fill:Color.RED
    content:[
        ShapeSubtract {a:[r1] b:[c1,c2] fill:Color.BISQUE},
        ShapeSubtract{
          a:a1
          b:[for(i in [0..3]){
              Circle {
                  centerX: 125 + (i*50),
                  centerY:149 radius:17}
              }]
          fill:Color.BISQUE
        }
    ]
}
```

The executed code renders the shape shown in the following figure:

How it works...

When you combine different basic shapes, you can create completely new ones. In this recipe, we used constructive geometry to create the dome in the previous figure. Let's see how it was constructed:

- *Building Blocks*—in the code, we declare a series of basic shapes that will be used to construct the dome. We have circles c1 and c2, rectangle r1, and arc a1.

- *Creating the tip of the dome*—the shape we are looking for can be formed by adjoining two circles (c1 and c2) without overlapping. The pointy area between the two circles is what we are interested in as shown in the next figure (A). The dome's top is created in two steps:

  - First, we create a shape to serve as a mask to provide the non-overlapping area between the two circles. In our example, we create a small rectangle (r1) that overlaps the area between the circles as shown in the next figure (B .

  - Next, we apply the Boolean expression r1 NOT (c1 AND c2) to create the shape needed. We use an instance of ShapeSubtract where property a = r1 and property b = [c1,c2]. This produces the curvy tip shape as shown in the next figure (C).

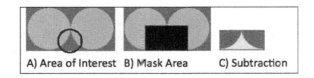

A) Area of Interest B) Mask Area   C) Subtraction

- *Shaping the base of the dome*—the dome rendered by the code shows four semi-circle cutouts at the base of the dome. This is accomplished by dynamically drawing four circles that are subtracted from arc a1. Here again, we use the ShapeSubtract class with property a = a1 and property b = [Circle1, Circle2,Circle3,Circle4].

There's more...

Here is some useful information to keep in mind when working with shape operations:

- `ShapeIntersect` is a diminutive operation where the resulting area is smaller than the original shapes. This will yield some interesting results when working with large number of shapes.

- Both `ShapeIntersect` and `ShapeSubtract` will automatically apply a union operation to all shapes assigned to sequence property a. You can omit property b when you want to apply the union operation.

- `ShapeIntersect` and `ShapeSubtract` both generate new shape objects. Therefore, color, effects, animation, transformation, and binding applied to the original members of the sets will be lost and will not be applied to the newly generated shape.

See also

- *Creating and using JavaFX sequences*
- *Drawing simple shapes*

Drawing letter shapes using the Text class

Beside geometric shapes (see the recipe *Drawing simple shapes*), one of the most fundamental node types available in JavaFX is the **Text** node. This node is used to draw letter shapes on the screen that can be manipulated just like other node types offered by the JavaFX platform. In this recipe, you will learn how to work with the `Text` class to display text on your application's screen.

Getting ready

Before you can draw text using JavaFX, you must know how to create a basic JavaFX application and know how to add content to the application's scene. To refresh your memory, see the recipe *Building a JavaFX application*. To display text, you will need to import the `Text` class found in the package `javafx.scene.text`. That package also contains additional classes to support text rendering in JavaFX including `Font`, `FontWeight`, `TextAlignment`, and `TextOrigin`.

How to do it...

When drawing text, you simply create a text node and attach it to the scene as shown in the next listing. You can get full listing of the code in `ch02/source-code/src/text/SimpleTextDemo.fx`.

```
Stage {
    title: "Text Demo"
    scene: Scene {
        width: 400
        height: 200
        content: [
            Text {
                x:50 y: 25
                wrappingWidth: 300
                font: Font {size: 28 name:"Arial Black" }
                fill:Color.BROWN
                letterSpacing:0.1
                oblique:true
                content: "This is a simple text demo."
            }
        ]
    }
}
```

This code snippet would render text content oblique as shown in the following figure:

This is a simple text demo.

How it works...

The Text class is a visual node intended to render textual shapes in the scene graph. It provides powerful low-level properties and behaviors, which afford developers control over raw text display. Let us explore the text properties used in this recipe:

- content:String—this is the actual text that will be displayed when the scene graph is rendered.

- font:Font—this is an instance of the Font class which is used to specify the font used for the rendered text.

- fill:Color—the fill property specifies the color or effect that is applied to the rendered font.

- Stroke:Color—this property controls the color of the outline stroke of the letter drawn. You can further control the stroke by applying property strokeWidth:Number to specify the size of the outer stroke around the letter.

- letterSpacing:Number—this property specifies the space increment between letters.

- oblique:Boolean—when set to true, this property attempts to algorithmically render the font italicized, whether there is an available italic version of the font or not.

There's more...

There are some interesting aspects of text rendering with which you should familiarize yourself before you leave this recipe.

Text origin

Unlike other node types, the text node has a variable coordinate system which can be changed dynamically to accommodate where the text is rendered relative to its y coordinate using the `textOrigin:TextOrigin` property. The following code snippet shows how this works. You can get the full list in `ch02/source-code/src/text/TextOriginDemo.fx`.

```
Line{startX:50 startY:0 endX:50 endY:200 stroke:Color.SILVER}
Line{startX:0 startY:25 endX:400 endY:25 stroke:Color.SILVER}
Text {
    x:50 y: 25
    font: Font {size: 20 name:"Arial Black"}
    fill:Color.BROWN
    textOrigin: TextOrigin.TOP
    content: "This text uses TextOrigin.TOP"
}
```

This text uses
TextOrigin.BASELINE

This text uses
TextOrigin.TOP

This text uses
TextOrigin.BOTTOM

The `TextOrigin` class includes the following options:

- `TextOrigin.BASELINE`—with this option (default), the coordinate system for the text originates from the bottom left-hand corner of the bounding box for the first line of the text. The bottom of all non-descending letters are drawn along the y coordinate as shown in the previous figure.

- `TextOrigin.TOP`—the reference coordinate for the text originates from the upper left-hand corner of the bounding box of the text, rendering the tallest letter of the first line below the y coordinate as shown in the previous figure.

▶ `TextOrigin.BOTTOM`—with this option, the reference coordinate system for the text starts from the lower left-hand side corner of the bounding box of last line rendering the descending tail of the most descending letter along the `y` coordinate as shown in the previous figure.

Text wrapping

By default when you use the `Text` class, it will render your text in a single line. If you want to render the text in multiple lines, you have two options:

▶ *New Line Character*—The text content can include the new line character '\n' to force the text to explicitly wrap to the next line. When you use this approach, the bounding box is as wide as the longest text segment.

▶ `wrappingWidth:Number` *property*—the `wrappingWidth` property allows you to specify the width of the bounding box for the text. The text will be wrapped at word boundaries at the specified width as shown in the output for the previous code snippet.

Text alignment

With the text `textAlignment` property, you can influence the text flow when the text is rendered. The next code snippet shows how to center the text within its bounding box. You can see all alignment options shown in `ch02/source-code/src/text/TextAlignmentDemo.fx`.

```
Text {
    x:50 y: 25
    wrappingWidth:300
    content: "This is a simple text demo."
        "It shows how the text is automatically"
        "centered using TextAlignment.CENTER"
    textAlignment:TextAlignment.CENTER
}
```

The code renders the text as shown:

This is a simple text demo.It shows how the text is automatically centered using TextAlignment.CENTER

Other supported alignments include `TextAlignment.LEFT`, `TextAlignment.RIGHT`, and `TextAlignment.JUSTIFY`.

Embolden your font

In its declarative form, `Font{name:"Arial Black" size:12}`, you have to depend on the name of the font to indicate the font's weight. However, you have the option of using `Font.font(name:String, weight:FontWeight, size:Number)` function to create an instance of the font where the font-weight can be specified as follows:

```
Text {
    x:50 y: 25
    font: Font.font("Arial", FontWeight.BOLD, 28)
    content: "This is a simple text demo."
}
```

Using the function to create the font, you are able to specify the font's name, the font's weight, and the size of the font in point. The `FontWeight` class is used to indicate the boldness of the type used to render the font.

Locating fonts

JavaFX is capable of using *True Type* fonts embedded in the JavaFX application or hosted on the target device. The JavaFX runtime will try to first find fonts by searching in the application's embedded fonts, followed by a search in the JavaFX's installed fonts, and then a final searching within the device-installed fonts. If the font is still not found, JavaFX will default to the runtime's default font. You can query fonts that are available for use in JavaFX using the following methods:

- ▸ `Font.getFontNames():String[]`—returns all fonts reachable by the JavaFX runtime.

- ▸ `Font.getFontNames(familyName:String):Object[]`—returns fonts that share the specified family name.

See also

- ▸ *Drawing simple shapes*

Handling user input

As a platform designed to build rich user interface applications, JavaFX provides many ways for users to interact with your applications. In order to implement user interactions in your applications, at a minimum, you will have to capture key presses on the keyboard and gestures from pointing devices. This recipe shows you how to capture keyboard and mouse events.

Getting ready

When a key from the keyboard is pressed or a mouse event occurs, the JavaFX application framework will generate input events information stored in instances of `KeyEvent` and `MouseEvent` respectively. These classes are found in the package `javafx.scene.input`.

Input events are sent to nodes attached to your scene graph. Therefore, in order to receive input events, you must have at least one node added to your scene. Review the recipe *Building a JavaFX application* for background information on how to do that.

How to do it...

To demonstrate how to handle user input, the abbreviated code given next creates a virtual terminal that captures user's keyboard input (think of a command shell). The full code listing for the code can be found in `ch02/source-code/src/input/KeyboardMouseEvent.fx`.

```
def w = 500;
def h = 300;
var text = Text {
    x: 10, y: 10
    fill: Color.LIMEGREEN
    font: Font {name: "Courier New" size: 12 }
    wrappingWidth: w  - 100
};
var rect: Rectangle = Rectangle {
    x: 0 y: 0
    width: w height: h
    onMouseClicked: function (e: MouseEvent): Void {
        rect.requestFocus();
        if (text.content.length() > 0) {
            text.content = text.content.substring(0,
                text.content.length() - 1);
        }
    }

    onKeyPressed: function (e: KeyEvent): Void {
        if (e.code.equals(KeyCode.VK_BACK_SPACE)
            or e.code.equals(KeyCode.VK_DELETE)) {
            if(text.content.length() > 0){
                text.content = text.content.substring(0,
                    text.content.length() - 1)
            }
        }else if (e.code.equals(KeyCode.VK_SPACE)){
            text.content = "{text.content} ";
```

```
        }else if (e.code.equals(KeyCode.VK_ENTER)){
            text.content = "{text.content}\n";
        }else{
            text.content = "{text.content}{e.text}";
        }
    }
};

rect.requestFocus();
```

When the application runs, you get a window that displays your text as you type, as shown in the next figure:

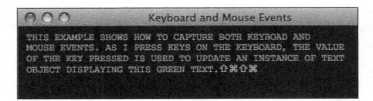

How it works...

The code in this recipe shows you how to set up a visual node in the scene graph to receive input events from the keyboard and the mouse. In the application, a black-filled rectangle receives both keyboard and mouse input events, which works as follows:

- The Text object—as the rectangle instance receives keyboard input events, the value of the character pressed is used to update the content of text.

- The Rectangle—as mentioned, the Rectangle is the node set up to receive input events. Calling the Rectangle's requestFocus() method causes it to receive keyboard events. For our example, we are using two event handling properties:

    - onKeyPressed:function(:KeyEvent)—the function assigned to this property is fired every time a key on the keyboard is pressed and receives an instance of class KeyEvent as an argument. KeyEvent contains all of the information captured about the key pressed. In this example, the function is used to process the pressed key and update the content of the text variable.

    - onMousePressed:function(:MouseEvent)—this function is invoked whenever the mouse button is pressed and receives an instance of MouseEvent as an argument. In this example, when the user clicks on the rectangle, it calls requestFocus() on the rectangle and allows it to receive keyboard events and update the text instance.

There's more...

All nodes can listen for a multitude of event types. Beside the events shown in the recipe, the next list shows additional event handlers that are common to all nodes. The name of the handler gives a hint on how and when the event may be fired.

- ▸ *Keyboard*—onKeyReleased and onKeyTyped
- ▸ *Mouse*—onMouseClicked, onMouseDragged, onMouseEntered, onMouseExited, onMouseMoved onMouseReleased, and onMouseWheelMoved.

See also

- ▸ *Creating a JavaFX application*

Arranging your nodes on stage

As your application grows in complexity, so you will find it tedious and (most importantly) imprecise to arrange your visual nodes directly using their x and y coordinates. This recipe shows you how to use JavaFX's built-in support for layout managers to arrange visual components on the screen.

Getting ready

As of version 1.2, JavaFX comes with several layout managers and each provides a different way of arranging visual nodes on the screen. You will find the layout managers in package javafx. scene.layout. Of course, you must know how to create an application in order to use a layout manager. See the recipe *Building a JavaFX application* for background information.

How to do it...

The following code snippet uses the the HBox and along with the VBox layout managers. The full code listing is available in ch02/source-code/src/layout/LayoutDemo.fx.

```
Scene {
    content: HBox {
        width: 400
        spacing: 20
        hpos: HPos.LEADING
        content: [
            VBox {
                spacing: 5 nodeHPos: HPos.CENTER
                content: [
                    Polygon {
                        fill: Color.MAGENTA
```

```
                        points: [
                            10.0, 10.0,
                            100.0, 100.0,
                            0.0, 100.0,
                            10.0, 10.0
                        ]
                    },
            Text { font: Font { size: 10 }
                    content: "3-sided Polygon" }
            ]
        },
        VBox {
            spacing: 5 nodeHPos: HPos.CENTER
            content: [
                    Arc {
                        radiusX: 45
                        radiusY: 45
                        startAngle: 90
                        length: 270
                        type: ArcType.ROUND
                        fill: Color.RED
                    },
                Text { font: Font { size: 10 }
                        content: "L-shaped red arc" }
            ]
        },
        VBox {
            spacing: 5 nodeHPos: HPos.CENTER
            content: [
                    Circle {
                        centerY: 100
                        radius: 45
                        fill: Color.SILVER
                    },
                Text { font: Font { size: 10 }
                        content: "A silver circle" }
            ]
        }
    ]
}
}
```

When the code is executed, it renders the following screen:

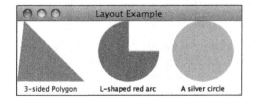

How it works...

The layout manager controls how components are arranged and laid out when rendered. A layout manager affords developers the ability to declaratively arrange nodes without having to worry about positional math and re-flow rules. The components are laid out according to the rules applied by the layout managers.

The code listing for the recipe uses the HBox in conjunction with the VBox layout managers to create the output shown in the previous screenshot. Let's examine how this works.

▶ *Splitting up the scene*—first, the HBox layout manager is used to split the scene horizontally into three cells (see next screenshot). This is done by placing an instance of the HBox class as the content of the Scene. Each item added to the content of the HBox layout manager is placed along the x-axis and is equally spaced (controlled by the spacing property).

▶ *Nesting layout*—the items placed in the HBox content can either be a visual node or another layout manager node (you have got to love scene graph!). This allows us to nest an instance of VBox in each cell of the HBox, as shown in the next screenshot. The VBox lays out its content vertically, and we use it to stack a shape and a text node that describes the shape.

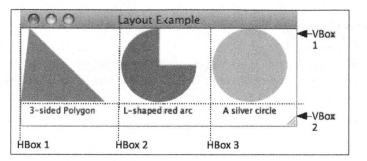

There's more...

JavaFX 1.2 offers several other managers to help developers quickly arrange nodes:

▶ Flow—lays out content vertically or horizontally (depending on the selected orientation). The manager automatically flows to the next column (or row).

▶ Stack—this layout manager stacks its content in z-plane going from back to front.

▶ Tile—lays out its content uniformly vertically or horizontally, where each node receives the same dimension in the tile (think of a HTML table).

Future versions of the platform will surely include more layout managers and options.

See also

▶   *Creating a JavaFX application*

Making your scripts modular

As your code grows in complexity, you will find it necessary to arrange your scripts into well-organized modular structures. This will help your codebase to scale in size to handle organizational complexities. This recipe addresses the facilities and practices available for JavaFX to implement code modularization.

Getting ready

The concepts presented here deal with logical modularity of your code (physical modularity, creating jars, is covered in *Chapter 7, Deployment and Integration*). JavaFX provides high-level abstractions to represent code organization including packages, modules, and classes. If you have written code in other high-level languages, you will be familiar with the concepts presented here. For background information, see `http://en.wikipedia.org/wiki/Modular_programming`.

How to do it...

To illustrate JavaFX modularization, we will create a script module and use its members to show how modules expose their members. The full code listing for this recipe can be found in `ch02/source-code/src/module/FooBarModule.fx`.

1. First, create a script file called `FooModule.fx`.

2. Next, add the members of the module as shown in the next listing:

```
public-read def size = Long.MAX_VALUE;
public var seed = Integer.MAX_VALUE;

class PrivateBar {
    function genId(): Number {
        new Random().nextInt(seed);
    }
}

public class Bar {
    def pb = PrivateBar{};
    public function print(): Void {
```

```
        println("This is a bar with id {pb.genId()}"};
    }
}

class Foo {
    public function print()  Void {
        println("The foo is {size} nibblets big!");
    }
}

public function makeFoo(): Void Foo ( {
    Foo { };
}
```

3. Once you have created the script module, you can reuse the module anywhere in your code. You can see the usage of the module in file `ch02/source-code/src/module/ModuleDemo.fx` as shown next:

```
println ("FooBar seed = {FooBarModule.seed}");
println ("FooBar size = {FooBarModule.size}");
FooBarModule.seed = 200000;

def bar = FooBarModule.Bar{};
bar.print();
FooBarModule.callFoo();
```

How it works...

A **module** is a standalone JavaFX script file that contains definitions for classes, functions, and variables. Let's examine the module presented in this recipe:

▶ **Script-level members**—a module is comprised of both public and script-scoped members, including variable declarations, class definitions, and functions. Public members can be reached by code outside of the module such as variables `size`, `seed`, and class `Bar`. Script-only members (those with *no access modifiers*) can only be accessed by members of the module (such as class `Foo`).

▶ **Class definitions**—classes marked as being `public` are reachable by client code both inside and outside of the module. A script-only class definition is accessible only by members in the same module. For instance, class `Foo` can only be accessed by other members in the module.

▶ **Function members**—JavaFX functions can also be defined as top-level members of a module. Functions marked `public` can be reached by client code outside of the module while script-only functions are only visible to members of the same module.

▶ **Module variables**—as a code unit, a module can also include top-level variable declarations. Beside the regular `public` scope, variables can also be marked `public-read` which indicates a read-only public variable (such as the `size` variable in the code). Script-only variables are only available to members of the module.

You can read more about access modifiers in the *There's more* section next.

There's more...

Before leaving this recipe, we should take a closer look at some important topics related to the material that we just covered.

Script versus module

How do you know when a file is a script or a module? Well, there are some rules that define the qualifications:

The following rules qualify a file as a regular script:

▶ A script can have classes, functions, and variable members

▶ A script can have dangling expressions (outside of a function or class code block)

▶ A script cannot have any public variable members

▶ A script can include the special function `run()` to launch it

A script file is a module that has the following:

▶ A module can have classes, functions, and variable members

▶ A module cannot have dangling expressions (all expressions are in classes or function code blocks)

▶ A module can have public variable members

▶ A well-designed module should not implement the function `run()`

Organize your code into packages

Similar to Java, JavaFX script files can be further organized as packages. A **package** is simply a directory structure where you can arrange your scripts, modules, and other resources in a way which provides separation and grouping structures. To create a package, you create the directory structure reflecting how you want your script files to be organized.

The structure of the directories translates into the dot notation of the package name. For instance, if you nest your directories as `com/mycompany/anim`, then your package is `com.mycompany.anim`. Scripts and modules that belong to a package must declare their membership with the statement `package com.mycompany.anim`. Client code interested in using items in the package must import the package using the statement `import com.mycompany.anim`.

Access modifiers

Let's take a closer look at the access modifiers supported in JavaFX. Access modifiers allow you to control the visibility of script-level and class-level members.

Access modifier	Description	Location
default	The default (or script-only) is applied when no modifier is specified. This means that the member is accessible by other members in the same script or module file. This applies to variables, functions, and classes.	Script, module.
public	This member is visible from anywhere in the application. The modifier can be applied to variables, function, and classes.	Module, class.
public-read	This member is public but it is read-only. This modifier applies to only variable members.	Module, class.
public-init	This member has public visibility. This modifier applies to only variables. It indicates that the member can be initialized in an object literal declaration.	Class.
protected	This member is visible to other code in the same package or sub-classed code. Modifier applies to variables and function members.	Script, module, class.
package	This members are visible to other code in the same package. This applies to variables, functions, and classes.	Script, module, class.

See also

▸ *Declaring and using JavaFX classes*

▸ *Creating and using JavaFX functions*

Creating your own custom node

Part of the fun in working with JavaFX is the ease with which you can create your own visual components. As your needs outgrow the basic nodes that are available, you will find it necessary to create new components that capture more complex interactivity behaviors and functionalities. In this recipe, we will explore how to create customized graphical nodes that can be used wherever you can attach a node to the scene graph.

Getting ready

Before you can create customized nodes, you must be familiar with the basic shapes and text nodes presented in previous recipes. If you are not familiar with the materials, review the recipes *Drawing simple shapes* and *Drawing letter shapes using the Text class*. Also, take a look at recipe *Handling user input* in this chapter to review how to handle user interactivity.

A custom node works just like any other JavaFX node and can be added to a scene graph. To create customized nodes, you will need to import the classes `Node` and `CustomNode` found in the package `javafx.scene`. You will also find it helpful to use the `Group` class (from the same package) to aggregate nodes that make up your custom node.

How to do it...

The code presented here shows you how to extend the `CustomNode` class to create a new node. In this case, the node is a simple button in the shape of a circle with mouse interactivity behaviors. You can see the full code listing in `ch02/source-code/src/custom/CustomNodeDemo.fx`.

```
class MessageButton extends CustomNode{
    public-init var message:String = "Hello!";
    public var xloc = 10;
    public var yloc = 10;
    public var size = 30;
    public var font:Font = Font{name:"Arial" size:12}

    override protected function create () : Node {
        def circle = Circle {
            centerX: bind xloc;
            centerY: bind yloc;
            radius:  bind size/2;
        }
        def text:Text = Text{
            font:font
            content:message
            textOrigin:TextOrigin.TOP
            wrappingWidth: bind size;
            fill:Color.WHITE
        };
        text.x = xloc - (text.boundsInLocal.width/2);
        text.y = yloc - (text.boundsInLocal.height/2);
        Group{
            content:[circle,text]
            onMouseEntered:function(e:MouseEvent){
                circle.scaleX = 1.25;
```

```
            circle.scaleY = 1.25;
        }
        onMouseExited:function(e:MouseEvent){
            circle.scaleX = 1.0;
            circle.scaleY = 1.0;
        }

    }

    }
}
```

Now, to use the custom node, we simply place it in the scene graph like any other node.

```
Scene {
    content: [
        MessageButton {xloc:100 yloc:100 size:50
                        message:"Hello, World!"}
        MessageButton {xloc:200 yloc:100 size:100
                        message:"We've Made It!"}
    ]
}
```

This would create two buttons as shown in the next figure:

How it works...

To create a customized node, you simply extend the abstract class CustomNode. As you may have guessed, CustomNode is a special class recognized by the JavaFX scene graph engine. You must implement (and override) function create():Node in your node class. During the rendering of the scene, the engine will invoke this function to get an instance of a node that represents your custom component to be rendered.

In our example, the create() method returns an instance of class Group a generic container node that lets you create a branch of leaf nodes (sub-tree) to be attached to a scene graph. Grouping your nodes allows you to treat all node members of the group as one unit. In our example, we define two mouse event handlers (onMouseEntered and onMouseExited) on the group. Therefore, all members of the group will respond to the mouse events.

There's more...

`CustomNode` and all other node types share a common ancestor, the `Node` class. Therefore, your custom node has access to all of the positional, effects, transformation, animation properties, and functionalities exposed by the `Node` class. Nodes can also receive keyboard and mouse events, including key up, key down, mouse up, mouse down, mouse pressed, and so on.

Defining your own node also means that you can place your custom component anywhere in the scene graph including directly on the scene, in a group, participate in layout, and be a branch node to other nodes. If you are building a composite node that consists of more than one node, group them in a branch node such as `Group`, `Layout`, `Panel`, and so on and the branch node from the `create()` function.

See also

- ▸ *Declaring and using variables*
- ▸ *Declaring and using JavaFX classes*
- ▸ *Handling user inputs*
- ▸ *Making your scripts modular*

Controlling your application's window style

As we have seen in the previous recipe, *Building a JavaFX application*, the Stage represents the outer-most window of a desktop application. The stage encapsulates many properties that control how the window is styled on the screen. This recipe explores how to control and change the style and behavior of your application's window.

Getting ready

Window style, in this recipe, refers to the border decoration that goes around the application window displayed on the screen. In this context, style does not refer to other attributes such color, size, and so on. Using the style attribute of the window, for instance, you can make a chromeless window: that is, when the border and all other window controls are removed from the window.

How to do it...

To change the style of your application's window, you set the value of the `style` property of the Stage as shown next. The full listing of the code for this recipe can be found in `ch02/source-code/src/application/StageStyleDemo.fx`.

```
Stage {
  title : "Stage Style"
  width: 300
  height: 200
  StageStyle.TRANSPARENT;
  scene: Scene {
    fill:Color.GRAY
    content: [
      Rectangle {
        x: 100 y: 50
        width: 100 height: 100
        arcWidth: 10
        arcHeight : 10
        fill: Color.RED
            },
          Text {
            content: "Stage\nStyle"
            x:110 y:60
            fill: Color.WHITE
            font:Font {size: 16}
          }
    ]
  }
  onClose: function():Void {
            Alert.inform("You are about to quit the application.");
    }
}
```

The given code produces an application within a window with transparent border, as shown in the next image:

How it works...

The `style` property of the Stage allows you to control the look of the window's border. The code in the recipe sets the style to TRANSPARENT. The transparent style removes all lines around the window's edge. This produces an application window with no controls and a zero pixel-width border around the window, as shown in the previous image.

Though the effect produced by this style is nice, there is, however, no way for the user to grab, move, or close the window. You must explicitly provide window controls yourself when you style the stage.

There's more...

The style property of the Stage class is of type `StageStyle`, which exposes two other predefined styles including:

▶ `StageStyle.DECORATED`—this style produces a normal window decorated with a border and window controls such as the minimize, maximize, and close buttons. This is the default style for the stage.

When the window's border is decorated, you can also control whether the window can be resized using the stage's Boolean property called `resizable`.

▶ `StageStyle.UNDECORATED`—this style is the opposite of decorated. It removes the window's border decoration leaving only a thin line around the window's edge.

When you use this style, ensure that you provide your users with a way to close and drag the application's window.

Controlling opacity

You can also control the opacity of your application's window on the desktop. Here's how to do it:

```
Stage {
   title : "Border Style"
   style: StageStyle.TRANSPARENT;
   opacity: 0.5
   scene: Scene {
     content: [
        ...
     ]
   }
}
```

The `opacity` property is a decimal value ranging from `0.0` to `1.0` where `0.0` means complete transparency and `1.0` means full opacity. The next screenshot shows a window with an opacity value of `0.5`. Notice the content of other application bleeding through the application's content.

See also

▶ *Building a JavaFX application*

Going full-screen

A popular way of running media-rich applications is the use of the full-screen theater mode. This is a great way to grab the user's attention by hiding all other applications and place the focus on your application's content. This recipe shows you how to accomplish the same effect by running your application in full-screen mode.

Getting ready

There is not much in prerequisite for this recipe. You do, however, need to know how to create a basic JavaFX application and know how to add content to the stage. To refresh your memory, see *Building a JavaFX application*.

How to do it...

To go full-screen, you simply set the Boolean value of the `fullScreen` property on the `Stage` object to `true` as shown in the partial listing given next. You can see the full code listing for this recipe at `ch02/source-code/src/application/FullScreen.fx`.

```
Stage {
    title : "Going Full Screen"
    width: 300
    height: 200
    fullScreen:true
    scene: Scene {
        content: [
            Rectangle {
                x: 100 y: 50
                width: 100 height: 100
                arcWidth: 10
                arcHeight : 10
                fill: Color.RED
            },
                Text {
                    content: "Full\nScreen"
                    x:110 y:60
                    fill: Color.WHITE
                    font:Font {size: 16}
                }
        ]
    }
    onClose: function():Void {
            Alert.inform("You are about to quit the application.");
    }
}
```

When you run this code, it will start the application immediately in full-screen mode, hiding all other content on your desktop.

How it works...

When you set the value of the `fullScreen` property of the stage to true, JavaFX will put the application in full-screen mode with an undecorated window (see *Controlling your application's window style* earlier in this chapter). Depending on the platform's implementation of the full-screen mode (desktop or mobile), JavaFX will attempt to go into **Full-Screen Exclusive Mode** (**FSEM**), where the application window covers the entire screen, and all other running applications are placed in the background. If the platform does not support FSEM, JavaFX will run the application in a simulated full-screen mode, where the window will be placed in the foreground and maximized to full-screen dimensions with an undecorated window.

Here are the application's behaviors when going full-screen:

▸ The application will be restored to its last (pre-full-screen) window size when the user presses the escape (*Esc*) key at any time in the application.

▸ When the application goes into full-screen mode, the following properties will keep their original (pre-full-screen) values:

  ❑ `width` and `height` values

  ❑ `x` and `y` coordinates

  ❑ `iconified` and `resizeable` states

  ❑ `style` and `opacity` values

▸ When the application goes into full-screen mode, the opacity value is ignored and the stage is set to 100% opacity.

▸ The application will retain its full-screen mode when made invisible. Changing the visibility value will bring the application back to visible mode.

There's more...

While in full-screen, your users have unrestricted access to all functionalities of your application. However, *unsigned applications* launched as WebStart or running as Applets (see *Chapter 7, Deployment and Integration*) will have the following limitations in full-screen:

▸ Only a mouse event (onMouseClick, onMousePressed, and so on) can put the application in true FSEM. This is a security measure ensuring that only an action from the user will put the application in full-screen.

▸ If the screen is placed in true FSEM, users will only be allowed to use certain keys limited to *up, down, left, right, Page Up, Page Down, Tab, Home, End, Enter*, and *Esc* (mouse gestures are still allowed).

See also

▸ *Controlling your application's window style*

3
Transformations, Animations, and Effects

In this chapter, we will cover the following topics:

- ▸ Modifying shapes with the Transformation API
- ▸ Creating simple animation with the Transition API
- ▸ Composing animation with the Transition API
- ▸ Building animation with the KeyFrame API
- ▸ Creating custom Interpolators for animation
- ▸ Morphing shapes with the DelegateShape class
- ▸ Using data binding to drive animation sequences
- ▸ Applying cool paint effects with gradients
- ▸ Creating your own customized Paint
- ▸ Adding depth with lighting and shadow effects
- ▸ Creating your own Text effect
- ▸ Adding visual appeal with reflection

Introduction

This chapter is about pure, unadulterated eye candies. In previous chapters, you were introduced to the fundamentals of the language and framework. Now, it's time to explore the fun side of JavaFX. You will learn how to use transformation techniques to manipulate the location and dimension of objects in the scene. You will learn how to use JavaFX's Animation API to animate objects in order to create compelling content. Finally, you will learn how to make your objects visually appealing by applying paint and effects to your objects.

The JavaFX animation framework

Let's take a quick look into the animation framework before we move on. The built-in animation framework allows developers to animate an object easily using JavaFX's declarative syntax. You simply describe the state of the object at certain keyframes in the sequence, and the animation engine fills in the rest of the frames.

JavaFX supports two types of animations including transition- and keyframe-based animations. **Transition animations** are prepackaged sequences that animate a given property (dimension, opacity, location, and so on). **Keyframe animation** provides total control over the animation by exposing a complete idiom to express the animated sequence declaratively with timelines and keyframes.

Lastly, JavaFX's Animation API makes use of the built-in `Duration` type to represent time periods used in animation sequences (see *Chapter 1, Creating and Using Variables*). The Duration type provides a literal that provides a natural representation of time by specifying a number and a time unit together as shown in the next code snippet. For instance, the following code snippet expresses two minutes (see full code at `ch03/source-code/src/DurationTest.fx`).

```
var twoMinutes = 0h + 1m + 30s + 30000ms;

if(twoMinutes != 2m) println("Assertion failed");
if(twoMinutes != 120s) println("Assertion failed");
if(twoMinutes != 120000ms) println("Assertion failed");
```

Modifying shapes with the Transformation API

There will be a time when you will want to modify the shape of your objects into something completely different. You can tediously update positional or dimensional properties one by one, or you can use the **Transformation API**. This recipe shows you how to use the Transformation API to transform a shape's physical properties declaratively and effortlessly.

Getting started

Before you can apply transformations to shapes, you must be familiar with the steps required to create simple shapes using JavaFX. See *Drawing simple shapes* from *Chapter 2, Creating JavaFX Applications* for background information on creating simple shapes.

The classes for the Transformation API are kept in the package `javafx.scene.transform`. You will find several classes there used for different types of transformation, including `Rotate`, `Scale`, `Shear`, and `Translate`.

How to do it...

To demonstrate the Transformation API, the next code snippet shows the usage of both the `Translate` and the `Scale` transformations on a `Rectangle` shape. You can get the full code listing from `ch03/source-code/src/transformation/TransformDemo.fx`.

```
def w = 400;
def h = 200;
def rect:Rectangle = Rectangle {
          x: 0 y: 0
          width: w - 300
          height: h - 150;

          fill: Color.BLUE;
          stroke: Color.WHITE;
          strokeWidth: 3
          onMouseClicked:function(e:MouseEvent){
              rect.transforms = [
                  Translate{x: e.x y:e.y}
                  Rotate{angle:45}
              ];
          }
      }
```

When the code runs and the Rectangle instance (Figure A) receives a mouse-click event, it applies both `Translate` and `Rotate` transformation operations as shown in Figure B.

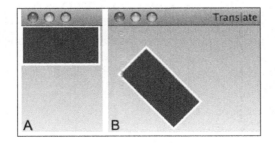

How it works...

The JavaFX Transformation API applies operations that transform the geometric properties of the target shapes relative to their current spatial attributes. All node instances in the scene graph are capable of receiving transformations. In the previous example, we are applying two transformation operations to the rectangle: **Translate** and **Scale**. As of version 1.2, the JavaFX SDK provides the transform operations listed next. You can find an example of their usage at `ch03/source-code/src/transformation/`.

- `Translate`—shifts all x and y points of the node to new co-ordinate space relative to its original co-ordinate space.
- `Scale`—stretches (scales) the dimension of a node by a specified factor. The number specified in the scale operation is a multiplier, not a dimension.
- `Shear`—all points along the specified axis remain constant while the parallel side is shifted by a given factor.
- `Rotate`—rotates a node for the specified number of degrees about a given pivot point.

You can instantiate transformation classes using the object literal form (as shown in the previous example), or you may use class-level functions from `Transform` including `Transform.translate()`, `Transform.scale()`, `Transform.shear()`, and `Transform.rotate()`.

In the code snippet for this recipe, we apply the transformation operations using the `transforms:Transform[]` property. This approach allows you to attach several transformations to the target shape. In this example, the transforms sequence is applied when the shape receives a mouse event.

There's more...

Besides the `transforms` sequence property discussed earlier in this recipe, the `Node` class (inherited by all shapes) also exposes individual properties to apply the transformation operations, shown next:

- `translateX` or `translateY`—these properties allow you to specify a value used to shift the node's co-ordinate space along the x or y axis
- `scaleX` or `scaleY`—this value is used as a factor to scale the dimension of the object along the x or y axis about the center of the object
- `rotate`—this value is the degree used to rotate the object about its center

See also

- *Chapter 2—Drawing simple shapes*

Creating simple animation with the Transition API

As you read this chapter, you will find out that JavaFX provides a powerful animation engine that lets you create complex sequences (see the *Introduction*). However, if your need is to create simple straightforward animated sequences, JavaFX has got you covered. In this recipe, we will explore how to create simple animations quickly using the JavaFX **Transition API**.

Getting ready

Before you can create transition-based animations, you must be familiar with the steps required to create simple shapes using the Shape API. See *Chapter 2, Drawing simple shapes* for background information on creating simple shapes.

All of the classes provided by the Transition API are located in the package `javafx.animation.transition`. There you will find several classes representing the type of animations they support, including `TranslateTransition`, `ScaleTransition`, `PathTransition`, `FadeTransition`, and `RotateTransition`.

The next code snippet shown will use an instance of `PathTransition` to demonstrate the simplicity and flexibility of the API. The `PathTransition` class makes use of the Path API, which was discussed in *Chapter 2*, under the recipe *Creating complex shapes using Path*, to animate an object along a specified path.

How to do it...

The next code snippet shows you how to use the PathTransition API to animate an object along a specified path. The full code listing can be accessed from `ch03/source-code/src/animation/trans/PathTransitionDemo.fx`.

```
def w = 400;
def h = 200;
def r = 30;
def mv = 60;

def circle = Circle {
    centerX: 0; centerY: 0 radius: r
    fill: Color.BLUE stroke: Color.WHITE strokeWidth: 3
}

var path = Path {
    elements: [
        MoveTo{x:0 y:0}
        HLineTo { x: mv}
```

```
            VLineTo { y: h }
            HLineTo { x: mv * 2}
            VLineTo { y: 0 }
            HLineTo { x: 3 * mv}
            VLineTo { y: h/2 }

            MoveTo{x: 3 * mv y: h/2}
            ArcTo {
                radiusX: 20
                radiusY: 20
                x: 5 * mv y:h/2
                sweepFlag:true
            }
        ]
    }

PathTransition {
    node: circle
    duration: 5s
    path:AnimationPath.createFromPath(path)
    repeatCount: FadeTransition.INDEFINITE autoReverse: true
}.playFromStart();
```

When the application is executed, the circle moves from the left-hand side of the screen to the right-hand side, following the path described by the path elements declared in the Path instance. The next figure shows an outline of the animated path that the circle follows.

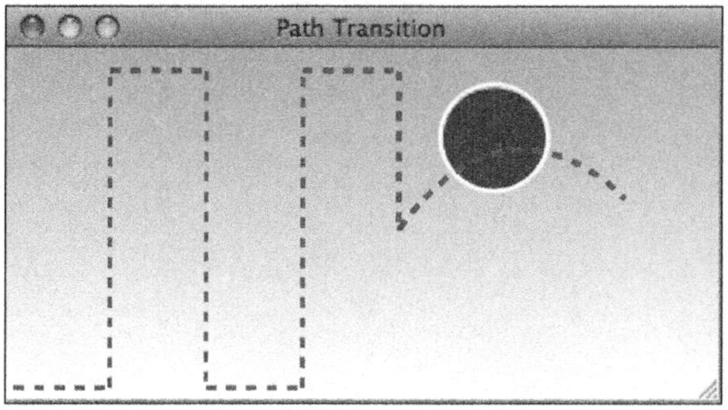

How it works...

Using transition-based animation is a simple and easy way to quickly get started with animation in JavaFX. A transition class provides a canned timeline that animates specific node properties including position and dimension over a given time period. All transition classes expose timeline controls by allowing playback, repeat count, and auto-reverse.

The code snippet makes use of the `Path` API and the `PathTransition` class to move the circle along a specified path. Let's take a closer look at the previous code.

- *Animated subject*—first, the code declares the node that will be animated. In this instance, it is a Circle. Notice that the node carries no information about the animation. There is a clear separation between the animated subject and the process that drives the animation.

- *Path description*—the `PathTransition` class makes use of the Path API to specify the path along which the animated subject will be displaced. The API provides an idiom to describe different segments of the path using path element classes. For more details about the Path API, have a look at the *See also* section following shortly.

- *Animation setup*—once we have an animation subject and animation path, we are ready to set up the animation. We declare an instance of `PathTransition` and use its `node` property to specify the subject being animated. Then, to resolve the path of the animation, we use an instance of another class named `AnimationPath` and its function `createFromPath(path:Path)` to transform the Path instance into coordinates for the animation sequence.

- *Animation control*—once the the instance of the transition class is declared, we can use the function `playFromStart()` to start playing the animation as shown in the code. When the property `autoReverse:Boolean` is set to `true`, it causes the play head to restart the animation when the end of the sequence is reached. The property `repeatCount:Number` is used to indicate the number of times the animation is repeated. A value of `PathTransition.INDEFINITE` causes the playback to repeat indefinitely, as exemplified in the code.

There's more...

Before we exit this recipe, let's take a look at the other transition classes provided by JavaFX. You can see examples of all of the transition classes in the package `ch03/source-code/src/animation/trans/`.

`TranslateTransition`—shifts the target node from its origin to the specified x and y coordinates	```TranslateTransition { node: circle duration: 3s toX:100 toY:300 }```
`ScaleTransition`—enlarges or shrinks the dimensions of the node by the specified factor	```ScaleTransition { node: circle duration: 3s fromX:0.5 fromY:0.5 toX:3 toY:3 }```

| RotateTransition—rotates the node using the specified angle value around a given pivot | ```
RotateTransition {
    node: circles
    duration: 1s
    byAngle:360
}
``` |
| FadeTransition—animates the node's opacity value over the specified time | ```
FadeTransition {
    node: circle
    duration: 3s
    fromValue: 1.0
    toValue: 0.25
}
``` |

The Timeline

The transition classes are an implementation of the `Timeline` class that provides ways to control keyframes generated during the animation. Here are some of the control functions which are available on all transition classes:

- ► `play()`—this function plays the animation from the last stopped time location and the last set direction.

- ► `playFromStart()`—similar to `play()`, this function plays back the animation. However, it resets the animation's playback time to zero (0) and plays in the forward direction.

- ► `pause()`—the `pause()` function stops the playback of the animation. The current time position is retained. The next call to `play()` will resume from the last paused time position.

- ► `stop()`—this function stops the animation's playback as well. However, it resets the time position to zero and sets the direction to forward.

The following are some important properties exposed by the Timeline class that you should be aware of when building animations:

- ► `rate:Number`—this property is a multiplier for the playback speed. A rate of 0.0 indicates normal playback, while 2.0 plays twice as fast, and so on. A negative rate (-0.0 for instance) plays the animation in reverse at the indicated rate.

- ► `framerate:Number`—this ratio indicates the number of frames played per second for an animation.

- ► `time:Duration`—this property indicates the position in time, in the sequence, where the animation will start when `play()` is invoked.

- ► `repeatCount`—the number of times the animation will repeat after the playback reaches the end. Setting this value to `Timeline.INDEFINITE` will repeat the animation until `pause()` or `stop()` is invoked.

- ► `autoReverse`—play the animation backward at the end of a sequence.

See also

  ▸ *Chapter 2—Drawing simple shapes*

  ▸ *Chapter 2—Creating complex shapes using Path*

Composing animation with the Transition API

In the recipe *Creating simple animation with the Transition API*, we explored how to animate an object using one of the transition classes. What if, however, you want to create more complex animation sequences composed of multiple transition steps? This recipe shows you how to use the Transition API in order to create more elaborate animation sequences composed of multiple transition classes.

Getting ready

In order to follow this recipe, you must know how to create shapes and animate them using the Transition API. For an introduction on the API, refer to the recipe *Creating simple animation with the Transition API*. Again, all of the transition classes provided by the Transition API are located in the package `javafx.animation.transition`. For this recipe you will use the class `ParallelTransition` to compose multi-step, transition-based animation sequences.

How to do it...

The abbreviated code snippet given next shows you how to use the `ParallelTransition` class to create animation sequences. You can get the complete listing of the code from `ch03/source-code/src/animation/trans/ParallelTransitionDemo.fx`.

```
def w = 400;
def h = 200;
def r = 25;
def circles = Group{
    content:[
        Circle {
            centerX:0   centerY:(h / 2) radius:r
            fill:Color.BLUE stroke:Color.WHITE
            strokeWidth:3
        }

        Circle {
            centerX:2*r   centerY:(h / 2) radius:r
            fill:Color.BLUE stroke:Color.WHITE
```

```
                        strokeWidth: 3
                }
        ]
}
def rect = Rectangle {x:10 y:10 width:50 height:20 fill:Color.RED}

ParallelTransition {
    content: [
        RotateTransition {
            node:circles   duration:1s   byAngle:360
            repeatCount:FadeTransition.INDEFINITE
            autoReverse:true
        }

        TranslateTransition {
            node:circles   duration:3s   byX:w/2
            repeatCount:FadeTransition.INDEFINITE
            autoReverse:true
        }

        TranslateTransition {
            node:rect   duration:3s
            byY:h-30
            repeatCount:FadeTransition.INDEFINITE
            autoReverse: true
        }
    ]
}.play();
```

When the application is executed, the circles are animated from left to right, while the rectangle moves from top to bottom simultaneously, as illustrated (as well as possible) in the next figure:

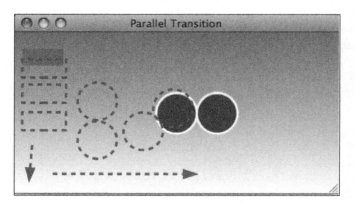

How it works...

Using transition-based animation is a simple and easy way to get started quickly with building animation sequences. Recall that a transition class provides a canned timeline that animates specific attributes on a node, including position and dimension. This recipe makes use of the `ParallelTransition` class. This is a special transition class used to compose animation sequences by animating simpler transition sequences in parallel. Let's examine how the code snippet works.

▸ _Animated subject_—in this recipe, there are two subjects being animated. The first one is a `Group` instance named `circles` that is composed of two adjoining circles. The other subject is a Rectangle (`rect`) instance.

▸ _Animation setup_—the animation is driven by an instance of `ParallelTransition`. This is a specialized transition class used as a container for other transition sequences. It provides a way to declaratively compose elaborate animation sequences by assembling together simpler animation transitions running in parallel.

▸ _Animation sequences_—the ParallelTransition class is used to drive three transition sequences on two objects:

  ❑ `circles`—the group of circles rotate 360 degrees using the `RotateTransition` for a period of one second. While the circles rotate, they are also translated for three seconds from the left-hand side to the right-hand side of the screen using the `TranslateTransition` method.

  ❑ `rect`—the other instance of `TranslateTransition` is used to animate the rectangle on the stage from the top of the screen toward the bottom for a period of three seconds.

▸ _Animation playback_—when the `play()` function is invoked on `ParallelTransition`, it starts the animation in parallel for each individual transition that it contains. Each transition element applies control properties from their own timeline, honoring its `repeatCount` and `autoReverse` properties respectively. This is to allow each timeline to move independently and in parallel.

There's more...

The JavaFX animation framework also offers a `SequentialTransition` class to compose animation sequences that are played serially (as opposed to parallel). Similar to the `ParallelTransition` class, the `SequentialTransition` class allows you to compose animation using a collection of simpler transition classes. Unlike the parallel animation sequence though, each sequence plays one after the other. The next snippet shows how we can animate the same objects presented in the recipe earlier using the `SequentialTransition` class. The full code can be found in `ch03/source-code/src/animation/trans/SequentialTransitionDemo.fx`.

```
SequentialTransition {
        content: [
            RotateTransition {
                node: circles
                duration: 1s
                byAngle:360
            }

            TranslateTransition {
                node: circles
                duration: 3s
                byX:w/2
            }

PauseTransition{duration:1.5s}

            TranslateTransition {
                node: rect
                duration: 3s
                byY:h-30
            }
        ]
    }.play();
```

You should note the following:

▸ The SequentialTransition class will play each animation in the order they appear in the content property.

▸ Individual transition class that is part of a SequentialTransition sequence should not control the playback with repeatCount=SequentialTransition. INDEFINITE. This will cause the transition to be stuck and not yield to other sequences.

▸ You can insert a pause time period in the sequence using the PauseTransition class. As its name implies, it allows you pause the playback sequence for the specified time.

See also

▸ *Chapter 2—Drawing simple shapes*

▸ *Chapter 3—Creating simple animation with the Transition API*

Building animation with the KeyFrame API

While transition-based animation classes provide a quick and easy way to animate objects in the scene graph, they expose little control over the way the animation steps are constructed. For instance, when you build an animation sequence with the `TranslateTransition` class, you can only specify the origin and the destination points of the object. The class automatically fills in the frames in between. This recipe covers keyframe-based animation techniques. Using this approach, developers are able to take full control over the animation sequence by specifying the keyframes that make up the animation.

Getting ready

Although optional, it is helpful to be familiar with the transition-based animation presented in the recipe *Creating simple animation with the Transition API,* as it includes valuable information about animation and animation controls. Creating keyframe animation involves two main classes, `Timeline` and `KeyFrame`, found in the package `javafx.animation`. Timeline provides overall control of the animation, while KeyFrame lets you assemble the granular steps that make up the animation.

How to do it...

To create keyframe-based animation, you can declaratively build your timeline by adding keyframes that describe the steps of your animation. To illustrate how to use keyframe animation, we will build a simple game where the objective will be to use a paddle that is moving from side-to-side on the screen to hit a ball. When the paddle hits the ball, you get one point. Since the code is rather long, it will be presented in chunks. You can get the full code listing from `ch03/source-code/src/animation/KeyFrameAnimDemo.fx`.

1. Let's first declare some variables to be used later in the code.
```
def w = 400;
def h = 200;
var rad = 15.0;
var cx = w / 2;
var cy = h - rad;
var scoreCounter = 0;
def paddleTime = 0.5s;
```

2. Next, we declare the objects used to display the score.
```
def score = Text {
    textOrigin: TextOrigin.TOP x: w / 2 y: h / 2
    font: Font.font("Helvetica", FontWeight.BOLD, 48)
    content: bind "{scoreCounter}"
```

```
            visible: false
        }
    def scoreAnim = Timeline {
        keyFrames: [
            at (1s) {
                score.scaleX => 3;
                score.scaleY => 3;
                score.opacity => 0.0;
                score.visible => false
            }
        ]
    }
```

3. Next, we declare objects to display and animate the paddle on the screen.

```
    def paddle: Rectangle = Rectangle {
        x: 10 y: 10 width: 50 height: 10
        fill: Color.BLUE stroke: Color.WHITE strokeWidth: 3
    }

    def paddleAnim = Timeline {
        autoReverse: true
        repeatCount: Timeline.INDEFINITE
        keyFrames: [
            KeyFrame{
                time:paddleTime values:paddle.translateX => 350
            }
        ]
    }
    paddleAnim.play();
```

4. Lastly, we declare the objects to display and animate the ball.

```
    def ball:Circle = Circle {
                radius: bind rad
                centerX: bind cx;
                centerY: bind cy;
                fill: Color.RED
                stroke: Color.WHITE
                strokeWidth: 3
```

```
                    onMousePressed: function (e: MouseEvent) {
                        ballAnim.playFromStart();
                    }
                }
    var ballAnim: Timeline = Timeline {
        keyFrames: [
            KeyFrame {
                time: 200ms
                values: [cy => 5 tween Interpolator.EASEIN]
                action: function () {
                    if(ball.intersects(paddle.boundsInParent)){
                        scoreCounter++;
                        score.visible = true;
                        scoreAnim.playFromStart();
                    }
                }
            }
            KeyFrame{
                time: 500ms
                values: [
                    cy => (h - rad) tween Interpolator.LINEAR
                ]
            }
        ]
    }
```

When all the objects are added to the stage and the code is executed, you should get something that looks like the next screenshot.

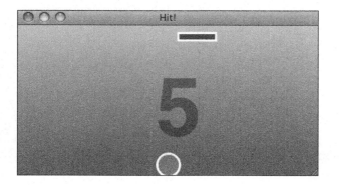

How it works...

As mentioned earlier, the two main classes involved in creating keyframe-based animation are `Timeline` and `KeyFrame`. These classes provide the necessary idiom to express the video-timeline metaphor, as shown in the next figure.

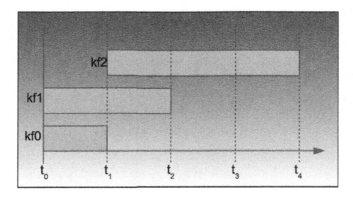

Each timeline is composed of a collection of one or more keyframes (kf1 to kfN). Each keyframe specifies a duration (t_i) and the values to be interpolated during that time. The animation engine automatically calculates the in-between values for interpolation. Because the time value of each keyframe may overlap each other, the length of an animation sequence is determined by the keyframe with the latest time period. Hence, in the previous figure, the animation length is t_4 (not the cumulative total).

The declarative syntax for creating timeline animation is as follows:

```
Timeline {
keyframes:[
KeyFrame:{
    time:animation_duration
    values:[interpolation_expression]
    action:function():Void
}
]
}
```

where

> ▶ *Timeline*—stores keyframe instances in its `keyframes` property. It also controls and manages the animation's playback.

▶ *KeyFrame*—this class represents a keyframe in the animation sequence with the following properties:

- ❑ `time:Duration`—the time period used for the extrapolation of in-between frames for the animation sequence.

- ❑ `values:KeyValue[]`—a collection of `KeyValue` classes that are used to express the initial and the terminal values of the key values for the animation sequence. That expression takes the form `initial_value => terminal_value`, specifying the key values that are interpolated by the animation engine over the specified time period.

- ❑ `action:function()`—is a function which can be attached to the keyframe. It is invoked when the keyframe's duration has elapsed.

Let's see how the recipe makes use of the keyframe animation constructs. The code uses three distinct timeline instances to animate the objects for the game. Let's also see how they are used:

▶ *The score*—the first animation sequence displays the game's score. This is accomplished through the `scoreAnim` Timeline instance. It is used to interpolate properties `scaleX => 3, scaleY => 3, opacity => 0`, and `visible => false` of the text node `score` text node `score` over a period of one second. When the animation is executed, the current score is animated showing the text for the score zooming in while fading simultaneously.

▶ *The paddle*—the paddle (an instance of `Rectangle` assigned to variable `paddle`) runs left and right on the top of the screen. It is animated by an instance of Timeline assigned to variable `paddleAnim`. The timeline has a single `KeyFrame` object that interpolates the `translateX` property of the paddle object to move it across the screen. The call to `paddleAnim.play()` runs the paddle's animation indefinitely because `repeatCount=INDEFINITE`, and the paddle goes back and forth because `autoReverse=true`.

▶ *The ball*—when the ball (an instance of `Circle` assigned to the variable `ball`) is clicked on, it travels from the bottom of the screen, moving upwards toward the paddle's trajectory. The ball is animated using variable binding where the `ball.centerY` property is bound to the variable `cy`. A Timeline instance, assigned to variable `ballAnim`, updates `cy` with two keyframes: at 200 ms variable `cy` is set to five (corresponding to the top of the screen); at 500 ms, `cy` is assigned an expression `(h - rad)` corresponding to the bottom of the screen. As `ballAnim` interpolates `cy`, `ball.centerY` is updated, thus animating the circle. To start the animation, `ball` includes an `onMousePressed` event handler used to call `ballAnim.playFromStart()`.

▶ *The hit*—the Timeline instance assigned to variable `ballAnim` contains a keyframe that gets executed over a period of 200 milliseconds (see previous bullets). At the end of the period, when the ball is at the top of the screen, the keyframe executes the function attached to its `action` property. That function:

- ❑ Detects when the ball hits the paddle with the expression
  `if(ball.intersects(paddle.boundsInParent)`

- ❑ Updates the score, increasing it by 1

- ❑ Plays the `socreAnim` animation sequence to display the score (see the previous score discussion)

There's more...

Building complex animations with several keyframes can get long and messy. To help with the syntax burden, JavaFX supports a shortcut notation of the KeyFrame declaration using the `at()` syntax. So the previous code snippet becomes:

```
def scoreAnim = Timeline {
    keyFrames: [
        at (1s) {
            score.scaleX => 3;
            score.scaleY => 3;
            score.opacity => 0.0;
            score.visible => false
        }
    ]
}
```

The `at()` syntax provides a simpler way of expressing keyframes on the timeline. Each `at()` is eventually mapped to a `KeyFrame` declaration and placed on the timeline.

Interpolation

The JavaFX KeyFrame animation API uses interpolation between keyframes to determine how to fill in the missing animated frames in between the keyframes. Each key value can receive an `Interpolator` type specified after the `tween` keyword (see code snippet). The interpolator in JavaFX provides the algorithm that figures out how to fill in the missing frames while maintaining synchronization with the timeline. There are several types of built-in interpolators with which you should be familiar:

▶ `Interpolator.EASEIN`—starts the sequence slow and accelerates it smoothly to a constant progression

▶ `Interpolator.EASEOUT`—decelerates the sequence from a constant progression, with smooth deceleration, and an eventual stop

▶ `Interpolator.EASEBOTH`—uses both `EASEIN` and `EASEOUT`

- Interpolator.LINEAR—maintains constant progression from the beginning to the end of the sequence (default)

- Interpolator.DISCRETE—this interpolator does no in-between animation

You can also create your own custom interpolator to specify how animated objects behave during animation. See the recipe *Creating custom interpolators for animation* in the next section.

Using the Timeline class as a timer

You can use the Timeline class to create general-purpose timers for your code. Declare an instance of the Timeline class having a single KeyFrame with the following:

- Set the keyframe's time property as the timer's time period.

- Define a callback function for the action property. It will be invoked on each expiration of the time period.

- Set the Timeline's repeatCount to INDEFINITE and turn off interpolation (interpolate=false) for discrete time progression.

The following snippet shows an example of how this would work (see full listing at ch03/source-code/src/animation/TimelineTimerDemo.fx).

```
var counter = 0;
var timer = Timeline {
            repeatCount: Timeline.INDEFINITE
            interpolate: false
            keyFrames: [
                KeyFrame {
                    time: 1s
                    action: function (): Void {
                        println(counter++);
                    }
                }
            ]
        }
timer.play();
```

The timer starts when timer.play() is invoked. The timer will run continuously until either the pause() or the stop() method is invoked.

See also

- *Introduction*
- *Creating simple animation with the Transition API*
- *Composing animation with the Transition API*
- *Creating custom interpolators for animation*

Creating custom interpolators for animation

The recipe *Building animation with the KeyFrame API* introduced the notion of keyframe animation using Interpolator instances to automatically calculate the in-between values between starting and ending keyframes. As of version 1.2, JavaFX comes with five interpolators including `Interpolator.EASEIN`, `Interpolator.EASEOUT`, `Interpolator.BOTH`, `Interpolator.LINEAR`, and `Interpolator.DISCRETE` (see *Building animation with the KeyFrame API* for details).

While these interpolators are adequate for most animation sequences, you may, however, encounter situations where you want your objects to behave differently than the ways offered by the built-in interpolators. In this recipe, we will show you how to create your own custom Interpolator class.

Getting ready

This recipe uses keyframe animation concepts supported by the `Timeline` and `KeyFrame` classes to create animation sequences. If you are not familiar with keyframe-based animation in JavaFX, review recipe *Building animation with the KeyFrame API*. This recipe will define a new interpolator class by extending base class `SimpleInterceptor`. If you are not familiar with defining and creating classes in JavaFX, please review *Chapter 1, Declaring and using JavaFX classes*.

How to do it...

To illustrate how to create your own custom interpolator, the recipe presents a simple interpolator class called `MagneticInterpolator`. As the name suggests, when using this interpolator, interpolated values briskly snap to the end value when a certain threshold (the attraction value) has been reached. You can access the full listing of the abbreviated code shown next in `source-code/src/animation/MagneticInterpolatorDemo.fx`.

```
class MagneticInterpolator extends SimpleInterpolator {
    public var attraction:Number = 0.05;
    override public function curve (t : Number) : Number {
        if(t >= 1 - attraction){
            1;
        }else if(t < attraction){
            0;
        }else{
            t;
        }
    }
}
```

```
def circ = Circle { centerX: 25 centerY: 100 radius: 25 };

var t = Timeline {
    autoReverse:true
    repeatCount:Timeline.INDEFINITE
    keyFrames: [
        at(2s) {
            circ.centerX => 375
            tween MagneticInterpolator{attraction:0.07}
        }
    ]
};
```

The next figure depicts how the circle's `centerX` property is interpolated using the `MagneticInterpolator` class.

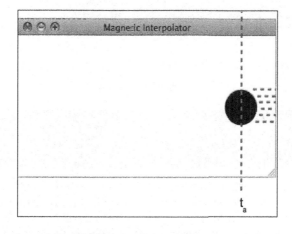

How it works...

Given a start and an end value, **interpolation** provides the ability to algorithmically deduce an in-between target value given ratio t where $0.0 <= t <= 1.0$. For instance when $t = 1.0$, most interpolators will return the end value. In JavaFX, to implement your own interpolator, you can either start from scratch and extend the `Interpolator` abstract class, where you will be responsible for providing your own interpolation algorithm. Or, you can extend the ready-made `SimpleInterpolator` class, which implements a simple linear algorithm.

For the implementation of the `MagneticInterpolator` class, we use the latter approach and extend `SimpleInterpolator`, because we expect values to be calculated in a linear fashion. The `MageneticInterpolator` class exposes a property called `attraction:Number` which, to keep things simple, is the t value beyond or below which (depending on direction) will snap to the final target value. As shown in the previous figure, when the Interpolator goes past time value t_a the location of the circle along the x-axis snaps to 375.

Usage of the `SimpleInterpolator` class requires the implementation of `function curve(t:Number):Number`, which is expected to emit the target value for a given `t`. The code snippet for this recipe implements the curve function where:

- If the `t` greater than `1 - attraction`, the function snaps to the end value
- If `t` is decreasing and goes below attraction, it snaps to the start value
- Otherwise, `t` progresses linearly

In our example, we use our magnetic interpolator in the `KeyFrame` instance to animate the displacement of the `Circle` instance along the x-axis over a period of two seconds. As the animation engine interpolates the location of the circle (`circ.centerX`) using the `MagneticInterpolator` instance, it will snap the end position of `375` when the time ratio `t` slides beyond the `attraction` property. When the animation is running in reverse, the interpolator snaps to 0 when `t` is less than `attraction`.

See also

- *Introduction*
- *Building animation with the KeyFrame API*
- *Morphing shapes with the DelegateShape class*

Morphing shapes with the DelegateShape class

You have seen these cool effects in movies and TV shows where an object smoothly transition from its current shape to another shape. The transition is known as morphing and you can easily achieve the same effect in JavaFX. In this recipe, we will explore how to use animation sequences and the `DelegateShape` class to morph shapes.

Getting ready

This recipe uses animation concepts presented in previous recipes. If you are not familiar with how to create animation sequences, review the recipe *Building animation with the KeyFrame API*. This recipe also uses the `DelegateShape` class, which is found in package `javafx.scene.shape`. This class, as you will see, can be used to create animation sequences of objects morphing from one shape to the other.

How to do it...

The following code snippet shows how to create a morphing animated sequence between three shapes. You can get the full code listing from `ch03/source-code/src/animation/ShapeMorphDemo.fx`:

```
def rect = Rectangle { x: 200 y: 100 width: 100 height: 50 };
def circ = Circle { centerX: 200 centerY: 100 radius: 50 };
def poly = Polygon { points: [200, 50, 300, 150, 150, 150] };

def morph = DelegateShape {
    shape:poly
    fill: LinearGradient {
        startX: 0, endX: 0, startY: 0, endY: 1
        stops: [
            Stop { offset: 0, color: Color.BLUE }
            Stop { offset: 1, color: Color.WHITE }
        ]
    }
    stroke:Color.NAVY
    strokeWidth:4
}

var t = Timeline {
    autoReverse:true
    repeatCount:Timeline.INDEFINITE
    keyFrames: [
        KeyFrame { time: 2s values: morph.shape => rect tween
                                        Interpolator.EASEBOTH] },
        KeyFrame { time: 4s values: morph.shape => circ},
        KeyFrame { time: 6s values: morph.shape => poly},
    ]
};

t.play();
```

When the animation is played, you will see the different shapes smoothly transition from the rectangle, circle, and the polygon, as shown in the following screenshot.

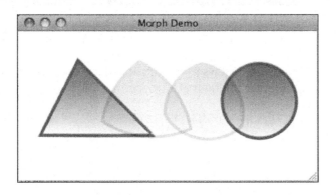

How it works...

This recipe shows you how to animate a shape to morph it to another shape smoothly using the `DelegateShape` class. This class is a descendent of `Shape`. It does not represent an actual shape itself, however, it uses its internal `Interpolator` instance to calculate the necessary in-between shapes between a start and an end shape.

In our code snippet, we declare three starting shapes: a `Rectangle`, a `Circle`, and a `Polygon`. Although these Shape instances are `Interpolatable`, it is impossible to interpolate between them, as they are of different types (Interpolators can only interpolate values of the same types). The `DelegateShape` class, however, can be assigned an object of type `Shape` through its `shape:Shape` property. That object instance can then be interpolated to another instance of `Shape` over time.

In the code snippet, the `ShapeDelegate.shape` property is initially assigned an instance of the `Polygon` shape. Using a `Timeline`, the `ShapeDelegate.shape` is interpolated to a `Rectangle` over a period of two seconds. At four seconds, `ShapeDelegate.shape` is interpolated from `Rectangle` to `Circle`. Lastly, `ShapeDelegate.shape` is interpolated from `Circle` to `Polygon` two seconds later. The entire animation produces a smooth animation of the shapes morphing from one figure to another.

See also

- ▶ *Introduction*
- ▶ *Creating simple animation with the Transition API*
- ▶ *Composing animation with the Transition API*
- ▶ *Building animation with the KeyFrame API*

Using data binding to drive animation sequences

As you create more elaborate animation, you will run into situations where you want to synchronize object movements in your animation sequences. You can do that by declaring several instances of `Timeline`, or you can automate the synchronization of your objects using bound variables. This recipe shows you how to use data binding to update object properties automatically during an animation sequence.

Getting ready

This recipe uses the `Timeline` and `KeyFrame` classes to create animation sequences. If you are not familiar with keyframe-based animation, review the recipe *Building animation with the KeyFrame API*. This recipe also includes the notion of data binding covered under *Using binding and triggers to update variables* in *Chapter 1, Getting Started with JavaFX*.

How to do it...

The next code snippet illustrates how to use data binding in keyframe-based animation. We will animate several objects synchronously using only one timeline. You can see the full code in ch03/source-code/src/animation/BoundAnimationDemo.fx.

```
def w = 400;
def h = 200;
def width = 50;
def rad = width/2;
def spacer = 30;
var locY = h - width;

def circ1 = Circle {
    centerX: rad + spacer centerY: bind (locY + rad)
    radius: rad
}
def rec1 = Rectangle {
    x: circ1.boundsInLocal.maxX + spacer y: bind locY
    width:width height:width
}

def circ2 = Circle {
    centerX: rec1.boundsInLocal.maxX + spacer + rad
    centerY: bind (locY + rad) radius: rad
}

def rec2 = Rectangle {
    x: circ2.boundsInLocal.maxX + spacer y: bind locY
    width:width height:width
}

Timeline {
    repeatCount:Timeline.INDEFINITE
    autoReverse:true
    keyFrames:[
        at(1s){locY => width tween Interpolator.EASEBOTH}
    ]
}.play();
```

Once the objects are placed in a Stage instance and the application is executed, you should see all four objects move up and down together on the screen, as shown in the next figure.

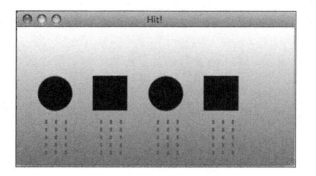

How it works...

The JavaFX data binding system provides an event-driven infrastructure which you can easily use to automate object property updates. When you bind the property of a node to a single value or an expression, the JavaFX binding system automatically registers your bound objects to receive updates as the value (or expression) is updated. In the context of an animated sequence, the bound object receives updates as the value (or expression), it is bound to is interpolated by the animation engine. You can leverage this mechanism to implement synchronized animation by binding several objects to interpolated values or expressions.

In our code snippet, we accomplish synchronized object animation with one `Timeline` instance as follows:

- *Declare variables*—in the first portion of the code, we declare all of the variables needed, including `locY`, which will be used to provide the trajectory for the animated objects.

- *Animated objects*—next, we declare four simple shapes, including two circles and two rectangles, that will be animated. Each shape has its y-coordinate bound to variable `locY` (or an expression that uses `locY`). As the value of `locY` changes, it will update the position of the object along the `y-axis`.

- *Timeline animation*—all four declared objects are animated using one `Timeline` instance with a single `KeyFrame` instance. The keyframe interpolates variable `locY` from the initial value of `(h - width)` to `width` over a one-second time period. As `locY` is updated by the interpolator, all four objects bound to variable `locY` are animated along the y-axis.

See also

- Chapter 1 —*Using binding and triggers to update variables*
- Chapter 3—*Building animation with the KeyFrame API*

Applying cool paint effects with gradients

In previous recipes, we have seen the `Color` class used to apply color to node instances through the `fill` property. You may have noticed in some recipes however, that instead of a simple color instance, you can apply color effects to the `fill` property. In this recipe, we are going to explore the gradient color effect.

Getting ready

This recipe uses the concept of gradient paint effects to demonstrate JavaFX's deep support for rich GUI functionalities. To use gradient paint effects presented in this recipe, you will need to import classes `LinearGradient`, `RadialGradient`, and `Stop` from the package `javafx.scene.paint`.

How to do it...

The abbreviated code listing below shows how to use the gradient classes. You can access the full code listing from `ch03/source-code/src/effects/GradientPaintDemo.fx`.

```
def w = 400;
def h = 200;

def linearGrad = LinearGradient {
    startX: 0.0, startY: 0.0, endX: 0.0, endY: 1.0
    proportional: true
    stops: [
        Stop {offset: 0.0 color: Color.RED},
        Stop {offset: 1.0 color: Color.BLACK},
    ]
}

def radialGrad = RadialGradient{
    radius:1; centerX: 0.5, centerY: 0.5
    proportional: true
    stops: [
        Stop {offset: 0.0 color: Color.BLACK},
        Stop {offset: 1.0 color: Color.WHITE},
    ]
}

def circ0 = Circle {
    centerX: w/2 centerY:h/2 radius: 90 fill:radialGrad
}
```

```
def rec0 = Rectangle {
    width: 100 height: 90
    x: 30 y: h - 90
    fill: linearGrad
    stroke:Color.SILVER
}
```

The code generates the objects shown in the next figure with a radial gradient applied to the circle and the linear gradient applied to the rectangle.

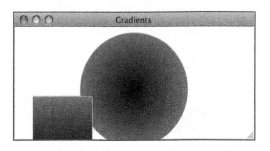

How it works...

The JavaFX GUI framework comes with two built-in gradient paint methods, the `LinearGradient` and the `RadialGradient`. The gradient is an extension of the paint class, meaning that it can be used anywhere that the paint class can be applied.

The gradient class fills the shape of their target nodes with two or more colors using a graded pattern between the colors. The gradient classes expose the `stops:Stop[]` property, which is a collection `Stop` instances. The `Stop` class is similar to the `KeyFrame` class, in that, it represents a key color participating in the gradient. The gradient class interpolates the graded colors between the specified stop colors. The `offset` property of the `Stop` class indicates the order in which the color is rendered in the gradient.

In the previous code snippet, each gradient instance uses two `Stop` instances to specify the colors participating in the gradient patterns. The `LinearGradient` creates a gradient between colors `Color.RED` and `Color.BLACK`; and the `RadialGradient` instance creates a gradient with the `Color.WHITE` and `Color.BLACK` colors. You can, however, have many more stops included in your gradient.

There's more...

JavaFX's gradient implementation uses the concept of proportionality to express the values of gradient properties. When proportionality is turned on through the `proportional:Boolean` property, the spatial and dimensional properties can be expressed as a ratio rather than an absolute value. For instance, the next code snippet uses proportional values to express the radius and the center location of the radial gradient as a fraction:

```
def radialGrad = RadialGradient{
    radius:1; centerX: 0.5, centerY: 0.5
    proportional: true
    stops: [ ...]
}
```

Here, radius = 1 means to stretch out the size of the radial gradient to 100% of the size of the target node. In our snippet, the centerX and centerY properties are expressed as fractional values of 0.5, which will cause the gradient to be generated at half the size of the circle.

See also

▸ *Introduction*

Creating your own customized Paint

In previous recipes (and chapters), we have seen the use of the Color class used to apply paint color to an object. In the recipe *Applying cool paint effects with gradients*, we explored how to use JavaFX's built-in gradient classes to apply paint effects to visual objects. But, what if you want to create your own customized paint? This is exactly what is covered in this recipe. You will learn how to create your own Paint instance, which can be used to fill in your objects.

Getting ready

This recipe makes use of the javafx.scene.paint.Paint class to create a customized Paint instance that can be used to paint any node object. We are also going to make use of additional classes, javax.imageio.ImageIO, java.net.URL, java.awt.geom.Rectangle2D, and java.awt.TexturePaint, that are used to load the image and create the paint texture.

How to do it...

Creating a customized paint involves extending class Paint. To illustrate how to accomplish this, the next code snippet creates the class CustomPaint to be used as textured paint. You can get the full listing of the code in ch03/source-code/src/effects/CustomPaintDemo.fx.

```
class CustomPaint extends Paint {
    public-init var url:String;
    override public function impl_getPlatformPaint () : Object
    {
        var buff = ImageIO.read(new URL(url));
```

```
               new TexturePaint(
                   buff,
                   new Rectangle2D.Double(0,0,64,52)
               );
           }
       }

   def w = 400;
   def h = 200;

   def circle = Circle {
       centerX:w/2 centerY:h/2
       radius:75
       fill:CustomPaint{url:"{__DIR__}texture.png"}
       stroke:Color.BLACK
       strokeWidth:3
   };
```

When the code is executed, it renders a circle that is painted with the textured paint returned by the CustomPaint class as shown in the following screenshot:.

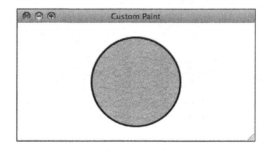

How it works...

The previous code snippet shows how to extend the Paint class to create a customized Paint class that can be used to fill shapes. In this recipe, we will create class CustomPaint to be used as textured paint. The class takes an arbitrary image file and use its content as the textured paint applied to the shape object. Let's examine how that is done in the code:

- CustomPaint *class*—is used to create our customized paint, we extend the abstract class Paint. Our class exposes the url:String property, which is a value that contains the URL location of the image to be used as the textured background for the paint.

- *Function* impl_getPlatformPaint—this is a required function that must be implemented when extending the Paint class. It is expected to return an Object instance that can be used as Paint instance.

- *Loading the image file*—inside the `impl_getPlatformPaint` function, the first thing that is done is to load the image file. We use `ImageIO.read()` function to read the image's content and return an instance of `java.awt.image.BufferedImage` stored in variable `buff`.

- *Creating texture*—once the image is loaded, it is ready to be handed off to create the `Paint` instance. This is done with an instance of the `TexturePaint` class. The constructor of that class takes two arguments, including a `BufferedImage`, stored in variable `buff`, and an instance of `Rectangle2D`, which provides the dimensions of the image being loaded.

- *Using the paint*—the paint can be used wherever a Paint instance can be applied. Here, we used the customized paint to fill an instance of the Circle shape:

```
Circle{...
    fill:CustomPaint{url:"{__DIR__}texture.png"} ...
}
```

When the texture paint is applied to a shape, it repeats the content of the image file across the surface of the shape, where it is applied automatically.

The {__DIR__} built-in variable returns to the location where the class being executed is found (in this case `source-code/src/effects/`). This is covered in more detail in *Chapter 5, JavaFX Media*.

See also

- *Applying cool paint effects with gradients*

Adding depth with lighting and shadow effects

All of the shapes we have used so far have been rendered pretty bland with boring solid colors. Let's say you want to enhance the look of your objects by adding depth for a more engaging look. This recipe shows you how to use the `Effect` classes to add lighting and shadow effects to visual nodes in the scene graph.

Getting ready

All Node instances can receive an effect through the `effect:Effect` property. You can find all effects in the package `javafx.scene.effect`. For this recipe, we are going to use effects classes `Lighting`, `DistantLighting`, and `DropShadow`.

How to do it...

The abbreviated code listing given next shows you how to use the Lighting and the DropShadow effects to enhance the appearance of a circle and a rectangle. You can find the the full listing in `ch03/source-code/src/effects/ShapeEffectDemo.fx`.

```
def shadow = DropShadow { offsetX:5 offsetY:5 }

def light = Lighting {
   light:DistantLight{azimuth:-45}
   surfaceScale:5
}

def circ = Circle {
    centerX: 125 centerY: 100 radius:50
    fill:Color.RED   stroke:Color.BLUE
    effect: light
}

def rect = Rectangle {
    x:200 y:50 width:125 height:100
    fill:Color.BLUE
    arcHeight:10 arcWidth:10
    effect:shadow
}
```

The code snippet produces the objects shown in the next figure.

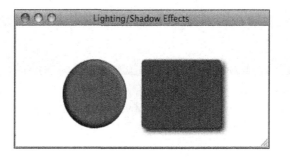

How it works...

As mentioned earlier, all `Node` instances expose the `effect:Effect` property. An `Effect` class provides algorithmic manipulation to the input source to produce new graphical elements with the applied effects during rendition of the scene graph. In this recipe, we use the `Lighting` and the `DropShadow` effects to add depth to the the objects on the scene. Let's see how these effects work.

The **Lighting effect** simulates a light source shining across the object, creating a slight shadow and reflection area on the surface of the object. This essentially generates an elevated 3D-like effect around the object (perfect for creating buttons). The `Lighting` effect exposes a number of properties including the `light:Light` property. The `Light` class provides further control over the direction and elevation of the light source being used to generate the effect.

In this recipe, the Lighting effect causes the circle to be re-rendered with a slight elevation and a surface shadow that falls around the edge of the new shape. The circle received an instance of `DistantLight`, through the `light` property, which represents a distant light source. The `DistantLight` instance provides control over the angle of the light source through the `azimuth` property (you can also control elevation). The `surfaceScale` property specifies the height of the surface elevation used to simulate the lighting effect.

The **DropShadow effect** re-renders the node with a shadow behind it. It automatically figures out the shape of the shadow and provides a default blur size. This gives the object the appearance of floating on the screen. The `DropShadow` effect offers several properties to control how the shadow is generated including the blur level of the shadow's edge, the shadow's color, the shadow's x/y offset, and the radius of the blur. For our example, we simply specify the `x` and `y` distance offset of the shadow, as shown in the previous screenshot.

 The algorithm which creates effects can be CPU intensive. If you have a scene graph containing hundreds of nodes with complicated effects, you will pay a penalty through performance degradation. Therefore, you should understand the implications of using a specific effect before applying it on a large scale.

There's more...

Though our recipe only covers two effects, JavaFX provides an extensive set of built-in effect classes located at `javafx.scene.effect`. The next table shows a list of all available effects as of version 1.2.

Blend	Blends two effects to create a third effect from the combination
Bloom	Makes bright portion of an input glow
BoxBlur, GaussianBlur, and MotionBlur	Available blur effects
ColorAdjust	Allows adjustment of hue, saturation, brightness, and contrast
DisplacementMap	A low-level effect that shifts each pixel by a specified value
Flood	Fills a rectangular region with a given paint

Glow	Makes the target appear to glow
Shadow, InnerShadow	Other classes that apply shadow effects
InvertMask	Renders a graphical inverse of the input
PerspectiveTransform	Modifies the perspective of an object to simulate 3D
SepiaTone	Renders a discoloration effect, producing an antique look

See also

▸ *Creating your own customized Paint*

▸ *Applying cool paint effects with gradients*

Creating your own Text effect

In the recipe *Adding depth with lighting and shadow effects,* we introduced several effect classes that are available in JavaFX. The Text node can receive any one of these effects to produce stunning text effects. You can, however, go beyond the available effects to produce your own text effects by combining available Node operations and effects. In this recipe, we are going to combine what we have learned in the second chapter's constructive area geometry operations, and the effects covered in this chapter, to create a text cut-out effect.

Getting ready

As mentioned in the introduction, this recipe combines concepts from constructive area geometry covered in the recipe *Creating shapes with constructive area geometry* from *Chapter 2, Creating JavaFX Applications*, and the Effect classes covered earlier in this chapter to create new text effects. Hence, if you are not familiar with any of these topics, it will be helpful to review them before continuing.

How to do it...

The next code snippet creates a text cut-out effect using `ShapeSubtract` to apply constructive area geometry operation and the `DropShadow` class to provide depth. The full code listing can be found in `ch03/source-code/src/effects/TextEffectDemo.fx`.

```
def w = 400; def h = 200;
def rw = w - 100; def rh = h - 50;

def bg = Rectangle {
    x: w/2-rw/2 y: h/2-rh/2 width: rw height: rh
    fill: LinearGradient {
        startX: 0, endX: 0, startY: 0, endY: 1
```

```
        }
    }
    def text: Text = Text {
        layoutX: bind (w - text.layoutBounds.width) / 2.0
        layoutY: bind (h - text.layoutBounds.height) / 2.0
        content: "Hello!"
        font: Font.font("Arial", FontWeight.BOLD, 100);
        fill: Color.SILVER
        textOrigin: TextOrigin.TOP
    }
    def txtfx = ShapeSubtract {
        a: bg
        b: text
        effect: DropShadow {
            color: Color.rgb(0, 0, 0, 0.9)
            offsetX: 5, offsetY: 5
            radius: 10
        }
        fill: LinearGradient {
            startX: 0, endX: 0, startY: 0, endY: 1
            stops: [
                Stop { offset: 0, color: Color.SILVER }
                Stop { offset: 1, color: Color.WHITE }
            ]
        }
    }
```

When the code is rendered, it produces the text effect shown in the following screenshot.

How it works...

The code illustrates how you can combine the built-in visual effects available in JavaFX to create new customized effects. In this recipe, we use the ShapeSubtract, DropShadow, and LinearGradient to build the cut-out text effect seen in the previous screenshot. Let's examine how this works.

- *Create the stencil*—first, we define a `Rectangle` instance (assigned to variable `bg`) from which the letters will be cut out. Next, we create the text shapes using a `Text` instance (assigned to variable `text`) that will be extruded from the rectangle shape.

- *Cut text out*—to extract the text shapes from the rectangle, we use the `ShapeSubtract` class to apply a shape subtraction operation, extracting the node assigned to property `a` (the text node) from property `b` (the rectangle).

- *Apply effects*—subtracting the shapes from one another does not create the desired effect. To make the effect more realistic, we apply a `DropShadow` effect to the subtracted shape (rectangle with cutout letters). This adds depth to the text, making the letters stand out as if they were cut out of the rectangle. To polish the effect, we apply a linear gradient to the surface of the rectangle giving it a dusty metallic look.

See also

- *Adding depth with lighting and shadow effects*
- *Applying cool paint effects with gradients*

Adding visual appeal with the Reflection effect

One of the appealing features of the Mac OS X operating system is its treatment of graphical reflection of objects on the desktop. As a modern development environment, JavaFX provides the tools and APIs to take advantage of popular effects, such as reflection. Before we conclude this chapter, we are going to explore how to use the Reflection class to create compelling graphical effects.

Getting ready

The `Reflection` effect can be found in the package `javafx.scene.effect` and is part of the `Effect` API covered in the recipe *Adding depth with lighting and shadow effects*. If you are not familiar with how effects work in JavaFX, review that recipe.

How to do it...

To keep things simple, the next code snippet shows you how to apply reflection effects to objects on the scene. You can see the full code listing from `ch03/source-code/src/effects/ReflectionEffect.fx`.

```
var grad =  LinearGradient {
    startX: 0.0, startY: 0.0, endX: 0.0, endY: 1.0
    proportional: true
```

```
        stops: [ Stop { offset: 0.0 cclor: Color.DARKBLUE },
                 Stop { offset: 1.0 cclor: Color.LIGHTBLUE } ]
    }

    var reflect = Reflection {
        fraction: 0.50
        topOpacity: 0.50
        bottomOpacity: 0.0
        topOffset: 2.0
    };

    var rect = Rectangle {
        x:130 y:50 width:100, height:80
        stroke:Color.RED strokeWidth:2
        arcHeight:10 arcWidth:10
        fill:grad
        effect:reflect
    }
    var circ = Circle {
        centerX:290 centerY:75 radius:50
        stroke:Color.BLUE strokeWidth:2
        fill:grad
        effect:reflect
    }
```

When the code is executed it places a rectangle and a circle with a reflection on the stage, as shown in the next figure.

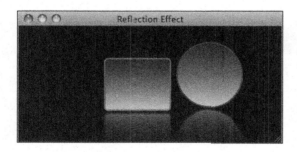

How it works...

Reflection, in JavaFX, is applied as an effect to a visual node in the scene graph. By default, the Reflection class uses the original node, to which it is attached, as its input and renders a new image with a reflection at the bottom. The top portion of the rendered image is the node, and the bottom is the generated reflection. The generated reflection is automatically blended with its surrounding's color, providing a clean rendition of the reflection effect.

For our example, we apply the reflection effect to a rectangle and a circle object. Both objects use a gradient paint against a black-filled scene. The `Reflection` class automatically blends the background color and the gradient from the original object to product a nice reflective effect.

The `Reflection` class makes several properties available that provide control over the way the reflections work. Here are some common properties that you may come across:

- `fraction`—a ratio between 0 to 1, which indicates how much of the original visual node is reflected. A value of 1, for instance, means that all of the original object is reflected. A value of 0 shows no reflection. For best results, apply this property with a value between 0.25 to 0.75.

- `topOpacity`—a ratio indicating how opaque the reflection is at the top of the reflected image. This number ranges from 0 to 1, where 0 is complete opacity and 1 is complete transparency.

- `bottomOpacity`—a ratio indicating how opaque the reflection is at its bottom where it starts to fade. This number has a range from 0 to 1, where 0 is complete opacity and 1 is full transparency.

- `topOffset`—this is the distance between the bottom of the original node and the top of the reflected image in pixels.

When you use the Reflection effect, the newly generated reflected image is attached to the original node. The reflection is updated accordingly with any spatial or visual changes that are applied to the properties of the original node.

 The reflected portion of the image does not respond to any mouse input gesture.

See also

- *Adding depth with lighting and shadow effects*

Components and Skinning

In this chapter, we will cover the following topics:

- ▸ Creating a form with JavaFX controls
- ▸ Displaying data with the ListView control
- ▸ Using the Slider control to input numeric values
- ▸ Showing progress with the progress controls
- ▸ Creating a custom JavaFX control
- ▸ Embedding Swing components in JavaFX
- ▸ Styling your applications with CSS
- ▸ Using CSS files to apply styles
- ▸ Using CSS files to declare your styles
- ▸ Skinning applications with multiple CSS files

Introduction

As a rich GUI application framework, JavaFX offers everything you will need to build applications that provide an engaging user experience. This chapter is about the GUI components that are available in the JavaFX application framework that you can use as building blocks to create applications quickly.

As of this writing, JavaFX's current version of 1.2 makes available more than a dozen JavaFX components (with the promise of more to come in future releases) located in the package `javafx.scene.control`. These are native JavaFX components designed from scratch to provide the level of rich properties and behaviors expected from a rich client platform. They include button, check-box, toggle buttons such as the radio button, hyperlink button, text box, label, and so on. See the recipe *Creating a form with JavaFX controls* for details.

This chapter also explores ways to integrate JavaFX and the venerable Java Swing GUI framework. Over the years, Swing has evolved into a stable and reliable GUI platform with a well-understood component model. Developers have been writing Swing components for well over a decade, producing a wealth of GUI components and knowledge. That fact did not escape the JavaFX engineers, so they have provided a bridge API, found in `javafx.ext.swing`, to let developers expose standard Swing controls inside JavaFX applications. If your needs go beyond the standard controls, you will learn how to wrap your custom Swing controls as JavaFX controls.

Finally, this chapter explores ways to customize the look and feel of your components using the JavaFX's implementation of Cascading Style Sheets (CSS) for skinning components. All visual nodes in a JavaFX scene can be injected with CSS styles similarly to web pages. You will learn how to style your JavaFX applications using inline or externalized CSS files.

I know you can't wait, so let's get started!

Creating a form with JavaFX controls

The previous chapters demonstrated the power of the JavaFX platform in creating engaging UI experiences with features such as animation, effects, and so on. Data capture is an equally important aspect for a great user experience. In this recipe, you will learn how to assemble standard JavaFX GUI controls to build a form to collect data.

Getting ready

This recipe attempts to use as many standard JavaFX controls as possible to create a form to collect data from the user. All of the controls used here are found in the package `javafx.scene.control`.

What is a Control anyway, you may ask? **Controls** provide a uniform graphical and interaction model with consistent and predictable behaviors. For instance, a button, a text input field, and a label, are all examples of standard controls available in JavaFX. All controls implement the `Control` class as the basis for all user interface controls that are part of the JavaFX application framework.

How to do it...

To illustrate how to use the standard JavaFX controls, we are going to create a data input form. Because the full listing of the code is rather long, the abbreviated version presented here shows the pertinent portion of the code. You can see the full version in `ch04/source-code/src/controls/DataFormDemo.fx`.

```
def rdoBtns = ToggleGroup{};
var nameRow = HBox {spacing:7
    content:[
        VBox{content:[Label{text:"First Name"},
            TextBox{id:"fName"}]}
        VBox{content:[Label{text:"Last Name"},
            TextBox{id:"lName"}]}
    ]
}

var addr1Row = HBox {
    spacing:7
    content:[
        VBox{content:[Label{text:"Address"},
            TextBox{id:"addr"}]}
        VBox{content:[Label{text:"Suite"},
            TextBox{id:"suite"}]}
    ]
}

var addr2Row =  HBox {
    spacing:7
    content:[
        VBox{content:[Label{text:"City"},
            TextBox{id:"city"}]}
        VBox{content:[Label{text:"Postal Code"},
            TextBox{id:"pcode"}]}
    ]
}

var titleRow = HBox {spacing:7
    content:[
        HBox{
            nodeVPos:VPos.CENTER spacing:7
            content:[
                Label{text:"Title:"}
                RadioButton{
```

```
                             text:"Programmer"
                             toggleGroup:rdoBtns id:"pgmr"}
                    RadioButton{
                         text:"Manager"
                         toggleGroup:rdoBtns id:"mngr"}
                    RadioButton{
                         text:"Janitor"
                         toggleGroup:rdoBtns id:"gntr"}
               ]
          }
     ]
}

var attndRow = HBox {spacing:7
     nodeVPos:VPos.CENTER
     content:[CheckBox{id:"isattnd" text:"Mark as Attendee"}]
}

var btnRow = HBox {
     spacing:7
     content:[
          Button{
               text:"Submit"
               action:function(){
                    // display data
               }
          }
          Button{text:"Clear"}
     ]
}

// form panel to display it all
def panel = VBox { spacing:5
     content: [
          nameRow,
          addr1Row, addr2Row,
          titleRow, attndRow,
          btnRow
     ]
}
```

When the `panel` variable is added to a scene and the application is executed, it wil create a form as shown in the next screenshot:

How it works...

The form created in this recipe uses several of the standard GUI controls found in JavaFX. Thought the code looks intimidating, each row in the form is organized as merely a series of repeating `VBox` and `HBox` layout managers assigned to a corresponding variable. Each row is then assembled in a `VBox` instance assigned to the variable `panel`. Let's take a closer look at the controls.

- ▶ `Label`—as you can guess, the `Label` control is normally used to affix a label for another control. Though basic in its functionalities, the `Label` class exposes a myriad of properties to control the font attributes, position, icon image, text behavior in constrained spaces, and text wrapping behaviors. In our example, we simply use the labels to label text boxes and other GUI controls the form.

- ▶ `TextBox`—this is the control designated to collect and display textual data using free-form text. The JavaFX `TextBox` class makes several useful properties available, including a watermark prompt (displayed prior to text entry), font attributes, the size of the text box, and the text that was entered.

- ▶ `RadioButton`—this control is designed to function as a toggle button when the user needs to select one item from two or more choices. Similar to other controls, the `RadioButton` exposes several properties to control the button's label, font, icon, and selection state. To get `RadioButton` instances to toggle as a group, you must specify a `ToggleGroup` instance through the `toggleGroup:ToggleGroup` property. In the recipe, we define variable `rdoBtns` as the `ToggleGroup` instance for all three instances of the radio button.

- ► CheckBox—similar to `RadioButton`, the `CheckBox` control is labeled entity, used to let the user make multiple selections. It exposes properties to control the CheckBox's label, font, icon, and, most importantly, the selection state.

- ► `Button`—the last controls used in the form is the `Button`. This class represents regular push button controls, used to execute an action when clicked. As a labeled entity, you can control the label's text, the font, and the icon for the button. The `Button` instances also expose the `action:function()` property to let developers specify what happens when the button is clicked.

There's more...

Once you have created a form using JavaFX, then what? How do you retrieve the data that is stored in the control? Fortunately, JavaFX offers an easy way to search for a control (or any node) you place in the scene graph. Recall that each control that receives input data has the `id:String` property. This property provides a reference for the control, where it can be searched in the scene graph tree.

The following code segment shows how to retrieve the text data stored in the TextBox instance identified as `city`:

```
var scene:Scene;
var city = (scene.lookup("city") as TextBox).text
Stage{
    scene: scene = Scene {...}
}
```

The code uses the `Scene.lookup(id:String):Node` script-level function to search for a given node in the scene graph. You can see the full example of how this is used in the source code from `ch04/source-code/src/DataFormDemo.fx`. When the **Submit** button is clicked, the function goes through and collects data from all of the input controls and displays it in a panel, as shown in the next screenshot:

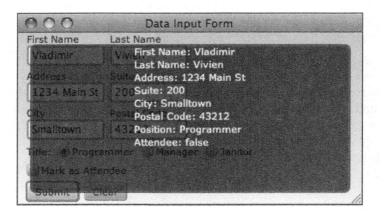

See also

▸ *Chapter 2—Arranging your nodes on stage*

▸ *Introduction*

Displaying data with the ListView control

In rich GUI frameworks, displaying data in a structured list is one of the fundamental GUI controls made available to users. In this recipe, we will discuss how to use the `ListView` component to collect and display data.

Getting ready

The `ListView` control is part of the GUI control collection offered by JavaFX in the `javafx.scene.control` package. If you have not used the JavaFX controls, it may be helpful to review the recipe *Creating a form with JavaFX controls* for some background information. Some of the code uses JavaFX constructs, such as for-loop expressions. If you need a refresher, review *Chapter 1, Getting Started with JavaFX,* which covers language fundamentals.

How to do it...

The `ListView` component has a simple mechanism. You provide it with a sequence of objects, and it will attempt to display those items in a list. In the next code snippet, we attach a sequence of String objects to the list to display. You can access the full code listing for this example from `ch04/source-code/src/ListViewDemoSimple.fx`.

```
var w = 400;
var h = 200;

var listView = ListView {
  width:w-200
  height:h-50
  effect:DropShadow{offsetY:3 offsetX:3}
  items:  for (i in [1..50]) "Cloud {%5s i}"
}

listView.layoutX = (w - listView.width)/2;
listView.layoutY = (h - listView.height)/2;

Stage {
  width: w
  height: h
```

```
scene: Scene {
    fill:LinearGradient {
        startX: 0, endX: 0, startY: 0, endY: 1
        stops: [
            Stop { offset: 0, color: Color.GRAY }
            Stop { offset: 1, color: Color.WHITESMOKE }
        ]
    }
    content: [listView]
}
}
```

When executed, the code produces the following list:

How it works...

The ListView control allows you to arrange and display data in a vertical list. This control makes available several properties, including selectedIndex and selectedItem, to access the currently selected item in the list. The ListView class also exposes the items:Object[] property as the list's data model displayed in the List instance. In our example, we dynamically generate the data model as a sequence of 50 strings using a for-loop expression and assign that sequence directly to the list's items property.

> As of version 1.2, the ListView component only displays textual items in the list. The component does not allow you to use, say, a Node class as its model. Therefore, you cannot create custom lists that display non-textual items. This will certainly be improved in future versions.

There's more...

Using a custom data model with ListView

While the previous code shows you how to use String sequences as the data model for a ListView, you are not limited to that. Here, we are going to modify the previous example to use a custom data model as the list item. The full listing of the code presented here can be found at ch04/source-code/src/controls/ListViewDemoExtended.fx.

To use a custom data model with the ListView, we use the following steps:

1. Define the model class. Below, we create class MyItem as the one to be used in the ListView instance. Make sure to override the function toString() to return a string representation of the data item to be displayed in the list. The MyItem class stores a shape along with a descriptive name.

```
class MyItem {
    public var id:Integer = new Random().nextInt(100);
    public var name:String;
    public var shape:Shape;
    override function toString():String {
        "Shape: {%5s name}"
    }
}
```

2. Add instances of the model to the ListView.items property. Here, we add four instances of the MyItem class to the ListView. Each MyItem instance has an id, name, and a shape stored in it.

```
var listView = ListView {
  width:200
  height:150
  items:  [
      MyItem{id:1 name: "Rectangle"
            shape:Rectangle{width:100 height:50}}
      MyItem{id:2 name:"Circle" shape:Circle{radius:25}}
      MyItem{id:3 name:"Line"
            shape:Line{startX:10 startY:10 endX:40 endY:50}}
      MyItem{id:4 name:"Round Rectangle"
            shape:Rectangle{
                width:100 height:50
                arcHeight:10 arcWidth:10}
        }
    ]
}
```

3. Use an `onMouseClicked` event handler to retrieve the item from the view. You can get the currently selected item using the `ListView.selectedItem` property when the mouse is clicked on the control.

```
listView.onMouseClicked = function(e) {
    var item = listView.selectedItem as MyItem;
    panel.content = [
        item.shape,
        Label{text:"You selected item {item.name}"}
    ]
}
```

When the code is executed, it renders the list as shown in the next screenshot.

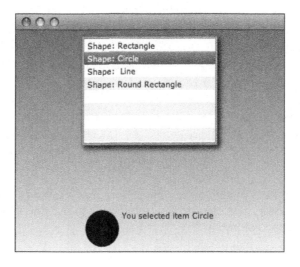

See also

▶ *Introduction*

▶ *Creating a form with JavaFX controls*

Using the Slider control to input numeric values

We have seen how to capture data input using traditional GUI controls such as TextBoxes and Buttons. The Slider control offers a different means of inputting data by sliding a knob along a groove. In this recipe, we use the Slider control to create a color picker application.

Getting ready

The Slider control is part of the standard GUI controls offered by JavaFX in the `javafx.scene.control` package. By sliding the slider along its track, users are both inputting data by selecting the slider's position on the track, and they are getting visual feedback confirming their input. If you have not used the JavaFX controls, it may be helpful to review the recipe *Creating a form with JavaFX controls* for some background information.

How to do it...

The following code snippet shows you how to use the Slider control as an input controller to update the color values of another object or the stage. You can get the full code listing from `ch04/source-code/src/controls/SliderDemo.fx`.

```
var rSlide = Slider {
    translateX:10 translateY:20 min:0 max:255 value:0
}
var gSlide = Slider {
    translateX:10 translateY:40 min:0 max:255 value:0
}
var bSlide = Slider {
    translateX:10 translateY:60 min:0 max:255 value:0
}

var circ = Circle {
    fill : bind Color.rgb(
        rSlide.value, gSlide.value, bSlide.value
    )
    stroke:Color.WHITE strokeWidth:3 radius: 70
    effect:DropShadow{offsetY:3 offsetX:3}
}

var panel = HBox{
    width:w
    spacing:20
    nodeVPos:VPos.TOP
    content:[
        VBox {content: [rSlide, gSlide, bSlide]},
         circ,
         VBox{
            spacing:20
            content:[
                Text{content: bind "R: {%.0f rSlide.value}"}
                Text{content: bind "G: {%.0f gSlide.value}"}
                Text{content: bind "B: {%.0f bSlide.value}"}
            ]
        }
    ]
}
```

When the variable `panel` is added to a `Scene` instance (not shown) and the application is executed, you will end up with what is shown in the next screenshot:

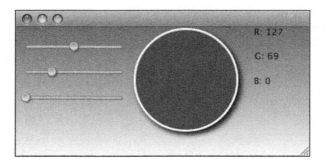

How it works...

The previous code shows how to use the Slider control to create a color picker. It declares three `Slider` instances to represent a color element including `rSlide` for red, `gSlide` for green, and `bSlide` for blue. The most pertinent properties of the Slider are `min:Number` and `max:Number`. These properties specify the range of values that the slider represents. In our code, each slider instance is declared with `min=0` and `max=255`, corresponding to the numeric ranges of the RGB color values. The user can only slide the knob between the `min` value and the `max` values (inclusive).

As the user drags the knob, the slider updates its `value:Number` property. This property indicates the currently selected value based on the knob position on the track. For instance, when the user slides the knob all the way to the right-hand side, the `value` property of the slider will be set to `255`.

The Circle instance `circ` is used to reflect the color changes as the slider values are updated. To do this, the `fill:Color` property of the circle is assigned a `Color` instance, where each element of the RGB color is bound to slider `rSlide.value`, `gSlide.value`, and `bSlide.value` respectively, as shown in the next code snippet. Whenever a color value changes, the bind generates a new `Color` instance to apply to the circle.

```
var circ = Circle {
    fill : bind Color.rgb(
        rSlide.value, gSlide.value, bSlide.value
    )
    ...
}
```

See also

- ▶ *Introduction*
- ▶ *Creating a form with JavaFX controls*

Showing progress with the progress controls

As a rich client platform, you will undoubtedly create long-running processes in JavaFX. You will, for instance, need to connect to a remote web server in order to download images or access large data set from a database server. In either case, it is imperative that the user's expectation is managed properly during the execution of these processes, or your application runs the risk of being labeled broken.

One of the most popular ways by which rich client applications manage the user experience during long-running processes is through the use of progress indicator widgets. This recipe shows you how to use JavaFX's built-in progress indicator controls to show progress of a long-running processes.

Getting ready

The progress controls are part of the standard GUI controls offered by JavaFX in the `javafx.scene.control` package. If you have not used the JavaFX controls, it may be helpful to review the recipe *Creating a form with JavaFX controls* for some background information. JavaFX offers two progress controls that you can use to provide feedback on the progress of long running processes: `ProgressBar` and the `ProgressIndicator`. Both controls function in the same way, but render their feedback to the user differently.

For this recipe, we are going to simulate a long-running process using a `Timeline` instance. The `Timeline` class lets us implement a timer that counts and pauses in-between counts, which is perfect for simulating long-running activities that can update a progress control. You can find out how to use the Timeline as a timer in the recipe *Building animation with the KeyFrame API* in *Chapter 3, Transformations, Animations, and Effects*.

How to do it...

The code presented here shows you how to use the `ProgressBar` component to track the progress of a long running process. As mentioned earlier, to keep things manageable, the long running process is simulated by a `Timeline` instance used as a timer. You can get the full listing of the code from `ch04/source-code/src/controls/ProgressBarDemo.fx`.

```
var w = 400;
var h = 200;
var total = 400;
var counter = 0;

def prog = ProgressBar {
    progress: bind ProgressBar.computeProgress(total, counter
    effect:DropShadow{offsetY:3 offsetX:3}
```

```
        width: w - 100
    }
    prog.layoutX = (w - prog.layoutBounds.width)/2;
    prog.layoutY = (h - prog.layoutBounds.height)/2;


    def timer:Timeline = Timeline {
        repeatCount: Timeline.INDEFINITE
        interpolate:false
        keyFrames:[
            KeyFrame{
                time:100ms
                action:function():Void {
                    if(counter <= total){
                        counter++;
                    }else{
                        //counter = 0;
                        timer.stop();
                    }
                }
            }
        ]
    }

    timer.play();

    def progTxt:Text = Text {
        layoutX:(prog.width)/2
        layoutY:prog.layoutY - 30
        content: bind "Progress: {%.0f prog.progress*100}%"
        font:Font.font("Arial", FontWeight.BOLD, 22)
        fill:Color.BLUE
        opacity:0.25
    }
```

When the code is executed, it shows a `ProgressBar` control on the screen being updated as shown in the next screenshot.

How it works...

The code in this recipe demonstrates an example of how to use the `ProgressBar` control to provide gradual feedback on a long-running process. The control works simply. It only requires the property `progress:Number` to be provided. This is a ratio, between `0.0` and `1.0`, of the completed activity. The control uses that value to draw the progress bar accordingly.

In the recipe, in order to continually update the progress bar, we bind the `progress` property to the convenience function `ProgressBar.computeProgress(total:Number, current:Number)` to calculate the progress ratio with the following code segment:

```
def prog = ProgressBar {
    progress: bind ProgressBar.computeProgress(total, counter)
...
}
```

In this recipe, the long-running process is simulated using an instance of `Timeline` named `timer`. In the code, the `Timeline` instance includes a KeyFrame which restarts repeatedly every `100ms` due to `repeatCount=Timeline.INDEFINITE`. At the end of each `100ms`, the KeyFrame executes the function attached to the `action` property. In our example, that function basically increments the variable `counter` by one if it is less than or equal to the variable `total`. Otherwise, it stops the timeline. With every increment of `counter`, it causes the `ProgressBar` instance to update itself because it is bound to the variable `counter` through the `progress` property (see previous code snippet).

There's more...

As mentioned earlier in the recipe, JavaFX also offers the `ProgressIndicator` control as another class, which can be used to provide users with feedback of progress during a long-running process. The `ProgressIndicator` operates in the exact same way as the `ProgressBar` and exposes the `progress:Number` property as a way to indicate the ratio of completion. `ProgressIndicator`, however, is rendered as a circular dial when displaying progress. `ProgressIndicator` class is suitable for cramped areas where the bar may take too much screen real estate. You can see an example of the progress indicator in `ch04/source-code/src/controls/ProgressIndicatorDemo.fx`. It is the same code as presented above; however, it uses a `ProgressIndicator` instead of a `ProgressBar`, as shown in the next screenshot.

See also

▶ *Chapter 2—Building animation with the KeyFrame API*

▶ *Introduction*

▶ *Creating a form with JavaFX controls*

Creating a custom JavaFX control

In previous recipes in this chapter, we have used the standard JavaFX controls to create application GUIs. Inevitably, you will have an idea for a component with specific behaviors and usage not offered by the standard set of controls. What do you do? Fortunately, creating your own control is as easy as creating a new class. In this recipe, you will learn how to create your own reusable GUI control.

Getting ready

As mentioned in the introduction for this recipe, creating a custom control is as easy as creating a new class. If you are not familiar with the topic of class creation and issues with accessibility and visibility of class members, review the recipes *Declaring and using JavaFX classes* from *Chapter 1*, *Creating your own custom node* from Chapter 2, and *Making your scripts modular,* also from Chapter 2. If you are not familiar with the JavaFX Control API, review the recipe *Creating a form with JavaFX controls* from this chapter.

How to do it...

The abbreviated version of the code for this custom control is shown next. It creates a class called Deck that stacks its content (a collection of nodes) from back to front. The control lets you shuffle the the content by shifting objects from the top to the bottom of the stack (or vice-versa). You can access the full listing of the code from ch04/source-code/ custom/DeckControl.fx.

Let's explore how the code works:

1. First, let's define the Deck class by extending the Control class:

```
class Deck extends Control {
    // properties
    override public var width = 200;
    override public var height = 100;
    public var roundCornerSize:Integer = 0;
    public var borderSize:Integer = 2;
    public var borderColor:Color = Color.BLACK;
    public var slideOffset:Integer=20;
    public var duration:Duration = 300ms;
```

```
public var enableReflection:Boolean = true;

public var fill:Paint = LinearGradient { ... }

def stack = Group{}

public function add(n:Node){
    insert createCard(n) into stack.content
}
...
public function remove(idx:Integer){
    def obj = stack.content[idx];
    delete obj from stack.content;
}

public function shiftBackToFront():Void {
    def node = stack.content[0];
    animate(node, 0);
}

public function shiftFrontToBack():Void {
    def node =
        stack.content[(sizeof stack.content)-1];
    animate(node, 1);
}
...

    override function create():Node {
        ...
        stack
    }

    function createCard(node:Node):Group { ... }

    function animate(node:Node, dir:Integer){
        TranslateTransition {
            ...
            action:function(){
                if(dir == 0)
                    node.toFront()
                else
                    node.toBack()
            }
        }.playFromStart();
    }
}
```

2. Next, we create an instance of `Deck` and add objects to its contents:

```
def w = 400;
def h = 320;
var scene:Scene;

def deck:Deck = Deck{
    width:w-100 height:h-100
    translateX:(w -(w-200))/2 translateY:(h-(h-100))/2
    slideOffset:50
    duration:300ms
    roundCornerSize:20
}
deck.add(Rectangle {width:150 height:100 fill:Color.RED});
deck.add(Circle{radius:70 fill:Color.BLUE});
deck.add(ImageView{
    image:Image{url:"{__DIR__}image1.png"}fitWidth:200
    preserveRatio:true
});
```

3. Lastly, we add interactions by creating buttons to animate the deck:

```
def leftBtn = Button {
    text:"<<"
    action:function(){
        deck.shiftBackToFront();
    }
}
def rightBtn = Button {
    text:">>"
    action:function(){
        deck.shiftFrontToBack();
    }
}
```

When the component is added to the stage, and the code is executed, you should see the application as shown in the next screenshot. When the buttons are pressed, it slides the top object (or bottom, depending on the button pressed) in the stack from the top to the bottom of the stack (hard to capture with the screenshot).

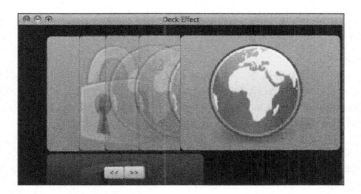

How it works...

The lengthy (yet abbreviated) code segment shows you how to implement a custom control class. This is done by extending the `Control` class from which our control will inherit several properties and behaviors. For our `Deck` control, let's explore how it works.

- ▶ *Defining the control*—the `Deck` class extends the `Control` class, which extends `CustomNode`. As a matter of fact, creating a custom control works in the same way as creating a custom node; you need `override function create():Node` to return the control you want to create. In our code example, we return an instance of `Group` as the container for our `Deck` class.

- ▶ *Class properties*—all public variables declared in the class definitions will be treated as class properties. Our custom `Deck` control will expose the following self-explanatory properties:

    - ❏ `roundCornerSize:Integer;`
    - ❏ `borderSize:Integer = 2;`
    - ❏ `borderColor:Color;`
    - ❏ `slideOffset:Integer=20;`
    - ❏ `duration:Duration = 300ms;`
    - ❏ `enableReflection:Boolean`

    The class `Deck` will also inherit properties from the base class `Control`.

- ▶ *The* `Deck.add()` *function*—the `Deck` class exposes the `Deck.add(node:Node)` function to add items to the stack (internally managed by an instance of `Group` assigned to variable `stack`). The function wraps the added node in a virtual card for the deck by calling `createCard()` which basically returns a Group instance containing the added node and a `Rectangle` instance as a background. The card is then added to the content sequence of the deck's internal `stack`.

▸ *The* Deck.remove() *function*—as a measure of convenience, a remove function is provided to remove node objects added to the stack easily.

▸ *The stack shuffle*—the Deck class exposes the public functions shiftBackToFront() and shiftFrontToBack() to trigger the shuffle animation sequence. Function shiftBackToFront() picks a card from the bottom of the stack and places it on top. Conversely, the function shiftFrontToBack() takes a card from the top of the stack and slides it to the bottom.

Both functions use the internal animate() function to create the animation sequence that slides the card out and back in the stack. This is accomplished by using a simple TranslateTransition class that moves the card away from the stack to a given distance (controlled by Deck property slideOffset), then reverses the animation sequence to bring the card back to the stack.

At the end of the initial slide sequence (away), the TranslateTransition calls its internal function attached to the property action:function() to change the Z-order of the card by moving it to the back using the toBack() function (or toFront(), depending on the operation invoked).

▸ *Using the Deck*—to use the Deck class you simply create an instance of it and place it in a scene graph. In the code, we assign an instance of Deck to the variable deck, with a literal declaration that sets the properties slideOff, duration, and roundCornerSize. Notice that we have access to Control-exposed properties such as dimensions, translations, and so on.

To add cards to the deck, we invoke the Deck.add() function. In the code example, we add several nodes to the deck including Shape instances and images using ImageView (covered in *Chapter 5, JavaFX Media*). The nodes are stacked from bottom to top, so the last node added is displayed and earlier nodes are hidden behind it. The class automatically centers the node instance on the rectangle.

Finally, we add two buttons to drive the animation. The button labeled **>>** calls the method Deck.frontToBack(), sliding the top card out and into the bottom of the stack. The button labeled **<<,** on the other hand, slides the card from the bottom and places it on top of the stack.

See also

▸ *Chapter 1—Declaring and using JavaFX classes*

▸ *Chapter 1—Creating and using JavaFX functions*

▸ *Chapter 2—Creating your own custom node*

▸ *Chapter 2—Making your scripts modular*

▸ *Introduction*

Embedding Swing components in JavaFX

As explained in the *Introduction* of this chapter, the Swing GUI framework has evolved into a set of rich GUI components, which developers have come to love over the years. Suppose, however, you want to continue using Swing in your JavaFX application; what do you do? This recipe shows you how to use the JavaFX wrapper APIs for Swing to embed Swing components in JavaFX scripts.

Getting ready

The JavaFX Swing wrapper classes let developers embed Swing components directly into JavaFX applications. The wrapper API can be found in the package `javafx.ext.swing`. For this recipe, it is assumed that you are familiar with using Swing components. It will also be helpful to be familiar with JavaFX's Control API. To illustrate how to embed Swing components in JavaFX, we have converted the data form introduced in the recipe *Creating a form with JavaFX controls*, to use all Swing components.

How to do it...

The next code snippet shows you how to embed Swing controls in JavaFX. Since this example is based on the data form introduced earlier in the recipe *Creating a form with JavaFX controls*, the code will be abbreviated down to the essentials. You can, however, get a full listing of the code discussed here from `ch04/source-code/src/controls/DataFormWithSwing.fx`.

```
def rdoBtns = SwingToggleGroup{};
var nameRow = HBox {spacing:7
    content:[
        VBox{content:[SwingLabel{text:"First Name"},
            SwingTextField{id:"fName" columns:10}]}
        VBox{content:[SwingLabel{text:"Last Name"},
            SwingTextField{id:"lName" columns:10}]}
    ]
}

...

var titleRow = HBox {spacing:7
    content:[
        HBox{
            nodeVPos:VPos.CENTER spacing:7
            content:[
                SwingLabel{text:"Title:"}
                SwingRadioButton{
                    text:"Programmer"
                    toggleGroup:rdoBtns id:"pgmr"}
```

```
                    SwingRadioButton{
                        text:"Manager"
                        toggleGroup:rdoBtns id:"mngr"}
                    SwingRadioButton{
                        text:"Janitor"
                        toggleGroup:rdoBtns id:"gntr"}
                ]
            }
        ]
    }

var attndRow = HBox {spacing:7
    nodeVPos:VPos.CENTER
    content:[
        SwingCheckBox{id:"isattnd"
        text:"Mark as Attendee"}
    ]
}

var btnRow = HBox {
    spacing:7
    content:[
        SwingButton{
            text:"Submit"
            action:function(){
                // display data
            }
        }
        SwingButton{text:"Clear"}
    ]
}
```

When the code runs, it will produce the form shown in the next screenshot. Compare this to the form produced by using JavaFX controls in the recipe *Creating a form with JavaFX controls*.

How it works...

The form built in this recipe uses the same layout structure as the form found in the recipe *Creating a form with JavaFX controls*. The controls are organized in the same manner, using `HBox` and `VBox` layout managers to arrange GUI controls in rows and columns. The difference, however, is in the controls that are used in the form. Instead of native JavaFX controls, their Swing counterparts are used.

JavaFX provides a collection of controls that serve as wrappers for standard Swing controls. The Swing components themselves are encapsulated in instances of `javafx.ext.swing.SwingComponent`, which is a Node instance that can be attached to the scene graph.

The code for the recipe uses several of these wrapper classes, including:

- ► `SwingLabel`—this class renders the Swing counterpart to the JavaFX `Label` control. It wraps and displays the Swing's `JLabel` control.

- ► `SwingTextField`—this wraps the Swing counterpart to JavaFX's `TextBox` control. Under the hood, the `SwingTextField` wrapper class renders the Swing's `JTextField` component.

- ► `SwingRadioButton`—this class represents Swing's counterpart to the JavaFX `RadioButton` control. Internally, the `SwingRadioButton` renders the Swing `JRadioButton` control. To get `SwingRadioButton` instances to toggle as a group, you must specify a toggle group through the property `toggleGroup:SwingToggleGroup`. In the recipe, we define variable `rdoBtns` as the toggle group.

- ► `SwingCheckBox`—this class represents Swing's counterpart to the JavaFX control `CheckBox`. Under the hood, `SwingCheckBox` class renders an instance of Swing's `JCheckBox`.

- ► `SwingButton`—this class represents Swing's counter part to JavaFX `Button` control. Under the hood, the `SwingButton` renders a `JButton` instance on the screen.

Swing controls wrapped in the `SwingComponent` classes behave as regular JavaFX nodes and can be added to the scene graph. To locate an instance of a `SwingComponent`, we use the `id:String` property and function `Scene.lookup(id:String)`, as is done with native JavaFX controls.

There's more...

Wrapping custom Swing controls into JavaFX node

What if you wanted to use an existing custom Swing component as part of your JavaFX application? Well, JavaFX provides an easy way to transform existing Swing components into JavaFX node instances, which can be graphed into the scene using a script-level utility function `SwingComponent.wrap(swing:javax.swing.JComponent)`. For instance:

```
var mySwingComponent = new CustomSwingComponent();
var fxNode = SwingComponent.wrap(mySwingComponent);
```

When using the `SwingComponent.wrap()` function, you should be aware of the following:

1. Your Swing component must be a descent of the `JComponent` class.
2. You lose the JavaFX idioms, such as class properties, function variables, and so on. You must use Java-style getter and setters accessors to access instance values, and you cannot use function variables to handle events.

Creating a Swing control façade from JavaFX

As we have seen previously, it is a rather easy exercise to wrap existing Swing components using the `SwingComponent.wrap()` function. A more elegant way is to wrap your custom Swing controls yourself by encapsulating them within a JavaFX façade class. The benefit of this approach is having full control over the way your Swing controls are initialized and exposed. Since you are wrapping your Swing components in a JavaFX class, you will be able to retain the JavaFX idioms for creating and managing object instances.

The (very) abbreviated code snippet next shows you how this can be done by extending a class `SwingComponent` and implementing `function createJComponent():JComponent`.

```
class PopupMenu extends SwingComponent {
    var button:JButton;
    var menu:JPopupMenu;
...
    override function createJComponent():JComponent{
        button = new JButton();
        menu = new JPopupMenu();
        menu.setBorderPainted(true);

        button.addActionListener(ActionListener{
            public override function
                actionPerformed(e:ActionEvent) {
                menu.show(button, 0,button.getHeight()-5);
            }
        });
        button;
    }
...
```

```
    }

// using PopupMenu in JavaFX
PopupMenu{
    items:[
        MenuItem{
            title:"Hello!",
            action:function({Alert.inform("Hi!")}
        }
    ]
}
```

Class `PopupMenu`, defined above, is a façade that encapsulates and manages two Swing components, mainly a `JButton` and a `JpopupMenu`. Function `createJComponent()` initializes the internal Swing components and returns an instance of the `JButton`. You can get the full code listing for this example from `ch04/source-code/src/custom/SwingFacadeDemo.fx`.

See also

▸ *Chapter 1—Declaring and using JavaFX classes*

▸ *Chapter 2—Creating your own custom node*

▸ *Introduction*

▸ *Creating a custom JavaFX control*

Styling your applications with CSS

In previous recipes, we have seen how to control the look and feel of JavaFX graphical nodes programmatically by setting property values on the node directly. Programmatic style manipulation works just fine, but is hard to externalize. If you want to update the look of your application, you must recompile. However, JavaFX also offers a way to declare styles using Cascading Style Sheets (CSS). This recipe shows you how to apply styles declaratively to JavaFX graphical nodes using CSS.

Getting ready

Before going through this recipe, you should have an idea of what CSS is and how it is used for designing HTML web pages. Similar concepts are discussed here and other CSS-related recipes in this chapter. CSS was created by the web governing body W3C and is traditionally used for markup development languages such as HTML and other XML-derivatives (XUL, SVG, and so on). For information about CSS, visit `http://en.wikipedia.org/wiki/Cascading_Style_Sheets`.

To illustrate how to use CSS concepts, we are going to reuse the form created in the recipe *Creating a form with JavaFX controls*. In this recipe, we will extend the code for the form to include CSS formatting. Since the form code has been discussed previously, we will concentrate on the CSS portion of the code.

How to do it...

The abbreviated code snippet given next shows instances where CSS is used to format GUI control elements in the data input form. You can see the full listing of the code in `ch04/source-code/src/styling/DataFormInlineCssDemo.fx`.

```
def heading = Text{
    content:"Employee Information"
    style:"font-family:\"Helvetica\";"
         "font-size:24pt;"
         "font-weight:bold;"
}

def nameRow = HBox {
    spacing:7
    content:[
        VBox{content:[
            Label{text:"First Name" style:"textFill:blue"},
            TextBox{
                id:"fName"
                style:"textFill:yellow; "
                     "backgroundFill:lightblue;"
                     "borderFill:lightblue"
            }
        ]}
    ]
}
...
def btnRow = HBox {
    spacing:7
    content:[
        Button{
            text:"Submit"
            style:"textFill:blue;fill:lightblue"
        }
        Button{text:"Clear"
        style:"textFill:blue;fill:lightblue"}
    ]
}
```

When the code for the form containing the CSS styling is executed, it will produce the form shown in the next screenshot:

How it works...

Cascading Style Sheets (CSS) facilitate the separation of visual content in the scene graph from the styling of that content. CSS provides a declarative language to express the presentation and formatting semantics of the associated content. All Node instances in JavaFX expose the property `style:String`, which lets you inject CSS directives directly in your JavaFX code, similar to the `style` attribute in an HTML document.

In our previous code snippet, we used the `style` property to format the GUI elements in the form. The first element formatted is the `Text` instance. As you can see, using the CSS, you can specify all formatting attributes about the text including font-family, size, and weight. The code also shows you how to apply inline CSS styling directives to controls such as `Label`, `TextInput`, and `Button` instances.

There's more...

JavaFX CSS

Due to its wide adoption, CSS has been ported to non-XML-based languages, such as JavaFX. CSS in JavaFX is similar to the W3C's CSS language only in functionality. The JavaFX's version of CSS works as a declarative meta-programming language that lets developers declare formatting and layout directives of JavaFX nodes. When you declare a style in CSS, the JavaFX runtime matches the CSS property name to the node's property with the same name. So, when you see:

```
var circle = Circle {
  style:"center-x: 140; "
}
```

JavaFX will match the style property `center-x` to the `Circle.centerX` property. The CSS parser substitutes the - and the following letter with an uppercase letter to form a camel-case notation. So, the style property `arc-width` maps to the node property `arcWidth`, and so forth. If you do not like the style property name with the dash, you can use the actual node's property name as the style name as follows:

```
var circle = Circle {
   style: "centerX:100,centerY:100"
}
```

The runtime module will set the circle's `centerX` and `centerY` property to 100.

Because the CSS parser maps node property names to style properties, as of version 1.2 of the SDK, you can use style declarations to set pretty much all node properties of type `Number` and `Integer`, `String`, `Paint`, and `Font`. At this time, other value types will cause a parsing exception.

Styling Text nodes with CSS

Font style names for the Text node do not map directly to properties attached to the `Text` class. Recall that text is styled as follows:

```
var txt = Text {
   content: "Hello!"
   font: Font {name: "Helvetica" size:12}
}
```

In order to support the semantics of the W3C's guidelines, the JavaFX CSS parser provides shortcuts which apply the CSS style properties for font directly to the **Text** instance. Hence, the following code will format and apply font styles to the text:

```
var txt = Text {
   content: "Hello!"
   style: "font-family:\"Helvetica\";"
          "font-size:24pt;"
          "font-weight:heavy;"
}
```

Two things that you should notice with this declaration:

1. The Text node does not have an instance of `Font {}` attached to it. However, Text still receives font styles from the CSS declaration.

2. The Text node does not have the properties `fontFamily`, `fontSize`, and `fontWeight`. The CSS engine figures out how to apply the font styles to the text node directly.

Styling Paint properties with CSS

JavaFX lets you declare color styles in three ways, including the RGB hexadecimal, the color name, and the RGB decimal values as shown in the following snippets:

```
Rectangle {
    style:"fill:#33FFCC;stroke:#0000FF;"


}
Circle {
    style:"fill:red;stroke:blue;"


}
MyCustomNode {
    style:"fill:rgb(150,44,96);stroke:rgb(255,55,148);"


}
```

The CSS engine also supports a shortcut notation that lets developers specify paint gradients:

```
Circle {
  style:"fill:linear(100%, 0%)"
           "to (0%,0%)"
               "stops (0.0, red), (1.0, white);"
}
Rectangle {
  style:"fill:radial (0%, 0%) , 50% focus(25%, 25%)"
            "stops (0.00, red), (1.0, white);"
}
```

For linear gradients, JavaFX's CSS has the `linear(startX,startY)`, `to(endX, endY)`, and `stops(offset,color)` directives to build the gradient. For radial gradients, JavaFX provides the `radial(centerX,centerY)`, `radius-value focus(focusX,focusY)`, and the `stops(offset, color)` directives.

See also

- *Chapter 3—Applying cool paint effects with gradients*
- *Introduction*
- *Creating a form with JavaFX controls*

Using CSS files to apply styles

As your application grows beyond a few GUI components, you will find it cumbersome and impractical to use inline CSS directives to apply styles. Similar to HTML documents, the JavaFX platform provides the necessary mechanism to externalize style declarations in one or more CSS files. In this recipes we will explore how to create and attach a CSS file to your applications.

Getting ready

Before you go through this recipe, you should have an idea of what CSS is and how it is used. Review the previous recipe *Styling your applications with CSS* to get an idea of how JavaFX CSS works. You will create a simple application and an accompanying stylesheet file. We will examine how the elements are styled using the declared styles in the CSS file.

How to do it...

For this recipe, we are going to create a simple application.

1. The following is the code for the application that will be styled. The full listing of the code for the application can be found in ch04/source-code/src/styling/ExternalCssDemo.fx.

```
def w = 400;
def h = 200;

def panel = VBox {
    width:w height:h nodeHPos:HPos.CENTER spacing:10
    content:[
        Text{content:"External CSS" id:"titleText"}
        HBox{
            width:w height:h nodeVPos:VPos.CENTER spacing:5
            content:[
                Circle{radius:50}
                Rectangle{
                    width:100 height:70 styleClass:"broad"
                }
                Line{startX:0 endX:100 styleClass:"broad"}
            ]}
        Text{
            content:"Pay Attention!"
            styleClass:"specialText"
        }
```

```
        Text{content:"All objects styled with CSS"}
    ]
}
Stage {
  title : "External CSS Example"
  scene: Scene {
      width: w
      height: h
          content: [ panel ]
          stylesheets:["{__DIR__}main.css"]
  }
}
```

2. Next, in a separate CSS file, we will declare the styles that are applied to the
   application. You can find the full listing of the CSS file in ch04/source-code/src/
   styling/main.css.

```
Scene {
    fill:linear (0%, 0%) to (0%,100%)
            stops (0.0, grey), (1.0, white)
}

Rectangle {
  fill:yellow;
  strokeWidth:2;
  arcWidth:10;
  arcHeight:10;
}
Circle {
  fill:silver;
  strokeWidth:2;
      stroke:black
}

Text {
  fill:blue;
  font-family:"Arial,Sans";
  font-size:12pt
}

#titleText {
  fill:white;
```

```
      font-family:"Arial Black";
      font-size:24pt
  }
  .specialText {
      fill:red;
      font-family:"Arial Black";
      font-size:16pt
  }

  .broad{
      stroke:red;
      strokeWidth:4
  }
```

When the code for this application is executed (given that the CSS file is located in the same directory as the JavaFX source file), you will get the result shown in the next screenshot:

How it works...

The beauty of styling with CSS becomes apparent when you define your styles in a CSS file and reuse your styles throughout your application. In this recipe, we created a simple application which uses styles declared in a separate file.

Let's explore the JavaFX code first. Reviewing the code, you can see that the shapes used in the application have little or no style properties defined in the code. However, as seen in the previous screenshot, they have plenty of visual properties applied. This is how:

> ▶   Circle—the Circle shape receives its styles due to the `Circle{}` type selector defined in the CSS file. The definition of the type selector `Circle{}` causes any `Circle` type defined in the code to be styled using that selector.

- Rectangle—the CSS engine injects two styles into the `Rectangle` instance. The rectangle inherits default style defined by CSS type selector `Rectangle{}` in the CSS file. In addition, the rectangle receives the styles defined by CSS class selector `.broad` because its `styleClass` property is set to "broad".

- Line—the `Line` instance is styled using CSS class selector `.broad` because its `styleClass` property is set to "broad".

- *Text 1*—the first text with content "`External CSS`" is styled using the CSS ID selector rule. The CSS engine applies styles defined for ID selector `#titleText` to the node instance with `id="titleText"`.

- *Text 2*—the text with content "`Pay Attention!`" is styled using the CSS class selector `.specialText` by setting the property `styleClass` to "specialText".

- *Text 3*—the last `Text` node receives its styles by default due to the CSS type selector `Text{}` defined in the CSS file.

The last and most important thing to note in the code is the way the CSS file is attached to the application. This is done by setting the property `Scene.stylesheets` to a sequence of the locations of the CSS files. In our example, the stylesheet is specified with the next code snippet:

```
Stage {
    Scene {

        stylesheets:["{__DIR__}main.css"]
    }
}
```

Now, let's examine the CSS file. Similar to W3C's stylesheet definition, JavaFX style declarations are made up of style selectors, followed by a rule block, which contains the style properties. In JavaFX, the selector can match a JavaFX class name, a node `id` property, or a node's `styleClass` property. In our previous example, the CSS file `main.css` defines all of our style selectors. Let's take a look:

- *Type selector*—the CSS file has several type selectors including `Scene`, `Rectangle`, `Circle`, and `Text`. When JavaFX nodes are being rendered, the CSS engine will apply the styles that match instances of JavaFX types with the same name. You can use the type's full name in the CSS file when defining the selector block.

- *ID selector*—in the CSS file, we have the `#titleText` selector block defined. This declaration defines a style using the ID selector rule. Only the node with property `id="specialText"` will receive styles defined by this selector.

- *CSS class selector*—the CSS file contains two CSS class selector definitions including `.specialText` and `.broad`. The styles defined by these selectors will be applied to any node instance that has its property `styleClass` set to "broad" or "specialText".

There's more...

Pseudo-classes

In CSS, the pseudo-class allows you to designate the behavior of the entity receiving the style when there is interaction with the user. JavaFX's CSS has out-of-the-box support for pseudo-classes including `:hover`, `:pressed`, and `:focused`. As you might imagine, you use these pseudo-classes to specify the styles when a component is hovered, pressed, or receives focus respectively, as demonstrated in the next code snippet:

```
.myButton:hover {
  fill:silver;
  strokeWidth:2
}
```

Cascading styles

JavaFX CSS supports styles that can be cascaded, using a combination of the selectors identified earlier:

- `Text#titleText{ }`—this selector defines styles to be applied only to a `Text` instance with property `id` set to `"titleText"`.

- `Rectangle.broad{ }`—applies the style only to Rectangle types with property `styleClass` set to `"broad"`.

- `.broad:hover{ }`—this selector defines the hover behavior only for node instances with their `styleClass` property set to `"broad"`.

These can be chained in any combination to define fine-grained style rules which will be applied to entities which meet the rule criteria.

See also

- *Introduction*
- *Styling your applications with CSS*

Skinning applications with multiple CSS files

The benefit of externalizing CSS is the ability to update the look and feel of your application without having to update the code or recompile. Another attractive aspect of externalizing CSS is to let your users select a preferred theme or applying a skin. In this recipe, we are going to extend the data input form example, used throughout this chapter, to add skinning capabilities with CSS.

Getting ready

The concepts presented here all deal with CSS and externalizing through CSS files. f you have not used CSS, or are unfamiliar with JavaFX's support for CSS, it is recommended that you review the recipe *Styling your applications with CSS* and *Using CSS files to apply styles* from this chapter to get acquainted with JavaFX 's implementation of CSS.

This recipe is going to reuse the data form example used throughout the chapter. Refer to the recipe *Creating a form with JavaFX controls* for a thorough background on this example. In this usage, we extend the code in the form to support skinning using JavaFX CSS. In this version, the user is able to apply one of two themes to update the look of the application.

How to do it...

Again, the code that creates the data form has been discussed in earlier recipes (see *Getting ready*). Hence, we are going to concentrate on how to update application's styles in real-time without a restart. If you want to see the full code listing of the application, refer to `ch04/source-code/src/styling/DataFormSkinnableCss.fx`.

The super abbreviated code snippet given next provides the part of the code that updates the CSS files. This is done as follows:

```
var cssFile = "bluemoon.css";
...
var btnRow = HBox {
    spacing:7
    content:[
        Button{
            text:"Bluemoon.css"
            action:function(){
                cssFile = "bluemoon.css"
            }
        }
        Button{text:"Autumn.css"
            action:function(){
                cssFile = "autumn.css";
            }
        }
    ]
}

...
Stage {
  title : "Skinnable Data Input Form"
  scene: scene = Scene {
```

```
        width: w
        height: h
        content: [Group{ layoutX:10 content:panel}]
                stylesheets: bind ["{__DIR__}{cssFile}"]
    }
}
```

The application uses two separate CSS files. One is named `bluemoon.css` and applies a blue theme to all controls on the form. `Autumn.css` applies a Fall-colored theme to objects that use its styles. We are not going to show the CSS files here. To get a full listing of the CSS files, refer to `ch04/source-code/src/styling/bluemoon.css` and `ch04/source-code/src/styling/autumn.css`.

The next screenshot shows the application using both themes:

Bluemoon Skin   Autumn Skin

How it works...

This recipe presents the technique to create a skinnable application using JavaFX CSS. The skin is implemented using CSS style directives encapsulated in a file. For our recipe, we use two CSS files `bluemoon.css` and `autumn.css`. Each CSS file has the same styling elements. However, each applies a different theme based on color. The `bluemoon.css` file uses the blue family of colors to style its components. The `autumn.css` file uses the same CSS elements, but paints everything using Fall-color theme (browns, gold, orange, and so on).

The application lets users select between the two stylesheets to update the skin for the application. In the code, we declare the variable `cssFile` to store the name of the currently applied CSS file. When the user clicks on the button labeled **Bluemoon.css** it sets the variable `cssFile = "bluemoon.css"`. When the user clicks on the button labeled **Autumn.css** it sets `cssFile = "autumn.css"`.

The `Scene.stylesheets` property is bound to variable `cssFile` using the expression `Scene{stylesheets: bind ["{__DIR__}{cssFile}"]}`. When the value of the variable `cssFile` is updated (by pressing one of the buttons), it automatically updates the stylesheet for the scene. That's it!

See also

- *Introduction*
- *Creating a form with JavaFX controls*
- *Styling your applications with CSS*
- *Using CSS files to apply styles*

5
JavaFX Media

In this chapter, we will cover the following topics:

- ▶ Accessing media assets
- ▶ Loading and displaying images with ImageView
- ▶ Applying effects and transformations to images
- ▶ Creating image effects with blending
- ▶ Playing audio with MediaPlayer
- ▶ Playing video with MediaView
- ▶ Creating a media playback component

Introduction

One of the most celebrated features of JavaFX is its inherent support for media playback. As of version 1.2, JavaFX has the ability to seamlessly load images in different formats, play audio, and play video in several formats using its built-in components. To achieve platform independence and performance, the support for media playback in JavaFX is implemented as a two-tiered strategy:

- ▶ *Platform-independent APIs*—the JavaFX SDK comes with a media API designed to provide a uniform set of interfaces to media functionalities. Part of the platform-independence offerings include a portable codec (On2's VP6), which will play on all platforms where JavaFX media playback is supported .

- ▶ *Platform-dependent implementations*—to boost media playback performance, JavaFX also has the ability to use the native media engine supported by the underlying OS. For instance, playback on the Windows platform may be rendered by the Windows DirectShow media engine (see next recipe).

This chapter shows you how to use the supported media rendering components, including ImageView, MediaPlayer, and MediaView. These components provide high-level APIs that let developers create applications with engaging and interactive media content.

Accessing media assets

In previous chapters, you have seen the use of variable __DIR__ when accessing local resources, but little detail was offered about its purpose and how it works. So, what does that special variable store? In this recipe, we will explore how to use the __DIR__ special variable and other means of loading resources locally or remotely.

Getting ready

The concepts presented in this recipe are used widely throughout the JavaFX application framework when pointing to resources. In general, classes that point to a local or remote resource uses a string representation of a URL where the resource is stored. This is especially true for the ImageView and MediaPlayer classes discussed in this chapter.

How to do it...

This recipe shows you three ways of creating a URL to point to a local or remote resource used by a JavaFX application. The full listing of the code presented here can be found in ch05/source-code/src/UrlAccess.fx.

Using the __DIR__ pseudo-variable to access assets as packaged resources:

```
var resImage = "{__DIR__}image.png";
```

Using a direct reference to a local file:

```
var localImage =
   "file:/users/home/vladimir/javafx/ch005/source-code/src/image.png";
```

Using a URL to access a remote file:

```
var remoteImage = "http://www.flickr.com/3201/2905493571_a6db13ce1b_d.jpg"
```

How it works...

Loading media assets in JavaFX requires the use of a well-formatted URL that points to the location of the resources. For instance, both the Image and the Media classes (covered later in this chapter) require a URL string to locate and load the resource to be rendered. The URL must be an absolute path that specifies the fully-realized scheme, device, and resource location.

The previous code snippets show the following three ways of accessing resources in JavaFX:

- *__DIR__ pseudo-variable*—often, you will see the use of JavaFX's pseudo variable `__DIR__`, used when specifying the location of a resource. It is a special variable that stores the String value of the directory where the executing class that referenced `__DIR__` is located. This is valuable, especially when the resource is embedded in the application's JAR file. At runtime, `__DIR__` stores the location of the resource in the JAR file, making it accessible for reading as a stream. In the previous code, for example, the expression `{__DIR__}image.png` explodes as `jar:file:/users/home/vladimir/javafx/ch005/source-code/dist/source-code.jar!/image.png`.

- *Direct reference to local resources*—when the application is deployed as a desktop application, you can specify the location of your resources using URLs that provides the absolute path to where the resources are located. In our code, we use `file:/users/home/vladimir/javafx/ch005/source-code/src/image.png` as the absolute fully qualified path to the image file `image.png`.

- *Direct reference to remote resources*—finally, when loading media assets, you are able to specify the path of a fully-qualified URL to a remote resource using HTTP. As long as there are no subsequent permissions required, classes such as Image and Media are able to pull down the resource with no problem. For our code, we use a URL to a Flickr image `http://www.flickr.com/3201/2905493571_a6db13ce1b_d.jpg`.

There's more...

Besides `__DIR__`, JavaFX provides the `__FILE__` pseudo variable as well. As you may well guess, `__FILE__` resolves to the fully qualified path of the of the JavaFX script file that contains the `__FILE__` pseudo variable. At runtime, when your application is compiled, this will be the script class that contains the `__FILE__` reference.

Loading and displaying images with ImageView

If you have already checked out recipes in previous chapters, you know by now that JavaFX provides classes, which make it easy to load and display images. This recipe takes a closer look at the mechanics provided by the Image API to load and display images in your JavaFX applications.

Getting ready

This recipe uses classes from the *Image API* located in the `javafx.scene.image` package. Using this API, you are able to configure, load, and control how your images are displayed using the classes `Image` and `ImageView`. For this recipe, we will build a simple image browser to illustrate the concepts presented here. The browser allows users to load an image by providing its URL. You will use standard JavaFX controls, such as text boxes and buttons, to build the GUI. If you are not familiar with the standard GUI controls, review the recipe *Creating a form with JavaFX controls* from *Chapter 4, Components and Skinning*.

How to do it...

The code given next has been shortened to illustrate the essential portions involved in loading and displaying an image. You can get a full listing of the code from `ch05/source-code/src/image/ImageBrowserSimpleDemo.fx`.

```
def w = 800;
def h = 600;
var scene:Scene;
def maxW = w * 0.9;
def maxH = h * 0.9;
def imgView:ImageView = ImageView{
    preserveRatio:true
    fitWidth: maxW fitHeight:maxH
    layoutX:(w-maxW)/2 layoutY:(h-maxH)/2
};
function loadImg(){
    imgView.image = Image{
        url:(scene.lookup("addr") as TextBox).text
        backgroundLoading:true
        placeholder:Image{url:"{__DIR__}loading.jpg"}
    }
}
def addrBar = Group{
    layoutX: 20
    layoutY: 20
    content:HBox {
        nodeVPos:VPos.CENTER
        spacing:7
        content:[
            Label{text:"Image URL:" textFill:Color.SILVER}
            TextBox{id:"addr" columns:80 promptText:"http://"
                action:function(){loadImg()}
            }
```

```
Button{id:"btnGo" text:"Get Image"
    action:function(){loadImg()}
}
]
}
}
```

When the variables `imgView` and `addrBar` are placed on the scene and the application is executed, you will get the results as shown in the following screenshot:

The image shown in this screenshot is licensed under creative common. For additional information and licensing details, go to `http://www.flickr.com/photos/motleypixel/2905493571/sizes/m/`.

How it works...

Loading and displaying images in JavaFX involves two classes, `Image` and `ImageView`. While class `Image` is responsible for accessing and managing the binary stream of the image, `ImageView`, on the other hand, is of the type `Node` and is responsible for displaying the loaded image on the scene. The code presented in this recipe lets the user enter a URL for an image and loads the image on the screen. Let's take a closer look at the code and how it works:

- *The ImageView*—the first significant item to notice is the declaration of an `ImageView` instance assigned to the variable `imgView`. This is the component that will display the image on the scene when it is fully loaded. We specify the properties `fitWidth`, `fitHeight`, and `preserveRatio`. These properties will cause `imgView` to stretch (if the image is smaller than specified) or shrink (if the image is larger than specified) while preserving the aspect ratio of the image.

- *Image URL bar*—the form that captures the URL of the image to load is grouped in the `Group` instance variable `addrBar`. The form consists of a `Label`, a `TextBox`, and a `Button` instance. The `TextBox` instance has several properties set, including `id="addr"`, which allows us to find a reference to it in the code. Both the `TextBox` and the `Button` instances have their action properties defined as a function that invokes function `loadImg()`. Therefore, when the `TextBox` has focus and the *Enter* key is pressed, or when the `Button` instance is clicked on, the image will be loaded.

- *Loading the image*—the image is loaded by calling the function `loadImg()`. It assigns an instance of `Image` to `imgView.image`. For the `Image.url` property, we use the `Scene.lookup(id:String)` function to retrieve an instance of the `TextBox` using its `id` of `addr`. For images that may take a while to load, we set up the following two properties:

    - To ensure that the application does not hang while the image loads, the property `backgroundLoading:Boolean` is set to true. This causes the GUI to remain responsive while an image loads.

    - The property `placeholder:Image` is used to specify a local image to use while the remote image is loading, as shown in the previous screenshot. For example, we use the local image `{__DIR__}` `loading.png`. It gets loaded immediately and remains on the screen while the remote image loads. When the remote image is loaded, it replaces the placeholder image.

There's more...

Format support

As of version 1.2, JavaFX has inherent supports for the most popular image formats (popularity here = web-supported), which includes *PNG*, *JPG*, *BMP*, and *GIF*. If you have requirements for formats other than these, such as TIFF for instance, you will have to take matters into your own hands and use external image libraries such as **Java Advanced Imaging** (**JAI**) API (not covered here).

Asynchronous loading issues

As mentioned in the previous section, when you are loading images from locations with high latency (over the network for instance), you can use the asynchronous background-loading option for your image. This causes the image-loading operation to occur in a separate execution thread to keep your GUI responsive.

This, however, presents an issue, whereby if you want to determine the dimensions of the image (which is available only after the image is fully downloaded), it will report zero when loading asynchronously, as shown in the next segment:

```
def img = Image{
    url:"http://someimage.com/img.png"
    backgroundLoading:true
}//does not wait here, it continues to next line

println (img.width); // prints 0
```

This is because the image is still being downloaded on the `Image` thread, and the main GUI thread did not wait for completion and continues with its execution. Therefore, when we query the property `width` of `Image`, it will be zero.

Unfortunately in version 1.2, the `Image` class does not offer event notification functions to know when image is done loading. If your code relies on the actual size of the image to be known, you must block with asynchronous loading (by setting `backgroundLoading = false`) to wait for the image to download and get the size. Another way around is to specify the size of the image yourself by specifying the dimensions (see next sub-section on *Image resize and aspect ratio*).

Image resize and aspect ratio

Another feature supported by `Image` and `ImageView` is the automatic resizing of the image. The `Image` class will attempt to resize the image when a value is provided for the properties. `width:Number` or `height:Number`. `ImageView` will attempt to do the same when the properties `fitWidth:Number` and `fitHeight:Number` are specified. Both classes support property `preserveRation:Boolean`, which forces the resize operation to maintain the aspect ratio of the original image while resizing to the specified dimensions as shown next:

```
def imgView:ImageView = ImageView{
    preserveRatio:true
    fitWidth: 200
};
```

The previous code will resize the image to a width of 200 pixels. Because the `preserveRatio` property is `true`, the height of the image is automatically calculated. This is useful especially if you do not know the actual size of the image ahead of time (see previous section).

See also

▸ *Chapter 4—Creating a form with JavaFX controls*

▸ *Introduction*

▸ *Accessing media assets*

Applying effects and transformations to images

Now that you have learned how to load images, what can you do with them? Well, since `ImageView` is an instance of the `Node` class, your loaded images can receive the same treatment you would ordinarily provide, shapes, for example. In this recipe, we are going to extend the example from the previous recipe, *Loading and displaying images with ImageView*, to add image manipulation functionalities.

Getting ready

In this recipe, we are going to reach back to some of the concepts learned in previous chapters to extend the image browser example presented in the previous recipe. We will make use of JavaFX GUI controls and node effects. If you are not familiar with either of these topics, please review the recipes from *Chapter 3, Transformations, Animations, and Effects*, and *Chapter 4, Components and Skinning*.

The example presented here extends the image browser from the previous recipe to add image manipulation capabilities. The new version adds GUI controls to scale, rotate, add effects, and animate the loaded image.

How to do it...

The code snippet presented next has been abbreviated to concentrate on the more interesting aspects of the code. You can access the full code listing from `ch05/source-code/src/image/ImageBrowserExtendedDemo.fx`.

```
def w = 800;
def h = 600;
def maxW = w * 0.7;
def maxH = h * 0.7;
var scene:Scene;

def slider = Slider{min:1 max:1.5 value:1}

def imgView:ImageView = ImageView{
    preserveRatio:true
    fitWidth:bind if((slider.value*maxW) < w)
        maxW * slider.value else w
    fitHeight:bind if((slider.value*maxH) < h)
        maxH * slider.value else h
};

var anim = TranslateTransition{
    fromX:0 toX:w - maxW
    node:imgView repeatCount:TranslateTransition.INDEFINITE
    autoReverse:true
}
var rotateAngle = 0;

... //Address Bar Group and loadImg() function not shown
```

```
def footer = Group{
    layoutX: 20
    layoutY: h - 60
    content:HBox {
        spacing: 12
        content:[
            slider,

            Button{text:"Rotate" action:function(){
                rotateAngle = rotateAngle + 90;
                imgView.rotate = rotateAngle;
            }}

            HBox{spacing:7 content:[
                Button{text:"Reflection"
                    onMouseClicked:function(e){
                        imgView.effect =
                            if(imgView.effect == null or
                            or not (imgView.effect instanceof
                                    Reflection))
                                Reflection{fraction:0.3 topOffset:0}
                            else null
                }}

                ... // Other effects omitted
                Button{text:"Sepia"
                    onMouseClicked:function(e){
                        imgView.effect = if(imgView.effect == null
                        or not (imgView.effect instanceof
                                SepiaTone)
                        )
                                SepiaTone{level:0.7}
                            else null
                }}
                Button{text:"Animate"
                    onMouseClicked:function(e){
                        if(not anim.running){
                            anim.play();
                        }else{
                            anim.stop();
                        }
                }}
            ]}
        ]
    }
}
```

When the `ImageView`, the `Slider`, and the other GUI controls are added to stage, and the application is executed, it will look like what is shown in the next screenshot. In it, you can see the reflection effect applied to the image.

How it works...

In the recipe *Loading and displaying images with ImageView* we have seen how to use the Image API to load and display local or remote images. This recipe extends the code in that recipe to not only load the image, but also apply effects and animations to it.

As shown in the previous screenshot, this version of the image browser includes a row of GUI controls at the bottom of the screen that are used to apply different transformations and effects to the loaded image. Let's take a closer look at how the code works:

> *Scaling the image*—using an instance of the `Slider` control you can dynamically grow or shrink the image. To do this, we bind the properties `ImageView.fitWidth` and `ImageView.fitHeight` to `Slider.value`. This causes the size of the image to grow or shrink dynamically, while maintaining proper image aspect ratio. The bound expression includes logic to ensure that the image does not grow excessively large when it is scaled up as shown below:

```
ImageView{
    fitWidth:bind if((slider.value*maxW) < w)
        maxW * slider.value else w
    fitHeight:bind if((slider.value*maxH) < h)
        maxH * slider.value else h

};
```

- ▸ *Image rotation*—the `Button` instance with the label `"Rotate"` rotates the image instance by 90 degrees with each click by setting the `imgView.rotate` property.

- ▸ *Image effects*—the next five buttons in the code apply effects reflected in their respective names. These buttons apply the `Reflection`, `Glow`, `GaussianBlur`, `Lighting` (using a `PointLight` effect), and `SepiaTone` effects to the image (only Reflection and Sepia are listed in the code). All buttons work in the same way: if the effect currently applied to the image is null or the effect is not of the desired type, then apply the desired effect, otherwise, if the effect is already being applied, turn it off. This makes the button toggle between its assigned effect.

- ▸ *Image animation*—the last `Button` control plays the `TranslateTransition` instance assigned to the variable `anim`. The transition animation moves the image from side-to-side indefinitely until the button is pressed again to stop the animation.

See also

- ▸ *Chapter 3—Transformation, animations. and effects*
- ▸ *Chapter 4—Components and skinning*
- ▸ *Loading and displaying images with ImageView*

Creating image effects with blending

In the previous recipe, we saw how easy it is to build an application that loads, displays, and applies effects to images. In this recipe, we are going to explore how to create new visual effects by blending two separate image sources.

Getting ready

For this recipe, you will need to be familiar with the concepts of loading and displaying images in your application using the Image API. If necessary, review the recipe *Loading and displaying images with ImageView*. Part of the code also uses transition animation to slide the images one on top of the other. If you need to review topics regarding animation, refer to the recipe *Creating simple animation with the Transition API* from *Chapter 3, Transformations, Animations, and Effects*. Lastly, the recipe makes use of GUI controls to capture image URLs and action buttons to apply the effects. If you are not familiar with JavaFX's GUI controls, review the recipe *Creating a form with JavaFX controls* from *Chapter 4, Components and Skinning*.

How to do it...

The code listing given next is abbreviated to show the essential portions that drive the application. You can get the full listing of this code from ch05/source-code/src/image/ ImageBlendDemo.fx.

```
var scene:Scene;
def w = 800; def h = 600;
def maxW = w * 0.4; def maxH = h * 0.5;

def img1 = ImageView{
    translateX:10 translateY:10
    preserveRatio:true
    fitWidth:maxW fitHeight:maxH
}
def img2 = ImageView{
    translateX:w - maxW translateY:10
    preserveRatio:true
    fitWidth:maxW fitHeight:maxH
}

def imgPanel = Group {content:[img1, img2]}

def anim = Timeline {
    keyFrames: [
        KeyFrame{time:1s
            values: [
                img1.translateX => (w - img1.fitWidth)/2
            ]
        }
        KeyFrame{time:1s
            values: [
                img2.translateX => (w - img2.fitWidth)/2
            ]
        }
    ]
}
// fn to load img
function loadImg(view:ImageView,url:String){
    view.effect = null;
    view.image = Image{
        backgroundLoading:true
        url:url
    }
```

```
}
// controls bottom of screen
def toggleGrp = ToggleGroup{}
def controls = Group{
    layoutY: h - 200
    content:[
        VBox{width:w spacing:12
            hpos:HPos.CENTER nodeHPos:HPos.CENTER content:[
            TextBox{id:"addr1" columns:60 promptText:"http://"
              action:function(){
                loadImg(img1,
                    (scene.lookup("addr1") as TextBox).text)
            }}

            TextBox{id:"addr2" columns:60 promptText:"http://"
              action:function(){
                loadImg(img2,
                        (scene.lookup("addr2") as TextBox).text)
            }}
            HBox{
                content:[
                    RadioButton{text:"ADD"
                      toggleGroup:toggleGrp selected:true
                    }
                    ...  // other blending modes omitted
                    RadioButton{text:"LIGHTEN"
                      toggleGroup:toggleGrp
                    }
                ]
            }
            HBox{
                content:[
                    RadioButton{text:"MULTIPLY"
                      toggleGroup:toggleGrp
                    }
                    ... //other blending modes omitted
                    RadioButton{text:"SRC_OVER"
                      toggleGroup:toggleGrp
                    }
                ]
            }
            Button{
                text:"Blend Images"
                font:Font.font("Sans Serif",
```

```
                              FontWeight.BOLD, 18)
            effect:DropShadow{offsetX:3 offsetY:3}
            onMouseClicked:function(e){
             def mode = toggleGrp.selectedButton.text;
             imgPanel.blendMode = BlendMode.valueOf(mode);
             anim.rate = 1.0;
             anim.playFromStart();
            }

            onMouseReleased:function(e){
                anim.rate = -1.0;
                anim.play();
            }
          }
        ]}
    ]
}
```

When the `Group` instances `imgPanel` and `controls` are placed on the stage, and the application is executed, it produces the next screenshot. The application lets users enter the URLs of two images and select a blend mode. When the **Blend Images** button is pressed, the images slide to overlap each other and apply the blend effect:

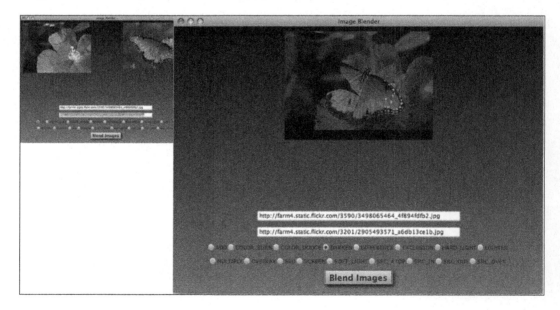

How it works...

The Group class (a node itself) allows the grouping of two or more nodes to be placed on the scene graph. One of the features of the Group node is its ability to apply a blending algorithm to the group's members. It applies its algorithm to all children in its `content` property when a blend mode is provided through the `blendMode:BlendMode` property.

In the previous sample code provided, we use `Group` instance `imgPanel` to apply blending effects to two images placed in the group. Let's take a closer look at how the application works:

- ▶ *The images*—the first thing we do in the code is to declare two instances of `ImageView`, `img1` and `img2`. To ensure that the images fit in a pre-determined dimension on the screen, we set the properties `fitWidth` and `fitHeight` on the two instances. Then, we place the two images in a `Group` instance called `imgPanel`, where they will receive blending effects.

- ▶ *The image animation*—to make things a little interesting, the code uses an instance of `Timeline` to animate the two images. The first `KeyFrame` instance slides `img1` from the left-hand side to the middle of the screen, and the second `KeyFrame` instance slides `img2` from the right-hand side to the middle of the screen. The two images stack up in the middle of the screen where you can see the selected blending effect applied.

- ▶ *Loading the images*—when the user types the URL location of the images in the `TextBox` instances, with property `id="addr1"` and `id="addr2"`, and presses *Enter*, this invokes the function `loadImg()`. That function loads and attaches the loaded image to instances of `ImageView` `img1` and `img2`, respectively.

- ▶ *Applying the blend*—`Group` variable `controls` contains two rows of `RadioButton` instances (not all shown in previous code). For each instance of `RadioButton`, the code assigns the name of a `BlendMode` as its text content (that is, `"ADD"`, `"COLOR_BURN"`, `"MULTIPLY"`, and so on). When the user clicks on the button titled **Blend Image**, it creates a `BlendMode` object using the text of the selected radio button, and applies it to the `imgPanel` Group containing the images, as shown:

```
def mode = toggleGrp.selectedButton.text;
imgPanel.blendMode = BlendMode.valueOf(mode);
```

`BlendMode.valueOf(:String)` returns an instance of `BlendMode` based on a String.

There's more...

JavaFX supports a multitude of blending options. The following table shows a list of the more interesting modes:

BlendMode.ADD—adds the color value of the top image to the bottom	BlendMode.DARKEN—the darker color values of the child images are displayed
BlendMode.DIFFERENCE—the darker color values are subtracted from the lighter colors	BlendMode.LIGHTEN—the lighter color values of the child images are displayed
BlendMode.MULTIPLY—the color values of the child images are multiplied together	BlendMode.SCREEN—the color values for the child images inverted, multiplied, and inverted again
BlendMode.OVERLAY—the color values can have the screen or multiplication mode applied to them depending on the bottom input	BlendMode.COLOR_BURN—the color values of the bottom layer are divided by that of the top and then inverted

The BlendedMode class offers more blended modes, including RED, GREEN, BLUE, COLOR_DOGE, HARD_LIGHT, SOFT_LIGHT, SRC_ATOP, SRC_IN, SRC_OUT, and SRC_OVER.

See also

- ▶ *Chapter 3—Creating simple animation with the transition API*
- ▶ *Chapter 4—Creating a form with JavaFX controls*
- ▶ *Loading and displaying images with ImageView*

Playing audio with MediaPlayer

Playing audio is another important aspect of any rich client platform. One of the celebrated features of JavaFX is its ability to easily playback audio content. This recipe shows you how to create code that plays back audio resources using the MediaPlayer class.

Getting ready

This recipe uses classes from the *Media API* located in the javafx.scene.media package. As you will see in our example, using this API you are able to load, configure, and playback audio using the classes Media and MediaPlayer. For this recipe, we will build a simple audio player to illustrate the concepts presented here. Instead of using standard GUI controls, we will use button icons loaded as images. If you are not familiar with the concept of loading images, review the recipe *Loading and displaying images with ImageView* in this chapter.

In this example we will use a JavaFX podcast from Oracle Technology Network TechCast series where *Nandini Ramani* discusses JavaFX. The stream can be found at `http://streaming.oracle.com/ebn/podcasts/media/8576726_Nandini_Ramani_030210.mp3`.

How to do it...

The code given next has been shortened to illustrate the essential portions involved in loading and playing an audio stream. You can get the full listing of the code in this recipe from `ch05/source-code/src/media/AudioPlayerDemo.fx`

```
def w = 400;
def h = 200;
var scene:Scene;
def mediaSource = "http://streaming.oracle.com/ebn/podcasts/media/
  8576726_Nandini_Ramani_030210.mp3";

def player = MediaPlayer {media:Media{source:mediaSource}}

def controls = Group {
    layoutX:(w-110)/2
    layoutY:(h-50)/2
    effect:Reflection{
        fraction:0.4 bottomOpacity:0.1 topOffset:3
    }
    content:[
        HBox{spacing:10 content:[
            ImageView{id:"playCtrl"
                image:Image{url:"{__DIR__}play-large.png"}
                onMouseClicked:function(e:MouseEvent){
                    def playCtrl = e.source as ImageView;
                    if(not(player.status == player.PLAYING)){
                        playCtrl.image =
                            Image{url:"{__DIR__}pause-large.png"}
                        player.play();
                    }else if(player.status == player.PLAYING){
                        playCtrl.image =
                            Image{url:"{__DIR__}play-large.png"}
                        player.pause();
                    }
                }
            }
            ImageView{id:"stopCtrl"
                image:Image{url:"{__DIR__}stop-large.png"}
                onMouseClicked:function(e){
```

```
              def playCtrl = e.source as ImageView;
              if(player.status == player.PLAYING){
                 playCtrl.image =
                    Image{url:"{__DIR__}play-large.png"}
                 player.stop();
              }
           }
        }
     ]}
  ]
}
```

When the variable `controls` is added to a scene object and the application is executed, it produces the screen shown in the following screenshot:

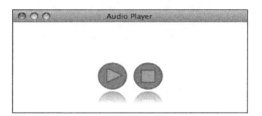

How it works...

The Media API is comprised of several components which, when put together, provides the mechanism to stream and playback the audio source. To playback audio requires two classes, including `Media` and `MediaPlayer`. Let's take a look at how these classes are used to playback audio in the previous example.

► *The MediaPlayer*—the first significant item in the code is the declaration and initialization of a `MediaPlayer` instance assigned to the variable `player`. To load the audio file, we assign an instance of `Media` to `player.media`. The `Media` class is used to specify the location of the audio. In our example, it is a URL that points to an MP3 file.

► *The controls*—the play, pause, and stop buttons are grouped in the `Group` object called `controls`. They are made of three separate image files: `play-large.png`, `pause-large.png`, and `stop-large.png`, loaded by two instances of the `ImageView` class. The `ImageView` objects serve to display the control icons and to control the playback of the audio:

  ❑ When the application starts, `imgView` displays image `play-large.png`. When the user clicks on the image, it invokes its action-handler function, which firsts detects the status of the `MediaPlayer` instance. If it is not playing, it starts playback of the audio source by calling `player.play()` and replaces the `play-large.png` with the image `pause-large.png`. If, however, audio is currently playing, then the audio is stopped and the image is replaced back with `play-large.png`.

❑ The other ImageView instance loads the `stop-large.png` icon. When the user clicks on it, it calls its action-handler to first stop the audio playback by calling `player.stop()`. Then it toggles the image for the "play" button back to icon `play-large.png`.

 As mentioned in the introduction, JavaFX will play the MP3 file format on any platform where the JavaFX format is supported. Anything other than MP3 must be supported natively by the OS's media engine where the file is played back. For instance, on my Mac OS, I can play MPEG-4, because it is a supported playback format by the OS's QuickTime engine.

There's more...

The `Media` class models the audio stream. It exposes properties to configure the location, resolves dimensions of the medium (if available; in the case of audio, that information is not available), and provides tracks and metadata about the resource to be played.

The `MediaPlayer` class itself is a controller class responsible for controlling playback of the medium by offering control functions such as `play()`, `pause()`, and `stop()`. It also exposes valuable playback data including current position, volume level, and status. We will use these additional functions and properties to extend our playback capabilities in the recipe *Controlling media playback* in this chapter.

See also

▸ *Accessing media assets*

▸ *Loading and displaying images with ImageView*

Playing video with MediaView

The previous recipe shows you how to play audio using the JavaFX Media API. This recipe builds on the versatility of the Media API and extends the previous recipe, *Playing audio with MediaPlayer*, and creates a video player with a few changes to the code.

Getting ready

This recipe uses classes from the *Media API* located in the `javafx.scene.media` package. As mentioned in the introduction of this recipe, the example presented here extends the code from the previous recipe to transform the audio player to now play video. We are going to reuse the same icons and the same logic to control the playback of the video. To review how to configure and use the Media API for playback, review the previous recipe *Playing audio with MediaPlayer*.

To illustrate video playback, the application plays back the award-winning, open-sourced, short, animated movie *Big Buck Bunny*. By default, the recipe will play the 854 x 480 H.264 version found at the address `http://mirror.bigbuckbunny.de/peach/bigbuckbunny_movies/big_buck_bunny_480p_h264.mov`.

How to do it...

Similar to audio, playing video is simple. The abbreviated code given next highlights the portion of the code that is changed to be able to display video. You can see the full listing of the code at `ch05/source-code/src/media/VideoPlayerDemo.fx`.

```
def w = 800;
def h = 600;
def maxW = w * 0.8;
def maxH = h * 0.7;
var scene:Scene;
def mediaSource =
"http://mirror.bigbuckbunny.de/peach/bigbuckbunny_movies/big_buck_
bunny_480p_h264.mov";

def player = MediaView{
    layoutX:(w - maxW)/2 layoutY:(h-maxH)/2
    mediaPlayer:MediaPlayer {media:Media{source:mediaSource}}
    fitWidth:maxW fitHeight:maxH
}

def controls = Group {
    layoutX:(w-110)/2
    layoutY:h-100
    effect:Reflection{
        fraction:0.4 bottomOpacity:0.1 topOffset:3}
    content:[
        HBox{spacing:10 content:[
            ImageView{id:"playCtrl"
                image:Image{url:"{__DIR__}play-large.png"}
                onMouseClicked:function(e:MouseEvent){
                    def playCtrl = e.source as ImageView;
```

```
            if(not(player.mediaPlayer.status ==
                MediaPlayer.PLAYING)){
                playCtrl.image = Image{
                    url:"{__DIR__}pause-large.png"
                }
                player.mediaPlayer.play();
            }else if(player.mediaPlayer.status ==
                MediaPlayer.PLAYING){
                playCtrl.image = Image{
                    url:"{__DIR__}play-large.png"
                }
                player.mediaPlayer.pause();
            }
        }
    }
}
ImageView{id:"stopCtrl"
    image:Image{url:"{__DIR__}stop-large.png"}
    onMouseClicked:function(e:MouseEvent){
        def playCtrl = e.source as ImageView;
        if(player.mediaPlayer.status ==
            MediaPlayer.PLAYING){
            playCtrl.image = Image{
                url:"{__DIR__}play-large.png"
            }
            player.mediaPlayer.stop();
        }
    }
}
        ]}
    ]
}
```

When the Group variable controls and the MediaView instance's player are placed on the scene, the application will create a window as shown in the next screenshot.

How it works...

While playing audio only requires the use of the classes `Media` and `MediaPlayer`, playing video requires an additional class called the `MediaView`. It is of type `Node` and can be used to display the content of a video on the screen. Let's take a closer look at the code:

- ▸ *The MediaView*—the first major component to be initialized is the `MediaView` assigned to variable `player`. The code uses the `MediaView` instance to configure the dimensions and the location where the video will be rendered. In order to control playback, the code assigns the `player.mediaPlayer` property an instance of `MediaPlayer,` used to control playback. MediaPlayer is then assigned an instance of `Media` (through the property `MediaPlayer.media`) to specify the location of the video resource we want to playback.

- ▸ *The controls*—the GUI controls in this example work the exact same way as described in *Playing audio with MediaPlayer*. We use a group of image icons to represent playback functions play, pause, and stop. When the play icon is pressed, it is starts playing the video by calling the `player.mediaPlayer.play()` function and toggles itself to the pause icon. When the pause icon is pressed, it pauses the video using function `player.mediaPlayer.pause()`. Finally, when the user presses the stop button, it makes a call to `player.mediaPlayer.stop()` to stop playback and toggles the play button back to the play icon.

There's more...

Processing video is expensive. The JavaFX `MediaView` class supports properties which can be used to provide rendering-time hints to maximize playback performance. These Boolean properties include:

- ▸ `compositable:Boolean`—if true, other nodes may overlay the `MediaView` node using transparency.

- ▸ `preserveRatio:Boolean`—if true, the aspect ratio of the video is preserved when the node is resized through the `fitWidth` or `fitHeight` property.

- ▸ `rotatable:Boolean`—when true, it allows the `MediaView` node to receive rotation requests through the `rotate` property.

- ▸ `transformable:Boolean`—the node will only apply transformations through the `transforms:Transform[]` property when this is set to true.

See also

- ▸ *Accessing media assets*
- ▸ *Playing audio with MediaPlayer*

Creating a media playback component

The previous two recipes, *Playing audio with MediaPlayer* and *Playing video with MediaView*, show you how to build applications quickly to playback media sources with basic controls, such as play, pause, and stop. However, the Media API supports more functionalities than what have been discussed so far. This recipe shows you how to build a custom media component to playback media sources providing extended functionalities such as fast forward, reverse, and timing information.

Getting ready

This recipe uses classes from the Media API located in the `javafx.scene.media` package. The example presented here extends the code from the previous recipe *Playing video with MediaView to create a playback component*. The component will take advantage of the functionalities and runtime data provided by the Media API to extend the features of the video player example. Before you continue, ensure that you are familiar with the materials covered in the recipes *Playing audio with MediaPlayer* and *Playing video with MediaView*.

How to do it...

The shortened code given next provides highlights of the more significant items involved in creating the playback component. You can access the full listing of the code from `cn05/source-code/src/media/MediaControllerComponent.fx`.

1. Let's define class `MediaController` as `CustomNode` that encapsulates the playback icons/buttons and control logic:

```
class MediaController extends CustomNode{
    public var mediaPlayer:MediaPlayer;

    var timestat = bind
        "{%02d mediaPlayer.currentTime.toHours()
          mod 12 as Integer}:"
        "{%02d mediaPlayer.currentTime.toMinutes()
          mod 60 as Integer}:"
        "{%02d mediaPlayer.currentTime.toSeconds()
          mod 60 as Integer}/"
        "{%02d mediaPlayer.media.duration.toHours()
          mod 12 as Integer}:"
        "{%02d mediaPlayer.media.duration.toMinutes()
          mod 60 as Integer}:"
        "{%02d mediaPlayer.media.duration.toSeconds()
          mod 60 as Integer}";
```

```
        // image icons
        def imgReverse = Image{url:"{__DIR__}reverse-small.png"};
        def imgPlay = Image{url:"{__DIR__}play-small.png"};
        def imgPause = Image{url:"{__DIR__}pause-small.png"};
        def imgFfwd = Image{url:"{__DIR__}ffwd-small.png"};
        def imgVolup = Image{url:"{__DIR__}volup-small.png"}
        def imgVolDn = Image{url:"{__DIR__}voldown-small.png"};

        def controls = Group {
            content:[
                HBox{spacing:10 content:[
                    // reverse button
                    ImageView{id:"reverseCtrl" image:imgReverse
                        onMousePressed:function(e:MouseEvent){
                            mediaPlayer.currentTime =
                            mediaPlayer.currentTime
                            - (mediaPlayer.media.duration * 0.01);
                        }
                    }

                    // play button
                    ImageView{id:"playCtrl" image:imgPlay
                        onMouseClicked:function(e:MouseEvent){
                            ... // starts media playback
                        }
                    }

                    // fast forward
                    ImageView{id:"ffwdCtrl" image:imgFfwd
                        onMousePressed:function(e:MouseEvent){
                            mediaPlayer.currentTime =
                            mediaPlayer.currentTime
                            + (mediaPlayer.media.duration * 0.01);
                        }
                    }

                    // volume up
                    ImageView{id:"voldn" image:imgVolDn;
                        onMouseClicked:function(e){
                            mediaPlayer.volume =
                            mediaPlayer.volume - 0.4;
```

```
            }
        }

        // volume down
        ImageView{id:"volup" image:imgVolup
            onMouseClicked:function(e){
                mediaPlayer.volume =
                    mediaPlayer.volume + 0.4;
            }
        }

    ]}

    // progress bar
    Line{
        startX:0 startY:40 endX:100 endY:40
        stroke:Color.MAROON
    }
    Circle{
        radius:5
        fill:Color.MAROON
        centerX:bind
          if(mediaPlayer.media.duration > 0ms)
            (mediaPlayer.currentTime /
             mediaPlayer.media.duration)*100
          else 5
        centerY:40
    }
    Text{
        x:105 y:35
        textAlignment:TextAlignment.LEFT
        textOrigin:TextOrigin.TOP
        font:Font.font("Sans Serif", 10)
        content: bind timestat
    }

    ]
}
override protected function create () : Node {
    return controls
}
}
```

2. The next code segment shows you how to use the `MediaController` class defined earlier:

```
def w = 800;
def h = 600;
def maxW = w * 0.8;
def maxH = h * 0.7;
var scene:Scene;
def mediaSource = "http://mirror.bigbuckbunny.de/peach/bigbuckbun-
ny_movies/big_buck_bunny_480p_h264.mov";

def video = MediaView{
    layoutX:(w - maxW)/2 layoutY:(h-maxH)/2
    mediaPlayer:MediaPlayer {media:Media{source:mediaSource}}
    fitWidth:maxW fitHeight:maxH
}


def controls = MediaController {
    mediaPlayer: video.mediaPlayer
    showReflection:true
    layoutX: (w - 200)/2 layoutY:video.fitHeight + 50
}
```

When we place variable `video` and the instance of `MediaController` in a scene and execute the application, we get a screen as shown in the next screenshot:

How it works...

The custom class presented in this recipe implements a `CustomNode` which encapsulates the icons and logic for media playback control functions including reverse, play, fast-forward, volume up, and volume down. The class also provides visual feedback on the length and current progression of the video playback. Let's take a closer look at the custom class:

▸ *Textual time progression*—before we look at the control functions, we will look at how the component reports time progression for the playback. The first item involved in time progression feedback is the variable `timestat` (to which a `Text` object that displays progression information is bound). `timestat` is itself bound to several expressions that return values containing current time and total time of playback, using values from `mediaPlayer.currentTime` and `mediaPlayer.media.duration`. Since time is reported as a `Duration` type, we have to pluck out each time subdivision (hour, minute, seconds) individually using the `mod` operator. Then, each unit is formatted to be printed as zero-padded values as shown in the snippet below:

```
var timestat = bind
        "{%02d mediaPlayer.currentTime.toHours()
          mod 12 as Integer}:"
        "{%02d mediaPlayer.currentTime.toMinutes()
          mod 60 as Integer}:"
. . .
```

▸ *Visual time progression*—to provide visual feedback of the progression of the playback, the media controller uses a custom progress bar composed of a `Circle` that slides along a `Line` instance. The line represents the total duration of the video, and the location of the circle (along the line) represents the current position of the playhead. To achieve this, the `Circle.centerX` property is bound to an expression that returns a ratio of `mediaPlayer.currentTime/mediaPlayer.media.duration`. This ratio is used to normalize the progress bar by multiplying it to the length of the line to get the current position of the circle, as shown in the snippet below:

```
Circle{
. . .
    centerX:bind
        if(mediaPlayer.media.duration > 0ms)
            (mediaPlayer.currentTime /
                mediaPlayer.media.duration)*100
        else 5
}
```

▸ *The controls*—as before, the control buttons consist of image icons displayed by instances of `ImageView`. The custom component loads six icons that represent functionalities such as reverse, play, pause, fast-forward, volume up, and volume down. The play and pause icons, assigned to `ImageView` instance with `id = "playCtrl"`, use the same logic from previous media playback recipes (consult the recipe *Playing audio with MediaPlayer* for details). Let's see how the others work:

- ❑ To fast-forward and reverse, we use `ImageView` instances with `id="reverseCtrl"` and `id="ffwdCtrl"` respectively. When the user clicks on these icons, the code adds one percent of the total duration to (or subtracts from) `mediaPlayer.currentTime` property. This has the effect of moving the playhead in the desired direction.

- ❑ To adjust the volume is even simpler. We use instances of ImageView with `id="volup"` and `id="voldn"` to control the volume. When the user clicks on the icon, it sets `mediaPlayer. volume` to the desired ratio. To increase the volume we add `0.4` to the current volume. To decrease the volume, we subtract `0.4` from the current volume level.

See also

- ▸ *Chapter 2—Create your own custom node*
- ▸ *Loading and displaying images with ImageView*
- ▸ *Playing audio with MediaPlayer*
- ▸ *Playing video with MediaView*

6
Working with Data

In this chapter, we will cover the following topics:

- ▶ Saving data locally with the Storage API
- ▶ Accessing remote data with HttpRequest
- ▶ Downloading images with HttpRequest
- ▶ Posting data to remote servers with HttpRequest
- ▶ Uploading files to servers with HttpRequest
- ▶ Building RESTful clients with the PullParser API
- ▶ Using the feed API to create RSS/Atom clients
- ▶ Visualizing data with the JavaFX Chart API

Introduction

All popular rich client platforms provide inherent support for local and remote data retrieval and persistence. JavaFX is no different. This chapter explores the tools that are available in JavaFX to access and manipulate data locally or remotely, and how to perform data visualization using the newly added JavaFX chart components.

Storage API

Part of the recent additions to version 1.2 of the SDK includes the Storage API. This API is designed to provide secure and uniform data storage and retrieval services for client applications working in offline mode. This chapter shows you how to use the Storage API to store and retrieve data locally.

REST-style development

Part of the main features of a rich client platform is its ability to connect to remote servers in order to retrieve data. Similar to the popular browser-based `XmlHttpRequest` object used to drive AJAX applications, JavaFX exposes the `HttpRequest` object, which lets developers connect asynchronously to web servers to exchange data over HTTP. This chapter shows you how to connect, retrieve data, and handle communication events during different phases of data exchange. You will also explore how to post data back to the server.

As a modern, rich application platform, JavaFX provides full support for popular data exchange and data representation formats, such as XML. Out-of-the-box, the JavaFX parser API can handle pure XML and specific XML-based formats, such as RSS and Atom. Additionally, JavaFX developers can leverage the wildly popular JavaScript-based data format named JSON, used extensively for data exchange on the Web. In this chapter, we look at how to access and parse XML-encoded and JSON-encoded data to build web-enabled JavaFX applications.

RSS and Atom are two of the most common data feed formats used around the Web for one-way content syndication. JavaFX provides full support of these formats through its Feed API. Later in this chapter, we will explore how to use JavaFX in order to build RSS and Atom clients.

Data visualization

In addition to accessing and manipulating data in JavaFX, as of version 1.2, you also have the ability to visualize your data using the Chart API. Built in JavaFX, you will find several different types of chart components, including area, bar, bubble, bar, bar 3D, line, pie, pie 3D, and scatter chart. This chapter shows you how to create and integrate charting as part of your JavaFX application.

Saving data locally with the Storage API

Although your JavaFX applications are expected to be able to connect to remote servers in order to persist or retrieve data, it is, however, also desirable to have the ability to save data locally on the user's device. Say, for instance, you have deployed a game. You may want to facilitate your gamers to save game settings, scores, and states locally, without having to connect to a server. This recipe shows you how to use the Storage API of JavaFX to save data on local devices.

Getting ready

The concepts presented here rely on classes found in the Storage API located in the `javafx.io` package. Prior to using the API, it is advisable that you have a working understanding of the low-level Java IO API classes used for data persistence and retrieval.

How to do it...

To illustrate how to save data locally, the following code snippet creates a simple application that reads and saves data, a list of US state capitals, locally. For a full listing of the code, refer to `ch06/source-code/src/localstore/StorageDemo.fx`.

```
var storage:Storage;
storage = Storage {
source: "statecaps.txt"
}
var data =
"Alaska:Juneau\n"
"Arizona:Phoenix\n"
"Arkansas:Little Rock\n"

"West Virginia:Charleston\n"
"Wisconsin:Madison\n"
"Wyoming:Cheyenne\n";

var res = storage.resource;
var output= res.openOutputStream(true);
output.write(data.getBytes());
output.close();

// read it and print it
var input = res.openInputStream();
var reader = new BufferedReader(new InputStreamReader(input))·
var line:String;
while((line = reader.readLine()) != null) {
  var record = line.split(":");
  println ("Capital of {record[0]} is {record[1]}");
}
```

How it works...

The Storage API allows developers to store and retrieve data locally on the user's device. In the previous code snippet, variable `data` is assigned a list (colon-separated) of United States capitals. Then, the Storage API's `resource` object is used to store the data on the user's local machine and subsequently read back from its stored location.

As mentioned, the Storage API provides two main classes as an abstraction of the local file system:

> ▸ The `Storage` class—this is a service class that exposes objects that facilitate the persistence and retrieval of remove it stored resources. Its property `Storage.source` provides reference to a stored resource needed to be accessed. In our example, `Storage.source` points to local storage resource `"statecaps.txt"`. All nput or output operations will be done against that resource for the associated instance of `Storage`.

- ▸ The `Resource` class—this class represents the stored item. As of version 1.2 of the SDK, a `resource` instance is mapped to an actual file in the user's local file system. You can use function `resource.openOutputStream()` to obtain an instance of `OutputStream` to write the data stream locally. The code uses the `resource.openInputStream()` function to get a reference to an `InputStream` object that is used to read the data from local storage.

As of JavaFX version 1.2.x, the Storage API exposes raw streams, (`java.io.InputStream` and `java.io.OutputStream`) for IO operations. Unfortunately, there are no JavaFX script syntax or API abstractions of the `java.io.*` classes. Therefore, you have to be familiar with low-level Java IO operations to read or write files.

There's more...

The `Storage` class provides several functions to manage the resources in which you may be interested:

- ▸ `list():Object[]`—a script-level function that lists all of the resources that can be accessed (or was created) by this application on the user's local file system
- ▸ `clearAll():Boolean`—this function deletes all of the saved resources from the local device
- ▸ `clear():Boolean`—this function is used to delete the resource associated with the instance of the `Storage` object

The `Resource` class exposes some useful properties of which you should be aware as well:

- ▸ `length:Long`—this property returns the size of the resource in bytes
- ▸ `maxLength:Long`—this is the maximum size that can be stored on a user's local file system
- ▸ `name:String`—the name of the resource at its stored location
- ▸ `readable:Boolean/writeable:Boolean`—these flags indicate the accessibility of the resource

Storage organization

When a user accesses your application as an applet, or runs it as a Java Web Start (see *Chapter 7*, Deployment and Integration) from the Web, JavaFX allows the application to store data locally even when the application runs as untrusted. The Storage API creates a sandbox storage area for each running application. This approach is similar to browser cookies (amusingly, in JavaFX, it's called a **muffin**). Each application is given its own, isolated storage space. By default, an application is reserved 1MB of storage. Total storage with each resource having a default size of 8KB (these defaults can be configured; see Local storage configuration, ahead).

The storage space for locally saved files is based on the domain from where the file was downloaded from (or the path where the app is executed for non-downloaded app). The following table shows the default location where a file will be stored, based on domain path.

Download Path	Local Storage Path
`http://www.myapp.com/`	/
`http://www.myapp.com/apps/`	/apps
`http://www.myapp.com/apps/version1`	/apps/version1/
Application executed locally from file:`/Users/vivien/JavaFX-Cookbook/ch006/`	/

When the application stores a resource using the Storage API, it will be saved locally at the storage space assigned to the application. Applications from the same domain and subpaths can share stored data. As a measure of security, however, applications from different domains (or same domain, different paths) cannot share data.

Local storage configuration

Clients can configure and control how the Storage API behaves using the `storage.properties` file. As of version 1.2 of the SDK, the file is located in:

- `%USER_HOME%\Sun\JavaFX\Deployment\storage.properties` (Windows)
- `$USER_HOME/.javafx/deployment/storage.properties` (*nix, MacOS)

By default, the content of this file is empty. The following can be used to control storage:

- `storage.enabled = [true | false]`—this configuration entry enables or disables the storage of a local file. When set to `false`, any attempt to write to local storage will result in an exception.
- `storage.limit.domain`—this configuration entry allows you to configure the number of bytes that can be saved manually per application domain (the default is 1 MB).

For further information on the Java IO API see:

- Java IO Tutorial—`http://java.sun.com/docs/books/tutorial/essential/io/`

Accessing remote data with HttpRequest

All modern rich client platforms provide ways to communicate with external servers. The Web and its associated protocols have become de facto technologies for building client-server applications. This recipe shows how to use JavaFX to communicate with web servers over HTTP using the `HttpRequest` object from JavaFX's IO API. You will learn how to submit a request to a remote web server and use HttpRequest's event-driven callback functions to handle responses from the server.

Getting ready

Prior to getting started with `HttpRequest`, you should have an understanding of the basic mechanics behind the Web and its HTTP protocol (see the HTTP reference at the end of this recipe). JavaFX's `HttpRequest` class, located in the `javafx.io.http` package, provides ways to manage communication between your JavaFX client application and a remote web server. To illustrate the use of the `HttpRequest` class, we will use it to pull down information from Wikipedia's entry about JavaFX programming language at the URL `http://en.wikipedia.org/wiki/JavaFX`. In future recipes, you will see how to use `HttpRequest` in conjunction with other data-specific APIs such as RSS. It is also a definite plus to be familiar with Java's IO API when working with the HttpRequest API.

How to do it...

The code snippet in this recipe shows you how to use the `HttpRequest` object to send a request to a server and handle the response using event-handler functions. The code segment given next show an abbreviated version of the code. Refer to `ch06/source-code/src/http/HttpRequestGET.fx` for a complete listing of the code.

```
var url = "http://en.wikipedia.org/wiki/JavaFX";
var http = HttpRequest {
    location: url
    method: HttpRequest.GET
    ...
    onInput: function(in: java.io.InputStream) {
        if(in.available() > 0){
            println ("Printing result from {url}");
            var reader:BufferedReader;
            try{
                reader = new BufferedReader(
                    new InputStreamReader(in));
                var line;
                while((line = reader.readLine()) != null){
                    println(line)
                }
            }finally{
                reader.close();
                in.close();
            }
        }
    }
    ...
}
http.start();
```

When the code is executed, it retrieves the data and prints it to the standard output stream as shown in the next screenshot:

```
<html xmlns="http://www.w3.org/1999/xhtml" lang="en" dir="ltr">
<head>
<title>JavaFX - Wikipedia, the free encyclopedia</title>
<meta http-equiv="Content-Type" content="text/html; charset=UTF-8" />
<meta http-equiv="Content-Style-Type" content="text/css" />
<meta name="generator" content="MediaWiki 1.16wmf4" />
<link rel="alternate" type="application/x-wiki" title="Edit this page" href="/w/inde
<link rel="edit" title="Edit this page" href="/w/index.php?title=JavaFX&amp;action=e
<link rel="stylesheet" type="text/css" href="http://bits.wikimedia.org/w/extensions/
<link rel="stylesheet" type="text/css" href="http://bits.wikimedia.org/w/extensions/
<link rel="apple-touch-icon" href="http://en.wikipedia.org/apple-touch-icon.png" />
<link rel="shortcut icon" href="/favicon.ico" />
<link rel="search" type="application/opensearchdescription+xml" href="/w/opensearch_
<link rel="copyright" href="http://creativecommons.org/licenses/by-sa/3.0/" />
<link rel="alternate" type="application/atom+xml" title="Wikipedia Atom feed" href="
<link rel="stylesheet" href="http://bits.wikimedia.org/skins-1.5/vector/main-ltr.css
<link rel="stylesheet" href="http://bits.wikimedia.org/skins-1.5/common/shared.css?2
<link rel="stylesheet" href="http://bits.wikimedia.org/skins-1.5/common/commonPrint.
<link rel="stylesheet" href="/w/index.php?title=MediaWiki:Common.css&amp;usemsgcache
<link rel="stylesheet" href="/w/index.php?title=MediaWiki:Print.css&amp;usemsgcache=
<link rel="stylesheet" href="/w/index.php?title=MediaWiki:Handheld.css&amp;usemsgcac
<link rel="stylesheet" href="/w/index.php?title=MediaWiki:Vector.css&amp;usemsgcache
<link rel="stylesheet" href="/w/index.php?title=-&amp;action=raw&amp;maxage=2678400&
<script type="text/javascript">
var skin="vector",
stylepath="http://bits.wikimedia.org/skins-1.5",
wgUrlProtocols="http\\:\\/\\/\\/|https\\:\\/\\/\\/|ftp\\:\\/\\/\\/|irc\\:\\/\\/|gopher\\:\\/\
```

How it works...

The HttpRequest object automatically handles all the network steps necessary to create a connection between your application and a remote web server. Here is what is going on in the code snippet:

1. *The URL*—the first item is the declaration of the URL location. The code sets up the variable url as the location of the Wikipedia entry that we want to retrieve.

2. *Connecting to the server*—next, we declare an instance of HttpRequest to handle the connectivity and manage the data. The location:String property of the HttpRequest instance is assigned the variable url. The other interesting property is the HttpRequest.method property, which specifies the HTTP method to use when interacting with the server. For the recipe's code, we set the HTTP method to HttpRequest.GET (see *There's more,* next).

3. *Handling the response*—finally, we define event-handler functions for the HttpRequest instance. These event handlers will get invoked at different phases of the request/response life cycle. In the code snippet, we are only showing the onInput event-handler function in detail. This function is invoked when all the bytes for the requested resource are received from the server. In the code, the function basically loops through the received bytes from the IO stream and prints the data, as shown in the previous screenshot.

There's more...

Specifying the `location` property for `HttpRequest` can be tricky, especially when composing URL with non-alphanumeric characters. These characters have to be encoded using the URL-encoding MIME format. To facilitate this, JavaFX offers the `javafx.io.http.URLConverter` class. This utility class provides several methods to convert string values into URL-encoded format. For instance, to pull down the Wikipedia page for the Java Platform, the following code snippet can be used:

```
var conv = URLConverter{};
var topic = conv.encodeString("Java_(programming_language)");
var url = "http://en.wikipedia.org/wiki/{topic}";
```

An instance of the `URLConverter` class is used to URL-encode string `"Java_(programming language)"`, which gets encoded as `"Java_%28programming_language%29"`. The non-alphanumeric characters are replaced with the `"%"` followed by the character's hexadecimal value in the ISO Latin-1 character set (ISO-8859-1).

HTTP methods

The `HttpRequest` API supports several HTTP methods, through the property `method:String`, including GET, POST, PUT, and DELETE. The `HttpRequest` class will behave differently, depending on the method set. For instance, GET is intended to retrieve the specified resource from the server, while POST is intended to submit data back on the server to be handled by the identified resource. You will see the use of both GET and POST throughout this chapter.

For further information on some of the topics covered see:

* HTTP—http://en.wikipedia.org/wiki/Hypertext_Transfer_Protocol
* Java IO Tutorial—http://java.sun.com/docs/books/tutorial/essential/io/

See also

▶ *Saving data locally with the Storage API*

Downloading images with HttpRequest

In the previous recipe, *Accessing remote data with HttpRequest*, we saw how to use the `HttpRequest` class to request and receive textual data from a remote server. How about the next most popular resources on the web: Images? The answer is a resounding yes. In this recipe, we will see how to pull down image binary data from the server specifically and display it in your JavaFX application.

Getting ready

In *Chapter 5, JavaFX Media*, we learned how to use the Image API to download images automatically. However, the API offers little control over the download process. In this recipe, we are going to use `HttpRequest`, which provides granular control over the content of the image downloaded. For some portions of the code, you will need to be familiar with the use of JavaFX data binding and triggers (see *Chapter 1, Getting Started with JavaFX* for details). For a background on how to display images in JavaFX, review the recipe *Loading and displaying images with ImageView* from *Chapter 5, JavaFX Media*.

To illustrate the use of `HttpRequest`, we are going to build a Google Map application. The application uses the Google Static Map API to download static map images based on a provided address. The example requires a Google API Key to run. You can get your own Google API Key at `http://code.google.com/apis/maps/signup.html`.

How to do it...

The abbreviated version of the code provided next shows the essential portions needed to show how to pull down an image from Google's map server. The code listing intentionally leaves out portion of the code used to assemble the GUI components (topics on GUI controls are covered in *Chapter 4, Components and Skinning*). Refer to `ch06/source-code/src/http/HttpRequestGoogleMap.fx` for a complete listing of the code.

```
var w = 640;
var h = 480;
var bytesToRead:Long;
var currentBytesRead:Long;

var imgW = w * 0.8;
var imgH = h * 0.7;
var converter = URLConverter{}
var loc  = converter.encodeString("Atlanta, GA");
var zoom:Number = 15;
var mapType="roadmap";
def apiKey="PLACE_YOUR_GOOGLE_API_KEY_HERE";

var gmapUrl = bind "http://maps.google.com/maps/api/staticmap?"
        "center={loc}"
        "&zoom={zoom as Integer}"
        "&size={imgW as Integer}x{imgH as Integer}"
        "&maptype={mapType}"
        "&format=png32"
                "&markers=color:blue|{loc}"
        "&sensor=false"
        "&key={apiKey}"
                on replace {
```

```
                        loadMapImage(gmapUrl);
                };

    var imgView = ImageView{
        preserveRatio:true
        effect: Reflection{fraction:0.25}
        layoutX:(w - imgW)/2
        layoutY:10
    };

    function loadMapImage(url:String):Void{
        var http:HttpRequest = HttpRequest {
            location: url;
            onInput: function(is: java.io.InputStream) {
                try {
                    if(is.available() > 0) {
                        var buffImg = ImageIO.read(is);
                        imgView.image = SwingUtils.toFXImage(buffImg);
                    }
                } finally {
                    is.close();
                }
            }
            ...
        };
        http.start();
    }
    // code to build the GUI omitted (see full listing)
```

When the GUI controls are added to the application's scene instance, it produces the Google Map mashup application shown in the next screenshot:

How it works...

The previous code listing has been trimmed to its bare essentials to show you how to download binary data of an image from a remote web server. There are two main places in the code where you should focus your attention:

- First, let's look at the declaration of the variable `gmapUrl`. This string composes the URL, which is sent to the server to retrieve the image data for the map. The string specifies all of the necessary URL parameters that the Google Map server is expecting to render and return the image properly (see the Google Map API documentation for details about expected parameters).

  The important portion of the declaration of `gmapUrl` is the `on replace` trigger. Any time that the expression for the URL value changes, the trigger automatically invokes the `loadImage(url)` function, which is used to retrieve the binary data from the server (see next bullet).

- The `loadImage(url)` method is responsible for submitting the request to retrieve the image from the remote web server using the `HttpResponse` object. Here again, we provide a callback event-handling function through the `onInput:function(:InputStream)` property. This function is invoked when all of the bytes for the binary resource have been downloaded. In the code, we first attempt to detect if the data is available using `InputStream.available() > 0`; if so, we generate the image, as follows:

  - The code uses the Java class `javax.imageio.ImageIO` to generate an instance of `java.awt.image.BufferedImage` from the received `InputStream` object.

  - Since we can't use `BufferedImage` directly to display the image, the code then uses the `javafx.ext.Swing.SwingUtils` to convert the buffered image into an instance of `javafx.scene.image.Imge` by calling `SwingUtils.toFXImage()`. The image is then made visible by assigning it to the `ImageView` instance, `imgView`, through its `image` property.

The omitted portion of the code is composed of the following GUI control elements:

- *Slider*—the slider is used to control the zoom level of the image
- *TextBox*—the text box captures the address or location for the map
- *Map button*—forces the application to request an illustrated road map
- *Satellite button*—requests a map with satellite image overlays

If you think this example could have been accomplished by simply using an instance of Image, you would be correct. However, the approach presented here gives you total control and access to the life cycle events generated by the interaction between your application and the server. You do not get this level of control when using the Image API directly to retrieve an image.

There's more...

You can get more information on the materials presented here:

- Java Image Tutorial—http://java.sun.com/docs/books/tutorial/2d/images/
- Java IO Tutorial—http://java.sun.com/docs/books/tutorial/essential/io/
- Google Static Map API—http://code.google.com/apis/maps/documentation/staticmaps/

See also

- *Chapter 1—Using binding and triggers to update variables*
- *Chapter 4—Creating a form with JavaFX controls*
- *Chapter 4—Using the Slider control to input numeric values*
- *Chapter 5—Loading and displaying images with ImageView*
- *Accessing remote data with HttpRequest*

Posting data to remote servers with HttpRequest

In the preceding recipes, we looked at how to get data from a remote web server. You may also wish to send data collected from your application to a web server for storage, for instance. Sending data to web servers is the other half of the rich interactions that are supported between JavaFX applications and remote servers. In this recipe, we explore how to post data to a web server.

Getting ready

You should have an understanding of the basic mechanics behind the Web and how HttpRequest interacts with the server to handle the request/response life cycle. You should also review materials from *Chapter 4, Components and Skinning,* for information on building data forms. For this recipe, let's assume that we have a web server running

an application that can accept the submission of an employee form at the address
`http://localhost:8080/webapp/employee/save`. In this section, we will see
how to use JavaFX to submit data to a web server using the `POST` method.

How to do it...

To demonstrate how to use HttpRequest to post data to a web server, we will create a simple
form in JavaFX which submits employee information to a backend web server. To do this, we
will use the `POST HTTP` method of the HttpRequest object to encode and send information
to the server. The next listing provides a shortened version of the code. You can get the full
version from `ch06/source-code/src/http/HttpRequestPOST.fx`.

1. The first portion of the code builds the GUI for the form. We have seen how to build
   GUI forms using standard JavaFX controls in _Chapter 4, Components and Skinning_.
   Hence, we won't spend too much time on that:

```
def w = 400;
def h = 200;
var scene:Scene;

var nameRow = HBox {
    spacing:7
    content:[
        VBox{content:[Label{text:"First
Name"},TextBox{id:"fName"}]}
        VBox{content:[Label{text:"Last
Name"},TextBox{id:"lName"}]}
    ]
}
...
var btnRow = HBox {
    spacing:7
    content:[
        Button{
            text:"Submit"
            action:function(){
                formData.visible = true;
                postData();
            }
        }
    ]
}
```

2. The second part of the code declares the function `postData()` to collect the data from the form's `TextBox` instances and send it to server:

```
function postData(){
    var conv = URLConverter{};
    var url = "http://localhost:8080/webapp/employee/save";
    var postData = [
        Pair{name:"firstName" value:(scene.lookup("fName") as
            TextBox).text},
        Pair{name:"lastName" value:{(scene.lookup("lName") as
            TextBox).text}},
        Pair{name:"title" value:(scene.lookup("title") as
            TextBox).text},
        Pair{name:"address" value:(scene.lookup("addr") as
            TextBox).text},
    ];

    var http = HttpRequest {
        location: url
        method: HttpRequest.POST

        onOutput:function (toServer: OutputStream){
            try {
                var data = conv.encodeParameters(postData);
                toServer.write(data.getBytes());
            }finally{
                toServer.close();
            }
        }
        ...
    }
    http.start();
}
```

When we put all of the GUI controls in a scene graph and run the application, it posts the data to the remote server as shown, to be saved in the database as shown in the next screenshot:

How it works...

The HttpRequest object works in similar ways when using the POST method as when using the GET method: you set up the HttpRequest.location property, then you call the HttpRequest.start() function to start the interaction between your application and the server. However, when posting, the data must be properly encoded in ways understood by the HTTP server. Let's take a look at the function postData():

▶ *Capture data in pair sequence*—each data item from the form to be sent to the server must be grouped in key/value pairs where the key is the name of a field in an HTTP form and the value is from the TextBox instances. To accomplish this, we place the data in a sequence of Pair instances. A Pair object is a tuple, where you can store name-value pairs. We declare variable postData as a sequence of Pair instances to store values for firstName, lastName, title, and address, respectively, as shown next:

```
var postData = [
        Pair{name:"firstName" value:(scene.lookup("fName") as
            TextBox).text},
        Pair{name:"lastName' value:{(scene.lookup("lName") as
            TextBox).text}},
        Pair{name:"title" value:(scene.lookup("title") as
            TextBox).text},
        Pair{name:"address" value:(scene.lookup("addr") as
            TextBox).text},
    ];
```

▶ *Sending data to server*—to communicate with the server, we instantiate HttpRequest and assign it to variable http. Next, the code sets the parameter location to point to the server that will receive the data. The code also sets the method property to HttpRequest.POST (instead of GET).

  ❑ The code defines the event-handler function onOutput:function (:OutputStream) as a callback function that provides access to an instance of OutputStream assigned to variable toServer. All values written to that stream will be sent to the server.

  ❑ Before data from the form can be posted to the server, the sequence of Pair instances must be converted into a format supported by the web server. The code uses function encodePa rameters(Pair[]):String from the URLConverter class to encode the values that will be sent to the server.

❏ Once the data is prepared in a manner that the web server can understand (see previous bullet), we attach it to the `OutputStream` instance as follows:

```
var data = conv.encodeParameters(postData);
toServer.write(data.getBytes());
```

There's more...

For further details, see:

▸ Java IO Tutorial—`http://java.sun.com/docs/books/tutorial/essential/io/`

See also

▸ *Chapter 4—Creating a form with JavaFX controls*

▸ *Accessing remote data with HttpRequest*

Uploading files to servers with HttpRequest

When creating fully connected rich client applications, part of the expected standard functionalities, sometimes, is the ability to exchange files with the server. We have already seen how to download an image from the server (see recipe *Downloading images with HttpRequest*). In this recipe, we will look at how to use `HttpRequest` to upload an image to the server.

Getting ready

The concepts presented here deals with HTTP and the `HttpRequest` object in JavaFX. You should already have an understanding of the basic mechanics behind the Web and how `HttpRequest` interacts with web servers to handle the request/response life cycle. Refer to the recipes *Accessing remote data with HttpRequest, Downloading images with HttpRequest*, and *Posting data to remote servers with HttpRequest*, in this chapter, for some background information on how to use the `HttpRequest` object to interact with a web server.

For this recipe, we will assume that we have a web server running an application which can process the submission of a multi-part form for image file upload running at the address—`http://java.sun.com/docs/books/tutorial/essential/iave`. JavaFX's `HttpRequest` object does not support file upload directly (as of version 1.2). However, in this recipe, we will use common (and publicly available) knowledge about multi-part web forms to create the low-level data stream required by HTTP for multi-part form submission for file upload.

How to do it...

The abbreviated code given next shows you the major components needed to achieve binary data upload to a remote web server. Refer to `ch06/source-code/src/http/HttpRequestFileUpload.fx` for a complete code listing.

1. The first portion of the code defines class `FormPart` used to encapsulate the binary data and the required HTTP multi-part boundary markers that are used to decorate the data so the server can parse it.

```
def MARKER = "--";
def CRLF      = "\r\n";
def BOUNDARY = "7d226f700d0';
def CONTENT_TYPE = "multipart/form-data; boundary={BOUNDARY}";

class FormPart  {
    public-init var name:String;
    public var value:String;
    public var file:File;

    var conv = URLConverter{}
    ...
    public function writeFileTo(out:OutputStream):Void {
        if(file != null){
            var header = new java.lang.StringBuilder();
            header
                .append(CRLF)
                .append(MARKER)
                .append(BOUNDARY)
                .append(CRLF)
                .append("Content-Disposition: form-data;
                        name=\'{name}\";
                        filename=\"{file.getAbsolutePath()}\"")
                .append(CRLF)
                .append("Content-Type: application/octet-stream")
                .append(CRLF)
                .append(CRLF);

            // write header to output stream
            out.write(header.toString().getBytes());

            // copy file content to out stream
            var byteRead:Integer;
            var input = new FileInputStream(file);
            try{
                while ((byteRead = input.read()) != -1){
                    out.write(byteRead);
                }
            }finally{
                input.close();
```

```
                           }
                       }
                   }
           }
```

2. The second part of the code utilizes `HttpRequest` in conjunction with the `FormPart` class to send the multi-part form to the the server.

```
def url    = "http://localhost:8080/webapp/upload/save";
def file = new File("image.png");
def fileLen = file.length();

// HttpRequest declaration which uses class FormData
var http:HttpRequest = HttpRequest {
    location: url
    method: HttpRequest.POST
    headers: [
        HttpHeader
            {name:HttpHeader.CONTENT_TYPE value:CONTENT_TYPE},
    ]

    onOutput:function(out: OutputStream){
        try {
            // write parts
            def filePart = FormPart{name:"file" file:file}
            filePart.writeFileTo(out);

            // close multipart with a footer
            var footer = new java.lang.StringBuilder();
            footer
                .append(CRLF)
                .append(MARKER)
                .append(BOUNDARY)
                .append(MARKER);
            out.write(footer.toString().getBytes());
        }finally{
            out.close();
        }
    }
    ...
}

http.start();
```

When this code is executed, it will invoke `HttpRequest.start()`, which will cause the content of the file `image.png` to be uploaded to the server.

How it works...

As mentioned earlier, as of version 1.2 of the SDK, JavaFX does not currently have a direct way to upload a file to a web server using the `HttpRequest` object. However, in this recipe we have manually crafted a multi-part form stream at the HTTP protocol level to achieve a file upload. Here is how the code snippet works:

> ▶ Firstly, the snippet declares a series of constants (`MARKER`, `CRLF`, `BOUNDARY`, and `CONTENT_TYPE`) that are used to construct the multi-part form header and footer byte sequences.

> ▶ Next, the code defines the utility class `FormPart`, which exposes a method that is used to assemble the multi-part form byte stream that is sent to the server. The function `writeToFile(out:java.io.OutputStream)` of that class will arrange the data by laying out the header marker bytes followed by the bytes of the file being uploaded into the output stream.

> ▶ The code then declares an instance of `HttpRequest`, used to communicate with the server for the file upload. The code sets the `location` and the `method` properties for the request.

> ▶ `HttpRequest.headers`—in the `HttpRequest` declaration, we are providing header information using the `headers` property. You can define one or more request headers, which will be sent to the server as metadata about the request. In our code, we send header `CONTENT_TYPE` to indicate the type of content (multi-part form) the server should expect.

> ▶ We define an event-handler function for property `HttpRequest.onOutput` to write the outgoing bytes to the server. In it, we do the following:

>> ❑ `FormPart`—we use an instance of `FormPart` to generate the byte sequence for the multi-part boundaries and markers needed for the file upload header information. Then, the content of the file is opened using a `FileInputStream` instance, whose binary stream content is written to `OutputStream` being set to the server through the `out.write(byte[])` call.

>> ❑ `footer`—to close out the stream, the code applies footer markers through the variable `footer`, to signal the end of the multi-part binary submission to the `OutputSream` instance.

There's more...

You can read more about the topics discussed here:

> ▶ Multi-Part Message—`http://en.wikipedia.org/wiki/MIME`

> ▶ Java IO Tutorial—`http://java.sun.com/docs/books/tutorial/essential/io/`

See also

- ▸ *Accessing remote data with HttpRequest*
- ▸ *Downloading images with HttpRequest*
- ▸ *Posting data to remote servers with HttpRequest*
- ▸ *Posting data to servers with HttpRequest*

Building RESTful clients with the PullParser API

Two of the more pervasive formats for information interchange in today's web-enabled environments are XML and (more recently) **JSON** (originally stood for **JavaScript Object Notation**, but has evolved into a general structured data format). These formats have seen nothing but growing adoptions with the explosion of the programmable web movement. Companies with content-driven services expose their offerings as platforms to clients of any types (web-based, desktop, mobile, and so on) to tap into the vast sea of data and services programmatically.

In this recipe, we will see how you can use JavaFX to process XML and JSON data from remote servers. To illustrate these capabilities, we will extend the example presented in the previous recipe *Downloading images with HttpRequest*, to create a REST-style real estate price estimator mashup application which uses services from both Google Map and the Zillow Real Estate engine (`http://www.zillow.com`).

Getting ready

To understand some of the concepts presented here, you should be familiar with the `HttpRequest` class. If not, review the recipe *Accessing remote data with HttpRequest* to learn how to request data from web servers. For this recipe, we are going to make web requests from both the Google Map API and the Zillow API to create the real estate price estimator mashup. You will also need to be familiar with the mechanics of downloading images from web servers using JavaFX. If you need to some help, see recipe *Downloading images with HttpRequest*.

To process XML or JSON payloads, JavaFX provides the PullParser API, located in the `javafx.data.pull` package. The PullParser is a fast, event-driven parser that lets developers quickly parse document nodes as they are encountered during document download. JavaFX provides a parser for XML and one for JSON. Both parsers use a common API to make it easy to learn and use.

To implement or run the code presented in this recipe yourself, you will need to get Google and Zillow API keys at http://code.google.com/apis/maps/signup.html and https://www.zillow.com/webservice/Registration.html, respectively.

Prior to jumping into the code, let's review the XML document, which is returned by the Zillow web service call. Zillow uses a REST-style API, whereby requests are sent to the server as an HTTP.GET method, and the server responses are returned as an XML document. For our needs, we will use the GetSearchResults web service to obtain information on a given location. The service returns an XML payload which looks like the following XML snippet (only showing used data elements):

```xml
<?xml version="1.0" encoding="utf-8" ?>
<SearchResults:searchresults xmlns:SearchResults="http://www.zillow.
com/vstatic/3/static/xsd/SearchResults.xsd">
...
<response>
  <results>
    <result>
      <zpid>48749425</zpid>
          ...
        <address>
              <street>2114 Bigelow Ave N</street>
          <zipcode>98109</zipcode>
          <city>SEATTLE</city>
          <state>WA</state>
          <latitude>47.637934</latitude>
          <longitude>-122.347935</longitude>
        </address>
            <zestimate>
              <amount currency="USD">1241162</amount>
              <last-updated>10/25/2007</last-updated>
            ...
          </zestimate>
      </result>
      </results>
</response>
</SearchResults:searchresults>
```

How to do it...

The code for this recipe is a little long. So, it has been segmented into chunks for easier readability and comprehension. For the full code listing of this recipe, see the script file available at `ch06/source-code/src/webservice/ZillowMashupDmo.fx`

1. Let us first declare some constant values and global variables used throughout the script file:

```
def w = 640;
def h = 480;
def imgW = w * 0.7;
def imgH = h * 0.6;

def ZILLOW_WS = "http://www.zillow.com/webservice/Get-
SearchResults.htm";
def ZILLOW_ZID = "PLACE_ZILLOW_KEY_HERE";
def GOOGLE_WS = "http://maps.google.com/maps/api/staticmap";
def GOOGLE_KEY = "PLACE_YOUR_GOOGLE_KEY_HERE";
def DEFAULT_ADDR  = createAddress("1600 Pennsylvania Ave, Washing-
ton DC");

def conv = URLConverter{};

var scene:Scene;
var imgView:ImageView;
```

2. Next, define two classes that are used as data model to represent addresses and Zillow listings:

```
// Address model
class Address {
    public var street:String;
    public var city:String;
    public var state:String;
    public var zip:String;
    override public function toString(){
        return "{street}, "
               "{city} {state} {zip}";
    }
}

// Zillow Listing Model
class ZillowListing extends Address{
```

```
    public var zpid:String;
    public var longitude:String;
    public var latitude:String;
    public var zestimate:Number;
    override public function toString(){
        return "[zpid:{zpid}, "
                "long:{longitude}, "
                "lat:{latitude}, "
                "addr:{street}, "
                "{city} {state} {zip},"
                " zestimate:{zestimate}]"
    }
}
```

3. Function `createAddress()` is used to create `Address` object from a string representation:

```
// creates an address object from a string
function createAddress(address:String):Address {
    var result = Address{};
    var addrParts = address.split(",");
    result.street = addrParts[0].trim();
    if(sizeof addrParts == 2){
        var subparts = addrParts[1].trim().split("\\s");
        result.city = subparts[0];
        result.state = subparts[1];
    }
    if(sizeof addrParts == 3){
        var subparts = addrParts[1].trim().split("\\s");
        result.city = subparts[0];
        result.state = subparts[1];
        result.zip = addrParts[2];
    }
    result;
}
```

4. Next, we declare a function `getZListing()` to set up the code that retrieves and processes Zillow pricing information for a given address instance:

```
// stores listing request
def zl = ZillowListing{}

// retrieves the zillow listing for given address
function getZListing(addr:Address){
    def citystatezip = "{addr.city} {addr.state} {addr.zip}";
    var url = bind "{ZILLOW_WS}?zws-id={ZILLOW_ZID}&"
```

```
        "address={conv.encodeString(addr.street)}&"
        "citystatezip={conv.encodeString(citystatezip)}";

var parser = PullParser {
    documentType:PullParser.XML
    onEvent: function(event:javafx.data.pull.Event){
        if(event.type == PullParser.END_ELEMENT){
            if(event.qname.name == "zpid"){
                zl.zpid = event.text;
            }
            if(event.qname.name == "longitude"){
                zl.longitude = event.text;
            }
            if(event.qname.name == "latitude"){
                zl.latitude = event.text;
            }
            if(event.qname.name == "street"){
                zl.street  = event.text;
            }
            if(event.qname.name == "city"){
                zl.city  = event.text;
            }
            if(event.qname.name == "state"){
                zl.state  = event.text;
            }
            if(event.qname.name == "zip"){
                zl.zip  = event.text;
            }
            if(event.qname.name == "amount"){
                zl.zestimate = Number.parseFloat(event.text);
            }
        }
    }
}

var http:HttpRequest = HttpRequest {
    method: HttpRequest.GET
    location : url
    onInput:function(in:java.io.InputStream){
        try{
            parser.input = in;
            parser.parse();
        }finally{
            in.close();
```

```
            }
        }
        onDone:function(){
            http.stop();
        }
    }
    http.start();
}
```

5. The next segment lists function getGMap() which retrieves a static map image for a given address. This is the same code used in the previous recipe *Downloading images with HttpRequest*. So, it will be abbreviated, if you need more details on how to download images using HttpRequest, see the aforementioned recipe.

```
function getGMap(addr:Address){
    var loc = "{addr.street}, {addr.city} {addr.state} {addr.
zip}";
    var url = bind "{GOOGLE_WS}?"
        "center={conv.encodeString(loc)}"
        "&zoom=13"
        "&size={imgW as Integer}x{imgH as Integer}"
        "&maptype=map"
        "&format=png32"
                    "&markers=color:blue|{conv.encodeString(loc)}"
        "&sensor=false"
        "&key={GOOGLE_KEY}";

    var http:HttpRequest = HttpRequest {
        location: url;
        onInput: function(is: java.io.InputStream) {
            try {
                if(is.available() > 0) {
                    var buffImg = ImageIO.read(is);
                    imgView.image = SwingUtils.toFXImage(buffImg);
                }
            } finally {
                is.close();
            }
        }

        ...

    };
    http.start();
}
```

The remainder of the code deals with creating the GUI for the application by arranging the image, the text box, and the button, as shown in the next screenshot. That code has been omitted as you are trusted to review the respective recipes that deal with GUI creation in previous chapters.

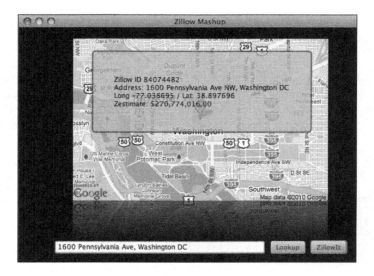

How it works...

In this recipe, we have built a RESTful mashup rich client application that displays a location on a Google Map and real estate data for that location using Zillow web service API. The previous code, snippet shows you how to pull down and parse an XML-encoded document from a remote web server using the PullParser API. Let's review what is going on in the code:

> *Global values*—the first segment of the code declares global values used throughout the code including the root URL's for the Google and Zillow services, API keys, a default address used when the application first started.

> *Data models*—to pass data around in the application, we create classes `Address` and `ZillowListing` as data model. The `Address` class provides a structured way to capture address data passed in as parameters to the web service requests. The `ZillowListing` class models the information returned by the Zillow web service. `ZillowListing` extends the `Address` class because the listing information from Zillow contains address data as well.

> Convenience function `createAddress(:String):Address` creates an `Address` object from a `String` value. This is valuable since both web services parameterize the address information differently. The `Address` class provides a normalized view of the address around the application.

▶ *Getting Zillow listings*—the third segment of the code shows the definition of the function getZListing(:Address). As you may expect, this function retrieves the Zillow listing based on the address parameters passed to the service. Here is what is going on inside the function:

  ❑ First, we defined the URL string to the Zillow service. To keep things simple, we use the global constants defined earlier to concatenate the web service location, the Zillow API ID, and the address parameters.

  ❑ Next, we instantiate a PullParser instance assigned to the variable parser. JavaFX's PullParser is an event-based parser, where an event cursor moves past the document as it is streamed from its source. Each node of the document raises an event (see *There's more* next) that is handled by the event-handler function attached to property onEvent of the parser.

    In the code, the onEvent function takes a simplistic approach to processing the node events. Basically, at the end of each element, detected with if(event.type == PullParser.END_ELEMENT), the code tests all expected element values and grabs the element that matches the expected name using a chain of if expressions.

  ❑ The next portion of the getZListing(:Address) function is the declaration of a HttpRequest instance assigned to the variable http. This is used to communicate with the server and retrieve the XML document. The event-handler function assigned to the http.onInput property connects the XML document's InputStream to the PullParser.in property. The code then calls the PullParser.parse() function to kickoff the parsing of the document.

▶ *Getting the Google Map image*—retrieving the Google Map image is done by the function getGMap(:Address). It uses the same technique covered in the recipe *Downloading images with HttpRequest*. It uses an instance of HttpRequest to download the binary data of the image and assign it to an instance of ImageView.image.

There's more...

JavaFX's PullParser class is designed to handle both XML and JSON structured data formats. The PullParser API uses a convention based on the **Document Object Model (DOM)** to identify the nodes in the document. As the parser encounters a document node during traversal, it generates a pull event and calls a user-defined event handler specified through parser property onEvent:function(:javafx.data.pull.Event). Both XML and JSON documents are handled in the same manner. The following table lists some common pull events generated by the parser:

DOCUMENT_START DOCUMENT_END	Generated when the beginning and end of the document have been reached (either XML or JSON)
START_ELEMENT END_ELEMENT	Generated at the start and end of an XML element (or JSON object) respectively
TEXT	Generated when textual value of an XML element (or of a JSON object) is encountered
START_VALUE END_VALUE	Generated when the value of a JSON object has been parsed
START_ARRAY END_ARRAY	Generates an event when the beginning and end of a JSON array have been reached, respectively
START_ARRAY_ELEMENT END_ARRAY_ELEMENT	Generated at the beginning and end of parsing a JSON array element, respectively

Custom parsing

The other way to use the `PullParser` API is to do a linear traversal across the document yourself, using methods to jump forward to specific locations in the document. To do this, you make use of the following methods:

`forward()`	Moves the event cursor forward to the next parsing event
`forward(level:Integer)`	Moves the event cursor forward by the given level into the document
`seek(element:Object)`	Moves the event cursor until the specified element is encountered
`seek(element:Object, level:Integer)`	Moves the event cursor until the element is found at the specified level

Referring back to the XML document from the Zillow request we saw earlier, we can access the address value with the following code:

```
var street = parser.seek(QName{name:"address"})
    .forward(2)
    .event.text;
```

The `seek()` method jumps to the address node, then skips two elements to get to the value node of the street address (refer to *Getting started for XML structure*).

When you are traversing the document manually as shown, it is important not to call the `parse()` method. This will cause the parser to move the event cursor all the way to the end of the document.

For details on some of the topics presented here, refer to:

- Java IO Tutorial—`http://java.sun.com/docs/books/tutorial/essential/io/`
- XML Document Object Model—`http://en.wikipedia.org/wiki/Document_Object_Model`

See also

- _Chapter 4—Creating a form with JavaFX controls_
- _Accessing remote data with HttpRequest_
- _Downloading images with HttpRequest_

Using the Feed API to create RSS/Atom clients

We have seen in the previous recipes that JavaFX is well-suited to handle XML data. One of the most pervasive usages of XML is the syndication of data made available through feed formats, such as the RSS and Atom formats. In this recipe, we explore JavaFX's inherent support for the RSS syndication format through the Feed API by building a simple weather reader application using RSS data from Yahoo.

Getting ready

To understand this recipe, you should be familiar with the notion of web content syndication, or web feeds. If not, have a quick look at `http://en.wikipedia.org/wiki/Web_feed` which provides background information about how feeds are used. You should also take a look at the previous recipe in this chapter, _Building RESTful clients with the PullParser API_.

In this recipe, we will show you how to parse RSS syndication feeds using JavaFX's RSS Feed API located in the `javafx.data.feed.rss` package. For this recipe, you will pull RSS-encoded weather data from Yahoo's weather services located at `http://weather.yahooapis.com/forecastrss`. We will use JavaFX's RSS API to create an application which displays weather conditions given a zip code. Unlike the other recipes presented earlier, you will not need an API key for this example.

How to do it...

The shortened code provided next shows how to retrieve and process RSS data using the Feed API. The omitted portion of the code deals with building the GUI elements, with which you should already be familiar. You can get the complete listing of the code from `ch06/source-code/src/webservice/YahooWeaherRSS.fx`.

```
// weather data model
class Weather {
    public var image:Image;
    public var title:String;
    public var city:String;
    public var region:String;
    public var country:String;
    public var condition:String;
    public var temp:String;
    public var windSpeed:String;
    public var humidity:String;
    public var visibility:String;
    public var pressure:String;
    public var sunsetTime:String;
    public var sunriseTime:String;
}

var zip = "33167";
var weather = Weather{}; // instance to hold weather info

// function to retrieve weather info based on zip code
function loadWeatherInfo(zip:String):Void {
    var rss:RssTask = RssTask {
        location: "http://weather.yahooapis.com/forecastrss?p={zip}";
...
    //handle Yahoo specific tags
        onForeignEvent:function(event:Event){
            if(event.type == PullParser.END_ELEMENT and
                event.qname.name.equals("location")){
                weather.city=event.getAttributeValue(
                    QName{name:"city"});
                weather.region=event.getAttributeValue(
                    QName{name:"region"});
                weather.country=event.getAttributeValue(
                    QName{name:"country"});
            }
            if(event.type == PullParser.END_ELEMENT and
                event.qname.name.equals("condition")){
                weather.condition =
                    event.getAttributeValue("text");
```

```
                weather.temp=event.getAttributeValue("temp");
                // assemble image
                var imgUrl = "http://l.yimg.com/a/i/us/we/52/"
                    "{event.getAttributeValue("code")}.gif";
                weather.image = Image{url:imgUrl};
            }
        if(event.type == PullParser.END_ELEMENT and
            event.qname.name.equals("wind")){
            weather.windSpeed=
                event.getAttributeValue("speed")
        }
        if(event.type == PullParser.END_ELEMENT and
            event.qname.name.equals("atmosphere")){
                weather.visibility=
                    event.getAttributeValue("visibility");
            weather.pressure =
                event.getAttributeValue("pressure");
            weather.humidity =
                event.getAttributeValue("humidity");
        }
        if(event.type == PullParser.END_ELEMENT and
            event.qname.name.equals("astronomy")){
            weather.sunriseTime =
                event.getAttributeValue("sunrise");
            weather.sunsetTime =
                event.getAttributeValue("sunset");
        }
        }
    }
    ...
    }
    rss.start();
}
```

When the code is executed, you will get a weather widget, as shown in the next screenshot.

How it works...

In this example, the code retrieves weather information from Yahoo Weather as RSS-encoded data. The steps needed to process RSS feeds are similar to those used in XML processing (see previous recipe). Let's examine how this is done:

- *Model the weather*—the first item listed is the definition of class `Weather`. It models the weather information that will be transferred from the server. A script-level instance of `Weather` is assigned to variable `weather`, which will be used to store information extracted from the RSS feed in function `loadRssInfo()` (see next bullet).

- *Retrieving RSS data*—function `loadRssInfo(zip:String)` encapsulates the code necessary to send a request to the feeds server and process the response. To do this, it declares an instance of `RssTask`, which is part of JavaFX's Feeds API.

  - `RssTask` uses the PullParser API internally to process RSS feeds. Therefore, it is an event-based parser that raises parsing events as the document is streamed from its source. To use the `RssTask`, you first set the `location` property to point to the RSS resource that you want to request. Property `onForeignEvent` is used to specify a callback function to handle streaming events used to extract weather information encoded in non-standard RSS tags, as is done in the Yahoo Weather format.

The same strategy used when processing XML in the previous recipe is used here. The code sets up a chain of `if` expressions designed to test when an expected element is encountered. When that happens, the code then retrieves the RSS element's attribute value, as shown in the following code snippet that retrieves attribute `"speed"` from element `"wind"`. The retrieved value is then assigned to the `weather` object.

```
if(event.type == PullParser.END_ELEMENT and
    event.qname.name.equals("wind")){
    weather.windSpeed=event.getAttributeValue("speed")
}
```

There's more...

The Feed API is used to process both RSS and Atom feeds. The API uses an asynchronous task-based approach to process incoming web feeds. For both types of documents, the API produces events that are mapped to high-level nodes found in these document types (that is, Channel in RSS or Entry in Atom). Let's look at how they parse that information.

Handling RSS

To get started with processing RSS data, you need to initiate an instance of the `RssTask`. As the internal parser processes the document, the `RssTask` object produces events for all high-level nodes as they are encountered during parsing. The following table shows the RSS document nodes and their associated events produced during parsing:

Node	Event Handler	Description
Channel	onChannel: function(:Channel):Void	RssTask calls this function after the RSS Channel node is successfully parsed. The callback function receives an instance of Channel, which contains all parsed nodes under Channel.
Item	onItem: function(:Item):Void	This function is invoked when the Item node on the RSS document is fully realized. The callback function receives an instance of Item, which contains all parsed nodes under Item.
Extension Nodes	onForeignEvent:function(:javafx. data.pull.Event)	This function is called when non-standard extension nodes are encountered in the document. The callback function receives an instance of the PullParser's Event class.

The instances of `Channel` and `Item` passed into each callback function (respectively) gives access to all of the additional nodes that make up a standard RSS document (that is: title, link, description, generator, category, pubDate, guid, and image).

Handling Atom

Similar to RSS, to get started with Atom, you must initiate an instance of the `AtomTask` class. The `AtomTask` class produces events for the `Feed` and `Entry` high-level nodes as they are encountered during parsing. The next table describes Atom nodes and the events they produced during parsing:

Node	Event Handler	Description
Feed	`onChannel: function(:Feed):Void`	This function is invoked after the `Feed` node of the document is successfully parsed. The method receives an instance of `Feed`, which contains data for all parsed sub-nodes.
Entry	`onItem: function(:Entry):Void`	This function is invoked after the `Entry` node and all of its child nodes are successfully parsed. The method receives an instance of `Entry`, which contains data for the parsed nodes.
Extension Nodes	`OnForeignEvent: function(:javafx.data.pull.Event)`	This function is called when non-standard extension nodes are encountered in the document. The callback function receives an instance of the PullParser's `Event` class.

The instances of `Feed` and `Entry` passed into each callback function (respectively) gives access to all of the additional nodes that make up a standard Atom document (that is: title, link, author, contributor, description, generator, category, rights, and logo).

Override default parsing behavior

Another feature of the Feed API is the ability to override the way the internal parser handles the documents. Both `RssTask` and the `AtomTask` classes use a `Factory` class to build parsed nodes from the document. You can provide your own Factory class to override how the nodes are parsed from the document. For instance, let's say we want to strip out any HTML tags embedded in the title of your Atom document. The following steps show you how to do it.

1. The first step is to create a new `Entry` class in order to gain access to the processing of the `title` node:

```
class SimpleTitleEntry extends Entry {
  public override function fromXML(parser:PullParser):Void {
    if(parser.event.qname == TITLE and
          parser.event.type == parser.TEXT) {
              title = parser.event.text.replaceAll(
              "<[a-zA-Z\/][^>]*>", "");
      }else{
      super.fromXML(parser);
      }
  }
}
```

2. Next, define a new `Factory` class, which will be responsible for building instances of the `SimpleTitleEntry` class during parsing:

```
class SimpleTitleFactory extends Factory {
  public override function newEntry(feed:Feed):Void {
    SimpleTitleEntry {feed: feed}
  }
}
```

3. Once your factory is defined, add it to your `FeedTask` instance as such:

```
var atom = AtomTask {
  location: "http://youratomlocation.com/file.atom"
  factory: SimpleTitleFactory{}
  ...
}
```

When the instance of `AtomTask` parses your document, it will automatically scrub the title of any extraneous HTML.

Refer to `http://en.wikipedia.org/wiki/Web_feed` for further information on web feeds.

See also

▶ *Chapter 4—Creating a form with JavaFX controls*

▶ *Accessing remote data with HttpRequest*

▶ *Downloading images with HttpRequest*

▶ *Building RESTful clients with the PullParser API*

Visualizing data with the JavaFX chart API

Up to this point, all of the recipes in this chapter dealt with retrieving, processing, or storing data. What about visualizing the data? As with other rich client platforms, JavaFX provides a wealth of data visualization tools in the form of the **Chart API**. This recipe shows you how to use the Chart API to create a visual rendition of your data in the form of charts.

Getting ready

This recipe involves discussion about JavaFX's Chart API located in package `javafx.scene.chart`. As of version 1.2 of the platform, the API offers support for more than half a dozen charts. All charts, however, share a common implementation design, which makes the creation of all charts a similar exercise. The example presented for this recipe will show you how to create a bar chart. However, the steps necessary to create other types of charts are similar.

How to do it...

The next code snippet shows you how to create a bar chart in JavaFX. As you will see, it is simple and straightforward. Refer to `ch06/source-code/src/chart/BarChartDemo.fx` for the full listing.

```
var categories = ["Q32009", "Q32008"];

var dataSeries = [
    BarChart.Series {
        name: "Nokia"
        data: [
            BarChart.Data {category: categories[0] value: 16.1},
            BarChart.Data {category: categories[1] value: 15.4}
        ]
    },
    BarChart.Series {
        name: "RIM"
        data: [
            BarChart.Data {category: categories[0] value: 8.5},
            BarChart.Data {category: categories[1] value: 5.8}
        ]
    },
    BarChart.Series {
        name: "Apple"
        data: [
            BarChart.Data {category: categories[0] value: 7},
```

```
                BarChart.Data {category: categories[1] value: 4.7}
          ]
      },
      ...  // omitted full list of data series
];

// put bar on stage for display
Stage {
   title: "Gartner Smartphone Sales"
   scene: Scene {
      content: [
        BarChart {
           title: "Gartner Smartphone Sales"
           titleFont: Font { size: 24 }
           categoryAxis:CategoryAxis {
               categories: categories
           }
           valueAxis:NumberAxis{
               label:"Sales (100K)'
               upperBound:20
               lowerBound:0
           }

           data: bind dataSeries
        }
      ]
   }
}
```

When the code is executed, it produces the bar chart shown in the next figure:

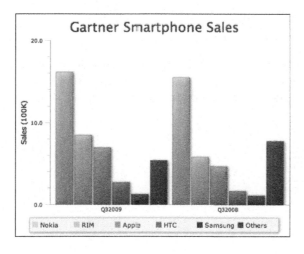

How it works...

As mentioned earlier, creating a chart is easy and straight forward. In this example, we use data from a Gartner report (see `http://www.gartner.com/it/page.jsp?id=1224645`) to display smartphone sales for Q309 versus Q308. The code to produce the chart from the tabular data provided in the report is deceptively simple. Let's see how the chart was produced:

- Categories—first, the code declares the data categories for the chart. A category is a broad, logical grouping of related data points. In the code snippet, variable `categories` is declared as a sequence of strings representation two categories "Q32009" and "Q32008".

- Data series—next, variable `dataSeries` is assigned a sequence of `BarChart.Series` instances. The `Series` class encapsulates the definition of one or more data points on the chart. Each `Series` instance has a name and contains a sequence of data points bound to a category (see previous bullet). The Chart API uses that information to generate each bar in the chart, select a color for the bar, and automatically generate the legend for the chart.

The last step is to place the generated chart on the stage. The chart automatically sizes itself to display the data properly. However, you can use the myriad of properties exposed by the Chart API to customize the look of your charts.

There's more...

Charts from the Chart API can be grouped in two major categories: XYChart, which represents charts with two-axis charts and PieChart (and its 3D version PieChart3D). As of version 1.2, XYChart classes can be further grouped as follows:

- `BarChart` and `BarChart3D`
- `LineChart` and `AreaChart`
- `BubbleChart` and `ScatterChart`

Each chart type listed shares similar properties, which makes it easy to switch between them. For instance, going from `BarChart` to `BarBarChart3D` involves a simple class substitution, which produces a 3D version of the chart, as shown in the following screenshot:

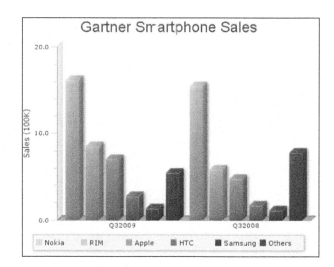

The `PieChart` class is actually simpler to use than the rest of the charts listed. `PieChart` uses a sequence of `PieChart.Data` to represent the data that will be plotted, where you provide `PieChart.Data.label` and `PieChart.Data.value` properties. Both `PieChart` and `PieChart3D` share the same properties and can be easily switched for one another.

Chart customization

The Chart API makes it easy to customize the look and behavior of your charts. Depending on the type of the chart you are creating, you have access to an assortment of properties that you can customize, including the data element's paint, effect, stroke, and node. You also have the ability to specify interaction behavior by providing an `action:function()` property for each data element on the chart using the `Data` class.

The `BarChart` class allows you to provide an instance of the `Node` class for each data item in the data series. To illustrate how to use this feature, we modify the code from the recipe (leaving only three data members) and define a function for the property `BarChart.Data.barCreator` as shown in the next code snippet. You can get the entire code listing from `ch06/source-code/src/chart/BarChartCustomDemo.fx`.

```
def width = 640;
def barWidth = (width/6) - 30;

var dataSeries = [
    BarChart.Series {
        name: "Nokia"
        data: [
            BarChart.Data {category: cats[0] value: 16.1},
            BarChart.Data {category: cats[1] value: 15.4}
        ]
```

```
barCreator:function(
        series:Series,
        pos:Integer,
        data:Data):Node{
    ImageView{
      image:Image{
        url:"{__DIR__}nokia.png"
        width:barWidth
      }
    }
  }
}

    . . .

}
```

The function assigned to `barCreator` is invoked for each data element in the series as the chart is rendered. In this version of the code, the function returns an instance of `ImageView`. The chart renders an image of a phone instead of the standard bar in the chart, as shown in the following figure:

7
Deployment and Integration

In this chapter, we will cover the following topics:

- ► Building and packaging your app with an IDE
- ► Building and packaging your app with javafxpackager
- ► Packaging your app to get Web Star(ed)
- ► Packaging your app as an applet
- ► Passing arguments to JavaFX applications
- ► Making your applets drag-to-install
- ► Controlling JavaFX applets from JavaScript

Introduction

Deployment and integration are critical steps in getting your application to its intended audience. Regardless of how polished or feature-rich your rich-client application happens to be, it will be tossed quickly to the side if its users are unable to access and run it with ease and no fuss. In this chapter, we will look at the many deployment options available to get your JavaFX applications to your audience.

The unified programming model

The JavaFX application framework supports a unified programming model. With this framework, you can write code that scales to target devices ranging from smart phones, set-top boxes, to entertainment systems, using the same code (with little or no changes). JavaFX's build and deployment systems determine how to wrap your code to target the proper runtime environments.

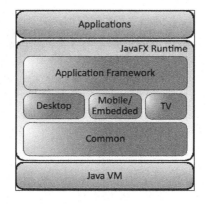

The JavaFX APIs are organized into profiles, which logically group the APIs into subsets of related functionalities that target one or more runtime environments. As of JavaFX 1.2, the supported profiles, as shown in the previous figure, include:

- ▶ **Common**—the APIs in this profile will run in any targeted runtime. Applications that use only APIs in this profile are guaranteed to be portable across all devices.

- ▶ **Desktop**—if you want your application to target only the desktop, with the full power of Java SE behind it, you would target this profile. It includes APIs, such as class reflection, Swing, and anything else supported by Java SE.

- ▶ **TV**—targeting the TV profile is similar to writing code for the desktop. However, for guaranteed portability, use the Common APIs as much as possible.

- ▶ **Mobile**—the mobile profile includes functionalities tied to a mobile environment with lighter functionalities available.

When you create JavaFX code, the deployment and runtime mechanism is responsible for determining how to run your application as either an embedded applet within a browser, a desktop application provisioned from the Web (see recipe *Packaging your app to get Web Start(ed)*), or a regular desktop application launched from the command line.

Building and packaging your app with an IDE

Before you can run your application using any of the profiles mentioned in the introduction, you must build and package it to target that profile. You can build your application using an IDE or the `javafxpackager` command-line tool (see the recipe *Building and packaging your app using javafxpackager*) that comes with SDK. In this recipe, we are going to explore how to build your application using NetBeans and Eclipse.

Getting ready

This recipe assumes that you are using either the NetBeans or the Eclipse IDE for your JavaFX development. If you are not familiar with either of the IDEs, refer to *Chapter 1, Getting Started with JavaFX*, for a discussion on how to get started with an IDE for JavaFX development.

How to do it...

Both IDEs (NetBeans and Eclipse) provide support for automatic building and packaging of your JavaFX applications. You can target different runtime environments supported by JavaFX right from the IDE.

In NetBeans, you can specify your packaging settings for your application from the project's properties dialog. Do the following in NetBeans:

1. Right-click on the project in the **Projects** window and select **Properties**.
2. Select **Run** to specify the application's main class.
3. Then, select the targeted execution environment as shown in the next screenshot.

Similarly in Eclipse, you can set up your project to assemble and build your applications automatically to target the desired execution environment automatically. To accomplish this in Eclipse, do the following:

1. Select **Run Configurations** from the **Run** menu for your project.

2. Then specify how you want to build your application by selecting the desired profile, as shown in the next screenshot.

How it works...

Both IDEs support functionalities that allow developers to build and package their applications to target the different runtimes or profiles supported by JavaFX. As shown in the previous figures, you have the ability to specify one of the following runtimes as a build setting:

NetBeans	Eclipse	Setting
Standard Execution	Desktop profile - Run as Application	Select this to deploy your application to run as a standalone raw jar with the javafx launcher (see next *Launch your application with the javafx launcher tool*).
Web Start Execution	Desktop profile - Run as Web Start	This setting packages the project to run within the Web Start runtime.
Run in Web Browser	Desktop profile - Run as Applet in a web browser	Select this to deploy your application as an applet.
Run in Mobile Emulator	Mobile profile - Run in Emulator	This setting is used to run an application within the Mobile runtime.
Run in TV Emulator	Not supported in Eclipse yet	Use this setting to target the TV runtime.

There's more...

Regardless of the targeted runtime, it is imperative that you specify the main JavaFX script file. So for instance, if your application's main entry class is `my.package.Main` (that is, the class where the Stage instance or the script-level `run()` function is declared), then you would enter the fully-qualified class name in the space provided in the IDE settings (check out the preceding two figures). That information will be added to the `manifest` file as:

```
Main-Class: my.package.Main
```

The runtime container uses this information to determine which class to use to boot up your application. If you fail to provide that information, your application will not start properly. If the class you specified is a code module (whereby it does not have a Stage declared nor does it have a script-level `run()` method), nothing will happen when you attempt to run the application.

See also

▶ *Chapter 1, Getting Started with JavaFX*

Building and packaging your app with javafxpackager

An IDE makes it easy to build and package your JavaFX application; however, driving the build process from a command-line interface may be the desirable approach (automated build comes to mind). In this recipe, we will see how to use the javafxpackager command-line tool to package and get your desktop application ready for deployment.

Getting ready

You should be familiar with using the command shell. We will assume that you have properly installed the JavaFX SDK with the `JAVAFX_HOME/bin` added to your shell's executable path. If you do not have the JavaFX SDK installed properly, you will not be able to run the javafxpackager tool. To ensure that you have your environment set up as expected, from a command prompt type `javafxpackager - version`, as shown next:

```
$> javafxpackager - version
$> javafxpackager 1.2.0_b233
```

You should get the version of the launcher currently installed (similar to the previous listing). If you get an error, refer to the recipe *Installing the JavaFX SDK* in *Chapter 1, Getting Started with JavaFX* for details on how to properly install the SDK.

How to do it...

For this recipe, let's assume the following:

▶ You have an application named "cookbook"

▶ The root directory for your source code is located in the folder `src`

▶ The main class is located in the package `cookbook.app.Main`, where script file `Main.fx` is designated as the entry point of the application

To package this application using JavaFX's packager tool, start a command prompt, and type the following:

```
javafxpackager -src src -appClass cookbook.app.Main
```

Upon completion, this command will generate a `dist/` directory where all the files are placed as shown in the next screenshot.

```
 418 Nov 21 08:39 Main.html
2883 Nov 21 08:39 Main.jar
 819 Nov 21 08:39 Main.jnlp
 861 Nov 21 08:39 Main_browser.jnlp
```

You will find the code as described for this recipe in `ch07/source-code/src/cookbook.app.Main.fx`. The code is immaterial for this recipe; however, it gives you a starting point to test the `javafxpackager`.

How it works...

Although the command issued at the prompt is simple, the JavaFX packager tool does several import tasks when packaging your application including the following:

▶ *Java and JavaFX code compilation*—the packager tool provides joint compilation services where it compiles Java source files and JavaFX script source files. It automatically resolves all interdependencies that may exist in the code structure between Java code and JavaFX code. In our scenario, all compilable code will be built into Java classes and placed in a temporary location during the build process to be assembled into a JAR file.

▶ *Assemble resources*—copies all non-compilable resources (that is, media files, fonts, and so on), that are on the source path (or explicitly specified using a build switch), for packaging. In the example, all resources found in the source path will be copied to a temporary build location until they are assembled as a JAR file.

▶ *Assemble JAR*—this step assembles the compiled class files and the media resources into the application's executable JAR file. For our example, the build process assembles all compiled resources and non-compiled resources into the `Main.jar` file.

- ▶ *Generate Web Start file*—creates a **JNLP** (Java Network Launching Protocol) descriptor file that you can use to distribute your application as a Java Web Start(ed) desktop application. In our example, the build step generates the `Main.jnlp` file.

- ▶ *Generate browser plugin file*—the packager also generates a `*_browser.jnlp` file, which is used to launch the application as an applet using the new Java Plugin architecture. For our example, the build step generated browser file `Main_browser.jnlp`.

- ▶ *Generate HTML and JavaScript stub*—finally, the packager creates a sample HTML which shows how to embed your application as an applet using JavaScript. In our example, the packager generated the `Main.html` file.

>
> The JNLP configuration and HTML code generated by the packager tool is intended to be a starting point. You are expected to edit and customize the content of these files to fit your deployment needs.

There's more...

The `javafxpackager` tool supports a myriad of options designed to control how it builds and packages your application. The following table lists some of the more commonly used packaging flags:

-profile | -p	Use this option to specify the target profile for the build. Valid values include `mobile` and `desktop` (default).
-sourcepath | -src	This required option specifies one or more top-level directories where project sources are located.
-classpath | -cp |-librarypath	This is a list of directories, classes, and jars that make up the application's classpath. Otherwise, the current directory is used as the classpath.
-resourcepath | -res	Use this option to specify the location of resources which will be packaged in the resulting jar. If none is specified, the packager will search your source path for resources.
-destination | -d	This option specifies the directory where all generated jar will be placed. The default is dist.
-appClass	This required option specifies the fully-qualified name of the class to use as the entry point for the application.
-appName	Use this option to specify your application's name. The files generated by the packager tool will use the name provided, rather than the name of the main class.

This is a partial list of the available options, there are many more available for you to customize your build. You will encounter more of them in other recipes as we explore the different execution environments.

Automating your JavaFX build with Ant

The simplest (and safest) way to integrate the JavaFX build process with your automated Ant build is to use the `exec` Ant task to invoke the `javafxpackager` tool as an out-of-process task. Assuming that both Ant and JavaFX SDK are installed properly and are a part of the command shell's execution path, you can invoke the javafxpackager tool to compile the code mentioned earlier in this recipe using the Ant build below. Refer to `ch07/source-code/fxbuild.xml` for the build file.

```xml
<?xml version="1.0" encoding="UTF-8"?>
<project name="JavaFX-Build" default="compile" basedir=".">
    <target name="compile">
        <echo message="Compiling JavaFX"/>
            <exec executable="javafxpackager" failonerror="true">
            <arg value="-src"/>
            <arg value="src"/>
            <arg value="-appClass"/>
            <arg value="cookbook.app.Main"/>
        </exec>
    </target>
</project>
```

Using the `exec` Ant task, we are able to invoke the `javafxpackager` tool and passing control parameters to it as if it is invoked from the command line. When the Ant build file is executed, you get the same result as described in the *How to do it* section.

The other way to do this is to use the `JavaFXAntTask` class found in the `com.sun.tools.javafx.ant` package. This approach, however, relies on the use of internal, non-documented Sun's private classes. Although it works today, there is no guarantee that it will work, or even be supported, later on. Nevertheless, it is there and can be used to achieve the same result as above.

See also

▸   *Chapter 1, Getting Started with JavaFX*

Packaging your app to be Web Start(ed)

You have couple of options when it comes to distributing your JavaFX desktop applications. The first option is to ship your app to your users as raw JAR files launched from the command line. While this gives the application full access to local resources. However, it is not officially supported (as of version 1.2) and will run the code unmanaged and unable to take advantage of the deployment services, such as auto-update, JRE detection, and so on.

The preferred option is to facilitate the down oad and seamless installation and execution of your application through Java Web Start, a deplcyment and execution container built on the Java platform. In this recipe, we will use the JavaFX packager tool to build and package our application to be distributed using Java Web Start.

Getting ready

This recipe will use the javafxpackager tool to build and package the sample application. If you are not familiar with javafxpackager, review the previous recipe. If you prefer to use an IDE for your build and deployment, that is OK. Ycu can still follow along, as both NetBeans and Eclipse support all the topics covered here.

We will package a sample application named "webstart-demo". We will use the `javafxpackager` tool to build the application and generate the Web Start assets, which we will place on a web server. This will allow us to web-launch and automatically install our application using Web Start.

How to do it...

We will go through several steps to demonstrate how to build and deploy your application with Web Start:

1. The first step is to create a small sample application. You can find the full code at `ch07/source-code/src/webstart/WebStartDemo.fx`:

```
package webstart.demo;

import javafx.stage.Stage;
import javafx.scene.Scene;
import javafx.scene.text.Text;
import javafx.scene.text.Font;

var msg:Text = Text {
    font : Font {
        size : 72
        embolden: true
        name: "sans-serif,Arial,Helvetica"
    }
    content: "I was Web Started!"
}
msg.translateY = msg.boundsInLccal.height;

Stage {
```

```
        title: "Application title"
        width: msg.boundsInLocal.width
        height: msg.boundsInLocal.height * 2
        scene: Scene {
            content: [msg]
        }
    }
}
```

2. Next, we use the `javafxpackager` tool to build and package the application as follows (note that the command line is wrapped for readability):

```
javafxpackager -src src -appClass webstart.WebStartDemo
               -appName webstart-demo
               -appVendor "Vladimir Vivien" -appVersion 1.0
               -appCodebase "http://my.server/path/to/app"
```

Upon completion, the packager tool will produce the following deployment assets in default distribution directory `dist/`, as shown in the next screenshot:

```
 455 Nov 24 03:34 webstart-demo.html
5628 Nov 24 03:34 webstart-demo.jar
 856 Nov 24 03:34 webstart-demo.jnlp
 907 Nov 24 03:34 webstart-demo_browser.jnlp
```

Since we are deploying our application as a Java Web Start, we need to review and update the application's JNLP file generated during the packaging process. That file contains configuration settings used by Web Start to run the application. Some configurations are based on arguments passed from the javafxpackager command line. Let's update the `title` and the `description` tags:

```
<?xml version="1.0" encoding="UTF-8"?>
<jnlp spec="1.0+"
    codebase="http://my.server/path/to/app/"
    href="webstart-demo.jnlp">
    <information>
        <title>JavaFX Web Start Demo</title>
        <vendor>Vladimir Vivien</vendor>
        <homepage href="http://my.server/path/to/app"/>
        <description>Run App from Web Start</description>
        <offline-allowed/>
        <shortcut>
            <desktop/>
        </shortcut>
    </information>
    <resources>
```

```
        <j2se version="1.5+"/>
        <extension name="JavaFX Runtime"
            href="http://dl.javafx.com/1.2/javafx-rt.jnlp"/>
        <jar href="webstart-demo.jar" main="true"/>
    </resources>
    <application-desc
      main-class="com.sun.javafx.runtime.main.Main">
        <argument>MainJavaFXScript=webstart.demo.Main</argument>
    </application-desc>
    <update check="background">
</jnlp>
```

3. Lastly, we upload the JNLP file along with the JAR to the web server location
    specified by the `-codeBase` argument. Now, you can launch the application from
    the Web by pointing your web browser to URL `http://my.server/path/to/app/`
    `webstart-demo.jnlp`. The following screenshot shows the Web Start runtime
    launching the application (from my Amazon S3 location).

To speed up local development, you can launch your JNLP file from your
local file system by specifying a local codebase as file:/path/to/jnlp/app/.
This eliminates the need for a web server upload every time.

After Web Start fully downloads the application on the client's machine, it gets
automatically started using the main class specified in the configuration, as shown
in the following screenshot:

The previous screenshot shows the Web Start-launched application running. Notice, however, that since the application is not signed (with a vendor certificate), it carries an advisory label located at the upper right-hand side corner of the window. Future versions of the SDK may remove this label to provide a less alarmist user experience.

How it works...

We will not discuss the JavaFX code itself here. It is simple and is designed to be used as an illustrative tool to show you how to build and package your code as Java Web Start using the `javafxpackager` tool. As we have seen in the recipe *Packaging your app using javafxpackager*, we use the packager's command-line interface to specify several parameters that were covered in the previous recipe about javafxpackager. However, the following parameters are worth mentioning:

- `-appVendor`—is a descriptive name for the application's vendor that gets displayed on the default Java Web Start splash screen.

- `-appVersion`—is the application's version. Web Start uses this number for incremental future updates.

The packager tool generates all necessary artifacts required for successful deployment. Upon close examination of the JNLP file, we see that the command-line arguments values appear in the JNLP file as parameters. In addition, the generated JNLP file include the following configuration parameters that will effect how the application is installed and launched:

- *Offline option*—specifying tag `<offline-allowed/>` will cause the application to be cached locally, with the ability to be launched by the Web Start manager, without requiring subsequent application download with future uses.

- *Shortcut integration*—by default, the packager tools turn on desktop integration through the `<shortcut><desktop/><desktop/>` tags. This will cause Web Start to create a shortcut icon on the client's desktop.

- *JavaFX class launcher*—the `<application-desc/>` tag specifies a Sun-provided class launcher, which loads the JavaFX main class. In our example, the launcher will launch our application using the main class specified by argument `MainJavaFXScript=webstart.demo.Main`.

There's more...

The Java Web Start technology has been part of the Java landscape for quite a while. Recently, however, it has become one of the main characters in the JavaFX story. Web Start makes it easy to deploy your desktop application by providing a uniform mechanism for deploying and installing applications on the user's local machine. Some of the more prominent features of Java Web Start include:

- ▶ _Uniform deployment_—Web Start makes it possible to distribute your desktop application and its resources using a uniform user experience. Once the application is packaged for Web Start distribution, it can be deployed wherever the desktop Java runtime is supported.

- ▶ _Browser-based provisioning_—with Web Start, applications can be automatically downloaded and installed using a web browser pointing to a URL. A properly installed JRE will automatically launch the Web Start runtime when a JNLP file is accessed through the browser.

- ▶ _Seamless integration_—after the initial install, applications are cached locally on the user's machine. It is possible to have Web Start create a program or launch menu shortcuts for the supported OS.

- ▶ _Automatic update_—Web Start will automatically check for updates when the user starts the application.

- ▶ _Security_—by default, unsigned applications installed with Web Start are restricted from accessing local network and file resources. As part of the application installation process provided by Web Start, the user can give permission to allow an application to access those resources.

- ▶ Java Web Start is part of the JRE and requires no additional download from the user.

For further details on Java Web Start, see
`http://java.sun.com/javase/technologies/desktop/javawebstart/`

See also

- ▶ _Building and packaging your app using an IDE_
- ▶ _Building and packaging your app with javafxpackager_

Packaging your app as an applet

The Java applet is a precursor to today's rich internet browser-embedded clients. While the applet has had its share of challenges, the new Java Plugin architecture, introduced in JDK 1.6u10, was completely rewritten to make applets a viable alternative to Flash and AJAX by allowing developers to create rich client applications that run on the Java Virtual Machine. In this recipe, we will see how to build and distribute JavaFX desktop applications as applets using the tools included in the JavaFX SDK.

Getting ready

JavaFX applets are deployed as part of the desktop profile. Therefore, applets are capable of using the JNLP for Web Start deployments. We will use the javafxpackager tool to generate deployment artifacts for the sample applet presented in this recipe. If you are not familiar with javafxpacakger, review the recipe *Building and packaging your app with javafxpackager* presented earlier in this chapter. If you prefer to use an IDE for your build and deployment, then refer to the recipe *Building and packaging your app using an IDE* from this chapter.

For this recipe, we will package a simple application named "applet-demo." We will use the `javafxpackager` tool to build the application and generate the deployment assets, which are expected to be provisioned from a web server using a web browser.

How to do it...

We will go through several steps to demonstrate how to build and deploy your application as a JavaFX applet. Again, the code is intentionally kept simple, so that you can concentrate on the packaging steps necessary to distribute the application as an applet:

1. The first step is to create your application. Here we have a small application listed below. Refer to the file `ch07/source-code/src/myapplet/SimpleApplet.fx` for complete code information.

```
package myapplet;

import javafx.stage.Stage;
import javafx.scene.Scene;
import javafx.scene.paint.Color;
import javafx.scene.text.Text;
import javafx.scene.text.Font;

var msg:Text = Text {
    font : Font {
        size : 52
        embolden: true
        name: "sans-serif,Arial,Helvetica"
    }
    content: "I am Browser-Embedded"
    stroke:Color.WHITE
}
msg.translateY = msg.boundsInLocal.height;
```

```
Stage {
    title: "Application title"
    width: msg.boundsInLocal.width
    height: msg.boundsInLocal.height * 2
    scene: Scene {
        fill:Color.BLUE
        content: [msg]
    }
}
```

2. Next, using the javafxpackager tool, build and package the application using the following command (note that command has been wrapped for readability):

```
javafxpackager -src src -appClass myapplet.SimpleApplet

        -appName applet-demo

        -appVendor "Vladimir Vivien" -appVersion 1.0

        -appCodebase "http://my.server/path/to/app/"

        -appWidth 640 -appHeight 75
```

Upon completion, the packager tool will produce the following deployment artifacts in the dist/ directory:

```
  444 Nov 30 01:49 applet-demo.html
 8362 Nov 30 01:49 applet-demo.jar
  829 Nov 30 01:49 applet-demo.jnlp
  877 Nov 30 01:49 applet-demo_browser.jnlp
```

3. Next, open the generated file **applet-demo.html**. You can use it as is, modify its content to fit your specific need, or copy the JavaScript snippet in the HTML file into your own file. Optionally, you can edit the JNLP file, **applet-demo_browser.jnlp**, to tweak the deployment information inside. Chances are, however, you will not need to (see the recipe _Packaging your app to be Web Start(ed)_ for information about JNLP file).

4. Finally, upload the files **applet-demo.jar**, **applet-demo.html**, and **applet-demo_browser.jnpl** onto a web server at a location matching the URL specified by flag -codeBase in the javafxpackager command line. If these values do not match, the applet will not work properly.

When the HTML file is accessed through the web, the browser renders the embedded applet inside the HTML page as shown in the following screenshot:

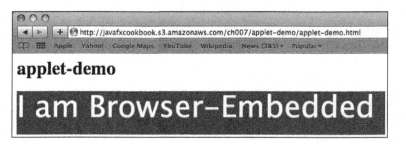

> If you are running 64-bit Windows 7, you must run your applets in a 64-bit browser for your applet to run properly.

How it works...

The applet runtime is designed to run Java desktop applications inside the browser. Unlike traditional desktop applications, applets are rendered directly within the web page using a frameless window, as shown in the previous screenshot. Users are not able to minimize, resize, or close the applet while within the browser.

Let's examine how we achieved this in our recipe:

- The JavaFX code—the code presented in the recipe is purely illustrative. There is nothing special about it. However, notice that we are not using any applet-specific APIs in the code that hints at the targeted environment. That is the power of the unified development and deployment model in JavaFX. The developer concentrates on creating the application and the tool chain handles building the code for the target environment.

- The HTML file—the packager tool generates a sample HTML file, which shows you how to use JavaScript to embed the JavaFX applet within the page. The generated JavaScript does a couple of things:

    - It loads a Sun-provided JavaScript library `http://dl.javafx.com/1.2/dtfx.js` that contains the code to bootstrap the applet within the HTML page.

    - It calls the function `javafx()`, which takes as parameter an associative array with configuration settings, including the JAR name, applet dimensions, main class, and name of application.

▶ The JNLP file—this file is also generated by the packaging step. The JNLP file contains descriptors for the deployment of the applet on the Web. It also contains directives for the applet's runtime, JAR dependency, and, if the applet is installed as a desktop application using the drag-to-install feature, the JNLP file contains directives for desktop behaviors (see *Deploying your applet for drag-to-install*).

There's more...

The JavaScript library that loads the applet on the page does more than what is listed above. It also provides the following services:

▶ *JRE detection*—the code will attempt to launch the proper JRE version capable of supporting the features of the new Java Plugin. It is also possible to detect a specific version of the JRE on the client's machine to run the application.

▶ *Graceful degradation*—the JavaScript attempts to gracefully fall back to a version of the JRE that can still execute the code.

▶ *Generate HTML tags*—the script generates the proper HTML tags (`<object>`, `<embed>`, or `<applet>`) to embed the code passing in the necessary attributes and parameters to the tags.

Overriding the JNLP file name

By default, the bootstrap JavaScript will look for a JNLP file name `{APP_NAME}_browser.jnlp`, where `APP_NAME` is the application name specified during the build. However, you can override the default JNLP file name in the bootstrap JavaScript as follows:

```
<script>
    javafx(
        {
                archive: "applet-demo.jar",
                width: 640,
                height: 75,
                code: "applet.demo.Main",
                name: "applet-demo"
                jnlp_href: "myapplet.jnlp"
        }
    );
</script>
```

Using the `jnlp_href` parameter, you can specify an arbitrary file name for your applet's JNLP. Ensure, however, that the `href` attribute inside the JNLP file (in the `</jnlp>` tag) matches the value specified with `jnlp_ref`, otherwise this will fail.

You can find out more about JNLP and Web Start at `http://java.sun.com/javase/technologies/desktop/javawebstart/`.

See also

- *Building and packaging your app with an IDE*
- *Building and packaging your app with javafxpackager*
- *Packaging your app to be Web Start(ed)*

Passing arguments to JavaFX applications

Often, it is desirable to pass in parameterized values as arguments to a running application. In regular Java applications, for instance, this is done by passing arguments through the command-line when an application is launched. This recipe shows you how to inject both application parameters and VM-level parameters into a desktop JavaFX application launched with the Web Start application.

Getting ready

This recipe shows how to pass in both applications and VM arguments to a JNLP-launched application via the Web Start or the new Java Plugin. If you are not familiar with JNLP, review the previous recipes *Building and packaging your app with javafxpackager*, *Packaging your app to Be Web Start(ed)*, and *Packaging your app as an applet*.

For this recipe, we will create a simple JavaFX application, which reads a parameter value passed in as an argument and displays it on stage. Simple, right? Right! Let's see how to do it.

How to do it...

1. To get started, we create a simple application that makes use of runtime parameters. The application will display a greeting, using a name passed in as a parameter. The full listing of the code can be found at `ch07/source-code/src/params/RuntimeArgsApplet.fx`.

```
var name = FX.getArgument("name");
var msg:Text = Text {
    font : Font {
        size : 52 embolden: true
        name: "sans-serif,Arial,Helvetica"
    }
        content: bind "Hello {name}!" fill:Color.WHITE
}
msg.translateY = msg.boundsInLocal.height;
Stage {
    title: "Application title"
```

```
        width: msg.boundsInLocal.width
        height: msg.boundsInLocal.height * 2
        scene: Scene {
            fill:Color.BLUE content: [msg]
        }
    }
```

2. Next, compile and package the application using the javafxpackager tool (or your favorite IDE). This will generate the JNLP, JAR file, and the HTML files used to deploy the application as a Web Start or as an applet.

```
javafxpackager -src src -appClass params.RuntimeArgsApplet
                -appName args-demo
                -appVendor "Vladimir Vivien" -appVersion 1.0
                -appCodebase "http://my.server/path/to/app/"
                -appWidth 640 -appHeight 75
```

3. To set the runtime parameter value for the Web Start application, edit the generated JNLP file, and add the `<argument>` tag in the `<application>` block as shown:

```
<jnlp>
...
   <application-desc
     main-class="com.sun.javafx.runtime.main.Main">
       <argument>MainJavaFXScript=param.demo.Main</argument>
       <argument>name=World</argument>
     </application-desc>
...
</jnlp>
```

If you are going to run the application as an applet, you have to set the parameter from within the bootstrap JavaScript code that launches the applet. Modify the JavaScript snippet generated during the build/packaging step as follows:

```
<script>
    javafx(
        {
            archive: "param-demo.jar",
            width: 400,
            height: 100,
            code: "param.demo.Main",
            name: "param-demo"
        },
        {
            name: "World"
        }
    );
</script>
```

When the application is launched as a Web Start app or as browser-embedded applet, we get the same result, shown in the next screenshot:

How it works...

The JavaFX application framework provides a uniform way to access application arguments. In the code above, function `FX.getParameter(name:String):String` is used to look up an argument by name passed into the application at runtime, either as a Web Start desktop application or as a browser-embedded applet.

The JavaFX application framework uses a key/value pair to represent the argument passed into an application at runtime. Let's see how that works:

▸ *Arguments through Web Start*—for Web Start desktop applications, arguments are specified in the JNLP descriptor file. All JavaFX arguments must take the form of `key=value` using the `<argument/>` tag. For our example, we specify `<argument>name=World</argument>`.

▸ *Arguments through Applet*—for applets, the Java Plugin reads runtime argument values from the JavaScript applet bootstrapping code embedded in the HTML. There, the argument is a `{key:value}` entry in an associative array passed as the second argument of the `javafx()` function (see code above). For our example, we pass in the argument as `{name:"World"}`.

There's more...

Accessing all arguments

The JavaFX runtime provides function `FX.getArguments():String[]`, which returns a sequence of Strings containing the "key=value" strings passed in using the method described previously.

Command-line arguments

When you run your application from the command line, you can still use the `key=value` mechanism to pass in arguments. The following command shows how you would launch the application packaged in this recipe using the JavaFX command-line launcher with runtime arguments:

```
javafx -jar dist/args-demo.jar name="World"
```

The `key=value` approach of specifying the command-line argument lets your application have uniform access to runtime argument values. However, if you know your application will always be launched from the command-line, outside of Web Start, you should simply access your parameters using the `run(args:String[])` function of your application's main class.

JVM arguments

When using Web Start or an applet, you can specify VM arguments in the JNLP file. To do this, locate the tag `<j2se/>` in the JNLP file and set the JVM arguments as follows:

```
<jnlp>
...
    <resources>
        <j2se version="1.5+" java-vm-args="-Xmx256M"/>
            ...
    </resources>
...
</jnlp>
```

See also

▶ *Building and packaging your app with javafxpackager*

Making your applets drag-to-install

So far, we have seen two ways to get your desktop applications deployed as either browser-embedded applets or desktop Web Start. However, none is cooler than *drag-to-install*. *What is that?* Well, it is a simple concept: enable the user to drag a running applet from the web page unto the desktop to install it automatically. In this recipe, we are going to look at how to create an application that can be deployed using the drag-to-install feature of the new Java Plugin for browsers.

Getting ready

For this recipe, we will create a simple JavaFX application, which we will build using the `javafxpackager` and deploy it as an applet. If you are not familiar with how to do this, review previous recipe *Building and packaging your app with javafxpackager*. Discussions in this recipe will also include topics covered in the recipes *Packaging your app to be Web Start(ed)* and *Packaging your app as an app et*.

How to do it...

To illustrate the techniques in this recipe, we will create a simple JavaFX application that displays the current time and deploy that application as a drag-to-install applet.

1. The first thing to do is create a simple JavaFX script that uses an instance of the `Timeline` class to drive a simple digital clock. The full listing of the code can be found at `ch07/source-code/src/draggable/DraggableApplet.fx`.

```
var currTime = function():String{
  new SimpleDateFormat("hh:mm:ss").format(new Date())
}
var time:String = currTime();
Timeline {
    repeatCount:Timeline.INDEFINITE interpolate:false
    keyFrames: KeyFrame {
        time: 1s
        action:function() {time = currTime()}
    }
}.play();


Stage {
    scene: Scene {
        fill:Color.BLUE
        content: [ ... //content omitted ]
    }

    extensions: [
        AppletStageExtension {
            shouldDragStart: function(e): Boolean {
                return true;
            }
            useDefaultClose: true
        }
    ]
}
```

2. Next, we compile and package the code using the `javafxpackager`. Notice that we are specifying the `-draggable` flag:

```
javafxpackager -src src -appClass draggable.DraggableApplet
                -appName draggable-applet
                -draggable
```

```
-appCodebase "http://my.server/path/to/app/'
-appWidth 200 -appHeight 75
```

2. Lastly, deploy `draggable-applet.jar`, `draggable-applet_browser.jnlp`, and `draggable-applet.html` files on a web server at the location specified by the `-codeBase` flag in the `javafxpackager` command line.

Now, notice when the applet is accessed from a browser that it looks as expected. It is unaltered with no indication that it is draggable, as shown in the next screenshot:

However, when you attempt to drag the applet you are able to move it outside of its original docked location in the page. You can drag the applet outside of the browser unto the desktop, as shown in the next screenshot:

How it works...

Drag-to-install is another nice feature, found in the redesigned Java Plugin architecture (made available as of version 1.6u10). It provides users with the ability to drag applets from their embedded location in the browser directly onto the desktop. Let's see how this is done:

► *The JavaFX code*—the application presented here is purely illustrative. It is a simple digital clock that displays the current time. Notice, however, that the `Stage` literal declaration includes a value for the property `extensions:StageExtension[]`. The `StageExtension` class is designed as an extension point for classes that provide profile-specific functionalities.

For this recipe, we use the `AppletStageExtension` class which provides integration support between browser-embedded applets and the JavaFX application Stage. Specifically, the `AppletStageExtension` is used here to define the behavior of the applet through callback functions when it is dragged off the browser page. The code defines a callback function for the property `shouldDragStart`, which returns `true` to indicate to the Java Plugin that the applet can be dragged.

- *The packaging of the code*—the javafxpackager tool necessitates using the `-draggable` flag so that it generates the applet artifacts accordingly. The command-line flag causes the code generated for the JavaScript launcher to include a `draggable` parameter set to `true` as shown next:

```
<script>
    javafx(
        {
                archive: "draggable-demo.jar",
                draggable: true,
                width: 200,
                height: 75,
                code: "draggable.demo.Main",
                name: "draggable-demo"
        }
    );
</script>
```

- *Running the applet*—the applet runs as would any normal applet. However, due to the Stage extension defined in the code, it will respond to the mouse's drag gesture. When a user starts dragging the applet body off the browser's page, the Java Plugin will invoke callback function `AppletStageExtension.shouldDragStart`. If the function returns true, then the applet will be allowed to be dragged off the page. Otherwise the drag gesture will be ignored.

There's more...

Before we leave this recipe, there are some additional items that we should address when implementing drag-to-install behavior for our applets.

AppletStageExtension Hooks

The JavaFX `AppletStageExtension` class provides a multitude of useful runtime information and event hooks for your applet. Here are some you will find useful:

`appletDragSupport:Boolean`	Use this flag to detect if the browser hosting the applet supports out-of-page dragging.
`useDefaultClose:Boolean`	When this flag is set to `true` (default), the applet will automatically receive a floating close box to its right-hand side (see previous figure). If set to `false`, the developer is responsible for providing a mechanism for closing the applet.
`onDragStarted:function()`	This is called after it has been determined that the applet is being dragged.

| `onDragFinished:function()` | This function is called when the drag gesture is finished. |
| `onAppletRestored:function()` | This function is called when the applet is closed by the user (or programmatically) while the original source web page is still opened. Then, the applet is restored back into the page. |

Preventing unintentional dragging

One technique used with draggable applets, to control unintentional dragging, is to detect the pressing of a control key while dragging. To do this, we can modify our sample app by changing the `shouldDragStart` function attribute:

```
Stage {
...
  extensions: [
    AppletStageExtension {
      shouldDragStart: function(e:MouseEvent): Boolean {
        return e.altDown and e.primaryButton;
      }
    }
  ]
}
```

With this change, the applet will only be dragged when the *Alt* key and the mouse's primary button are both pressed together while dragging.

Control post-installation behavior

Let's discuss one last important point about applet dragging, then we are done. Recall that an applet is rendered as an undecorated borderless window without any drag handles. So, when you set up your app as drag-to-install, you must provide windowing controls (close, move, minimize, maximize, and so on) to your users, so that when the application is subsequently launched as a desktop application through Web Start, it can also be closed or moved around the desktop.

One way to handle this situation is to use the `AppletStageExtension` properties, coupled with the `{__PROFILE__}` pseudo variable, to determine how and when to display window handles and decoration. You can use that value to properly set up windowing controls based on the profile. For instance, when `{__PROFILE__}` = `"desktop"`, display windowing controls in the application.

See also

▸ *Building and packaging your app with javafxpackager*

▸ *Packaging your app to be Web Start'ed)*

▸ *Packaging your app as an applet*

Controlling JavaFX applets from JavaScript

Part of the appeal of JavaFX as a browser-based deployment platform is its complete integration support between the browser and your JavaFX applets. When you deploy an applet, the new Java Plugin (see *Packaging your app as an Applet*) provides full two-way programmatic integration between your applet and JavaScript. In this recipe, we will see how you can use JavaScript to update attributes and invoke functions from an embedded applet.

Getting ready

Before you embark on the techniques presented in this recipe, you should be familiar with the deployment of your JavaFX applications as browser-embedded applets. If you are not, review the recipe *Packaging your app as an Applet,* presented earlier in this chapter. Secondly, since applets are embedded in HTML pages, you will need to have working knowledge of basic HTML and JavaScript. If you are not familiar with either, there are numerous resources online, including `http://www.w3schools.com/html/` for HTML and `http://www.w3schools.com/js/` for JavaScript.

To demonstrate how you can use JavaScript to control and interact with an embedded JavaFX applet programmatically, this recipe presents an application that allows users to use an HTML form to control the attributes and appearance of a text message displayed in a JavaFX applet.

How to do it...

To accomplish this recipe, we need to break down the solution into several steps as shown next. For the sake of saving space and keeping this chapter to a manageable length, the code is abbreviated, highlighting the more interesting portions. You can get the full listing for all recipe resources at location `ch07/source-code/src/js2jfx/`.

1. *The JavaFX code*—this is a simple JavaFX application that uses a `Text` node to display a text message on the stage. The code also exposes several script-level attributes and a script-level function designed to be accessed by JavaScript. The following snippet is an abbreviated version of the JavaFX code; you can get the full code from the file `ch07/src/source-code/js2jfx/JavaScript2JavaFXDemo.fx`.

   ```
   // public script-level properties
   public var textContent = "Text Commander";
   public var textColor = "blue";
   public var textColorEnd = "blue";
   public var textStrokeColor = "blue";
   public var textStrokeWidth = "1";
   public var textFont = "Helvetica";

   var w=800;
   ```

```
var h=100;
var text:Text; // text node

// call this fn to apply affect to text node
public function applyEffect(effect:Integer) {
    if(effect==0){
        text.effect = null;
    }
    if(effect==1){
        text.effect = Reflection{fraction:0.50};
    }
    if(effect==2){
        text.effect = DropShadow{offsetY:4}
    }
    if(effect==3){
        text.effect = Lighting {
            light: DistantLight { azimuth: -135 }
            surfaceScale: 5
        }
    }
}


// entry point
public function run() {
    text = Text {
        content: bind textContent
        style: bind "fill:{textColor};"
            "font-family:\"{textFont}\";"
            "font-size:64pt;"
            "font-weight:bold;"
            "fill:linear (0%, 0%) to (0%,100%)
             stops (0.0, {textColor}),
                    (1.0,{textColorEnd});"
    }

    ...
}
```

2. *Packaging for browser deployment*—to get the application deployed as a JavaFX applet, it must be packaged as such. To do this, we will use the `javafxpackager` tool (see the recipes *Building and packaging your app using javafxpackager* and *Packaging your app as an applet* in this chapter). As we have seen in the previous recipes, this step will yield a JAR file, a HTML file with the bootstrap JavaScript, and a browser JNLP file.

3. *The HTML page*—create an HTML file which will embed both the applet and an HTML form that controls the applet. Copy the bootstrap JavaScript stub, generated in previous step, and add it to the HTML file, as shown next. Modify the JavaScript code by adding an `id` attribute to the `javafx()` parameter. Also, create a new function named `update()` that will control the interaction between the JavaScript and the JavaFX applet:

```html
<html>
...
<body>
<script src="http://dl.javafx.com/1.2/dtfx.js"></script>
<script>
    // stub from packaging step
    javafx(
        {
                archive: "js2jfx.jar",
                width: 800,
                height: 100,
                code: "JavaScript2JavaFXDemo",
                name: "js2jfx",
                id:"js2jfx"
        }
    );

    // added function to control JavaFX
    function update(color) {
        var js2jfx = document.getElementById("js2jfx");
        js2jfx.script.textContent =
                document.getElementById("msg").value;
        js2jfx.script.textFont =
                document.getElementById("font").value;
        ...
        js2jfx.script.applyEffect(
            document.getElementById("effect").selectedIndex
        );
    }
</script>
<hr/>
<form>
```

```
<table>
    <tr><td>Text</td>
        <td><input id="msg" value="Text Commander"></td>
    </tr>
    <tr><td>Font</td>
        <td><input id="font" value="sans-serif"></td>
    </tr>

    ...
    <tr><td>Apply Effect</td>
        <td><select id="effect">
                <option value="0">None</option>
                <option value="1">Reflection</option>
                <option value="2">Drop Shadow</option>
                <option value="3">Lighting</option>
            </select>
        </td>
    </tr>
    <tr><td colspan="2">
        <input
        type="button"
        value="Set"
        onclick="update()"/>
    </td></tr>
</table>
</form>
</body>
</html>
```

4. The last step is to deploy the HTML file along with the JNLP and the JAR file to a web server. When you access the web page, you will see the applet and the HTML form rendered on the same web page, as shown in the following screenshot:

How it works...

In the code presented in this recipe, we are using the JavaFX-JavaScript bridge mechanism, provided by the new Java Plugin, to create programmatic interactions between a JavaFX applet and the JavaScript code embedded within a web page. The JavaScript code on the web page can do the following:

- ▶ Access JavaFX resources by calling functions
- ▶ Access and update variable values
- ▶ Pass in complex types
- ▶ Traverse JavaFX's scene graph

Let us examine how the JavaFX script is set up in order to accept programmatic interaction with the JavaScript

- ▶ *The JavaFX script*—the JavaFX-JavaScript bridge accesses the JavaFX applet through public script-level variables and functions declared in the main application class. Therefore, our code declares several script-level members that can be reached by JavaScript:
  - ❏ JavaFX public variable `textContent` is bound to the `content` property of the Text object. When a value is assigned to it, it will update the content of the Text node.
  - ❏ Public variables `textColor:String`, `textColorEnd:String`, `textStrokeColor:String`, `textStrokeWidth:String`, and `textFont:String` are bound to the `style` property of the `Text` object. This will allow the appearance of the Text node to be updated when any of these variables are updated from the JavaScript code. For instance, when the `textColor = "red"`, this will cause the Text instance color to be updated to red.
  - ❏ The public function `applyEffect(number):Void` applies an effect to the `Text` instance. The function can apply three effects to the text including reflection, drop shadow, and lighting. Each effect is associated with a number, where 0 = no effect. This makes easy for the function to be invoked from JavaScript to update the effect on the Text object.

The HTML Page that displays the JavaFX applet contains the JavaScript code and the HTML form used to interact with the applet. Let's see how things operate in there:

- ▶ *The JavaScript* `javafx()` *function*—the JavaScript function `javafx()`, found in the `<script/>` block, is used to initialize the applet on the web page. We have added `id:"js2jfx"` to the parameter map as a value that will be used as a reference identifier for the JavaFX applet object. This makes it easy to look up the object representing the applet from the JavaScript document object model (DOM).

Once the applet has been initialized, we can ask for an instance of the applet object using the JavaScript function `document.getElementById("js2jfx")`.

▶ *The JavaScript* `update()` *function*—the other function in the `<script/>` block is the `update()` function. This is where the JavaScript code interacts with the applet, so let's take a look:

  ❑ `var js2jfx = document.getElementById("js2jfx")`—this line obtains a reference to the JavaFX applet (see previous bullet). This object is used to communicate with the JavaFX applet directly.

  ❑ Accessing JavaFX public properties—Now that we have a reference to the JavaScript applet object, we can use `js2jfx.script` to update or access the value of any JavaFX script-level property. For instance, `js2jfx.script.textContent = document.getElementById("msg").value` assigns the value of JavaScript object `msg` to the JavaFX script-level property `textContent`.

  ❑ Calling JavaFX functions—similar to accessing JavaFX properties, `js2jfx.script` can also be used to invoke JavaFX public script-level functions. In our example, the JavaScript call `js2jfx.script.applyEffect(...)` invokes the JavaFX public script-level function `applyAffect(number)` declared in the JavaFX code.

▶ *The HTML form*—the remainder of the HTML source code contains the HTML form used to control the applet. When the `Set` button is clicked, it invokes the `update()` JavaScript function defined in the `<script>` block, which in turn passes all the collected values to the JavaFX code through the JavaScript applet object (see previous bullet).

> As of version 6, update 18 of the Java's consumer runtime (JRE) when this was tested, the features presented here only worked with the next generation Java Plugin running on the Windows platform. By the time you read this, support may be available for browsers on other platforms.

There's more...

As discussed above, the JavaFX-JavaScript bridge lets you access JavaFX script-level public variables and functions. This mechanism offers much more than depicted in the recipe above; let's explore some additional capabilities.

Type crossing JavaScript to JavaFX

When updating JavaFX script-level properties or invoking a parameterized function, the Java browser plugin framework will conduct an automatic type conversion to handle data representation from JavaScript to the JavaFX environment. Here is is chart showing how JavaFX types are mapped to JavaScript values.

JavaFX Type Expected	Compatible JavaScript Type			
	String	*Number*	*Boolean*	*Array*
Object	Yes	Yes	Yes	No
String	Yes	No	No	No
Integer	Yes—with valid numeric	Yes—float precision lost	No	No
Number	Yes—with valid numeric	Yes—integer converted to double	No	No
Boolean	Yes—empty string = false, all others = true	Yes—0 = false, all other values converted true	Yes	No
Sequence	No	No	No	Yes—with strict type match on member values.

Accessing the Scene graph

The JavaFX-JavaScript bridge lets you access the scene graph structure directly from JavaScript using the `js2jfx.stage.scene` proxy object (assuming the applet id is `"js2jfx"`). This implies that we could have written our JavaScript to update the content of the text in the recipe,:

```
js2jfx.stage.scene.content[0].content = "some text";
```

The code snippet accesses the first object in the Scene's `content` sequence which is the `Text` object and updates its content to text value.

Accessing JavaScript from JavaFX

Throughout this recipe, we have seen how to interact and control JavaFX from JavaScript. However, with the Java plugin architecture, it is also possible to do the opposite, where JavaFX script can access JavaScript code embedded on the web page. To access JavaScript from JavaFX, you must import the `javafx.stage.AppletStageExtension` class which, as the name implies, provides an interaction point between your applet and the JavaFX stage. Using `AppletStageExtension`, you can:

▶ Launch a new web page
▶ Evaluate JavaScript code

For instance, you can open a new browser window with:

```
javafx.stage.AppletStageExtension.showDocument("http://www.google.
com/");
```

Or, if you have a JavaScript function named `addTotal()` defined on the web page, you can invoke it using

```
javafx.stage.AppletStageExtension.eval("addTotal();");
```

See also

▸ *Building and packaging your app with javafxpackager*

▸ *Packaging your app to be Web Started)*

▸ *Packaging your app as an applet*

8

The JavaFX Production Suite

In this chapter, we will cover the following topics:

- ► Loading multiple images dynamically
- ► Exporting Adobe Photoshop graphics to JavaFX
- ► Exporting Adobe Illustrator graphics to JavaFX
- ► Exporting Scalable Vector Graphics (SVG) to JavaFX
- ► Using graphics loaded from FXZ Files

Introduction

Creating compelling and engaging user interfaces is an art best left to the professionals. The JavaFX engineers understood this fact. That is why they released tools that make it possible for graphics artists to work side-by-side with developers, allowing creative content to be easily integrated as a part of the development workflow.

In this chapter, we are going to explore the different options available to developers to integrate creative content into their JavaFX code using the JavaFX Production Suite. These tools, distributed separately from the JavaFX SDK, include plugins for best-of-breed graphics packages, such as Adobe Photoshop and Adobe Illustrator. Designers can export their artwork directly from these graphics packages into a JavaFX file format, FXZ, consumable within JavaFX projects.

The Production Suite includes:

► *Adobe Photoshop plugin*—a plugin that exports graphics objects from PSD files to the FXZ file format.

► *Adobe Illustrator plugin*—a plugin that exports graphics objects from Illustrator files to the FXZ file format.

► *SVG File Converter*—a utility that converts scalable vector graphics objects into the FXZ file format.

► *Graphics Viewer*—a standalone viewer utility that lets you view the FXZ file content. Note that NetBeans also includes an FXZ file viewer as well.

The following figure shows the path of integration that designers may choose to integrate their creative content into JavaFX projects.

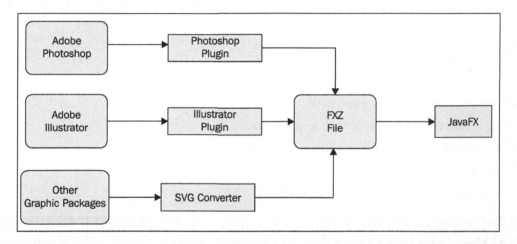

Loading multiple images dynamically

In *Chapter 5, JavaFX Media,* we have seen how to load a single image from a given location. However, in certain situations (think of game development, or dynamically building a GUI), you will find it necessary to load multiple images into your application. If you are loading three or four images, then there are no issues. If however you have, say, 30 or 100 images to load on the scene graph, that will definitely be a motivator to find an easy way to load them (yes, good developers are lazy and will look for ways to keep things simple, repeatable, and efficient).

This recipe shows you how to load multiple images into your application easily, and make them available for programmatic manipulation and display. Although this recipe does not use JavaFX's Production Suite tools, it presents an alternative approach for working with a large set of image assets that may have been imported or generated by your creative team for your JavaFX project.

Getting ready

This recipe uses techniques to load images using the `ImageView` component that were covered in *Chapter 5, JavaFX Media*. If you are not familiar with the `ImageView` component, refer to the recipe *Loading and displaying images with ImageView* for details on how to embed images in your JavaFX application. Other topics presented here include use of the `Sequence` type to store a list of `ImageView` objects. Refer to *Chapter 1, Getting Started with JavaFX* for further details on the `Sequence` type and its uses.

How to do it...

In this recipe, we are going to load 26 images, one for each letter of the alphabet. The code is presented in an abbreviated form. Refer to `ch08/source-code/src/alphabet/Main.fx` for a complete listing of the code and the images used in this recipe.

1. To get started, create one image file for each letter, using your favourite designer tool. For this recipe, you can use a commercial tool, such as Adobe Photoshop. However, if you do not have access to Photoshop, you can use an open source alternative such as GIMP (or anything that can create a PNG file).

2. Save each image as a PNG file, using the naming pattern `X.png`, where X represents the letter associated with the file (`A.png`, `B.png`, `C.png`, and so on). You should end up with 26 image files. Place all of the images in the same package (or sub-package) directory as the JavaFX script that will be using them. For our recipe, the images are placed in the `alphabet/images` folder, which is a level below where the script is located.

3. Next, we start with the JavaFX script code. In the first portion of the code, we declare the sequence object, `alphabet`, representing the letters of the alphabet:

```
def imgW = 214;
def imgH = 182

// sequence with alphabet
def alphabet = [
        "A", "B", "C", "D", "E", "F",
        "G", "H", "I", "J", "K", "L",
        "M", "N", "O", "P", "Q", "R",
        "S", "T", "U", "V", "W", "X",
        "Y", "Z"
];
```

4. Then, we create another sequence instance, `images`, into which we are going to load instances of `Image` class representing the PNG files:

```
// load each image and add to sequence
var images:Image[];

for (letter in alphabet){
    insert Image {
        url: "{__DIR__}images/{letter}.png"
        backgroundLoading: false
        width:imgW height:imgH
    } into images;
}
```

5. Once the images are loaded, the code declares an instance of `ImageView` that will be used to display the image on the screen:

```
var imgView = ImageView {
    x: (w - imgW)/2 y: (h - imgH)/2
    preserveRatio: true
    image: null
}
```

6. The last code segment requests input focus for the `ImageView` object. Then, we define a keyboard event-handler function to display the letter when a letter key is pressed:

```
imgView.requestFocus();
imgView.onKeyPressed = function (e:KeyEvent) {
    imgView.image = {
        var img:Image = imgView.image;
        for(i in images){
            if(i.url.contains("{e.text}.png")) {
                img = i;
                break;
            }
        }
        img
    }
}
```

The remainder of the code (not shown) builds the Stage and places the `ImageView` object in the scene graph. Once the application is compiled and executed, it shows an image of the letter when the corresponding letter is pressed on the keyboard, as shown in the next screenshot:

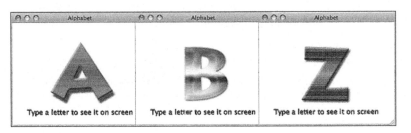

How it works...

This recipe demonstrates the techniques involved in loading multiple images for display and programmatic manipulation. Let's examine how it's done:

- ▶ *Image file format*—part of what makes this technique easier is that all images are of the same format. This reduces the size of the code by assuming that all images are of one type (PNG format here).

- ▶ *Image location*—another important trick that makes this approach work is a uniform location for all images. The images in this recipe are all located in the same directory, `source-code/src/alphabet/images`. The JavaFX packager will automatically add the images in the generated JAR file and thus be available from the classpath for easy access.

- ▶ *The alphabet sequence*—lastly, using a natural series as the naming strategy for the images makes it easy (not necessary) to load the images quickly. In the recipe, the first portion of the code declares a sequence of strings, named `alphabet:String[]`. This `Sequence` instance contains all of the letters of the alphabet. Recall that each image is named using a single letter of the alphabet (that is, `A.png`, `B.png`, and so on). This sequence can be mapped directly to the collection of image files representing the alphabet.

- ▶ *Loading the images*—next, the code does the following:
  - ❑ It declares variable `images[]` as a Sequence, used to store `Image` instances that are created when the image files are loaded.
  - ❑ *The* code loops through the `alphabet` sequence using the `letter` variable. For each `letter` in the sequence, the code creates an `Image` instance for the PNG file that matches the current value of `letter`, using the expression `url: "{__DIR__}images/{letter}.png"`. Then, the Image object is inserted in the sequence `images[]`

▶ *Display and add interaction*—once the images are loaded in the `images[]` sequence, we can now create the `ImageView` object assigned to variable `imgView` that will display the images.

    ❑ The `ImageView` instance requests focus using the `imgView.requestFocus()` function call. This causes the `imgView` component to receive keyboard events.

    ❑ A keyboard input event-handler function is attached to `imgView` to handle keyboard key presses. The code loops through the sequence of `images` to look for an `Image` instance whose `url` property contains the value of the key pressed, as shown in the following snippet:

```
for(i in images){
        if(i.url.contains("{e.text}.png")) {
            img = i;
            break;
        }
    }
```

    ❑ When the image is found, the value is assigned to `imgView.image` for display.

There's more...

A general approach to loading multiple images automatically is to use a predictable sequence to name your image files. For instance, for this recipe, we can use a numeric sequence of integers as a part of the file name instead of just the alphabet sequence of letters. So, the image for letter A is named `letter_0.png`, the image for letter B is named `letter_1.png`, and so forth, with the image for letter Z named `letter_25.png`. By doing this, our code gets even smaller, where we no longer need the sequence `alphabet[]` to store the image names. We can load the images as follows:

```
for (id in [0..25]){
    insert Image {
        url: "{__DIR__}images/letter_{id}.png"
        backgroundLoading: false
        width:imgW height:imgH
    } into images;
}
```

See also

▶ *Chapter 1—Creating and using JavaFX sequences*

▶ *Chapter 5—Loading and displaying images with ImageView*

Exporting Adobe Photoshop graphics to JavaFX

Say, for instance, you are heading a commercial JavaFX project. You decide to hire some designers to create an exceptionally well-designed GUI with rich and creative content for a compelling user experience. How do you integrate the work of your designers with the code being created by your developers? Your integration route can take you in one of the following directions:

▶ Your designers can export a multitude of individual image pieces, which you have to manage manually, and stitch into your application (see previous recipe). Although this will work for a moderate number of items, it may not scale well for larger, more complex UIs.

▶ The other option is to provide your creative team with a way to integrate their work directly into JavaFX code development.

In this recipe, we will explore the second option. We will see how to use JavaFX's _Production Suite_ tools to export graphics objects from the Adobe Photoshop to be integrated with JavaFX.

Getting ready

To be able to convert graphics objects from Adobe Photoshop to JavaFX graphics objects, you must first download the Production Suite from `http://javafx.com/downloads/` and install it.

JavaFX 1.2 Production Suite

A suite of tools and plugins that enables a collaborative workflow between designers and developers. Designers use familiar tools to exchange visual assets with developers building JavaFX applications.

Release Notes | Installation Instructions | System Requirements

Production Suite is a set of tools that are part of the JavaFX platform that includes a plugin for Adobe Photoshop CS3/CS4, a plugin for Illustrator CS3/CS4, an SVG converter, and a JavaFX viewing tool named _Viewer (see Introduction for further detail)._

This recipe assumes that you have a working knowledge of Adobe Photoshop. The recipe does not show you how to get started and create graphics content in Photoshop, but rather how to export the content to be used in JavaFX. This recipe uses a simple set of artwork as an illustrative tool to demonstrate the power of the Production Suite tools. However, the techniques covered here will work for more complex creative work as well.

How to do it...

For this recipe, we are going to walk through the steps of exporting graphics objects from a Photoshop project as JavaFX graphics objects.

1. First, you should ensure that you have installed the Production Suite tools properly. Go to menu **File | Automate**, and you should see menu choice **Save for JavaFX**, as shown in the following screenshot:

Automate	▶	Batch...
Scripts	▶	Create Droplet...
File Info...	⌥⇧⌘I	Crop and Straighten Photos
Page Setup...	⇧⌘P	Save for JavaFX...

2. Next, create a new or open an existing Photoshop project. For this recipe, we will be using the Photoshop project located in `ch08/source-code/resources/Symbols.psd`. The previous screenshot shows the Photoshop file used in this recipe. It consists of several iconic symbols, where each symbol is assigned to a Photoshop layer as shown below:

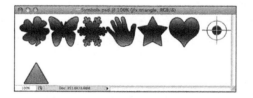

3. Each layer in the Photoshop artwork will be exported as a single image when converted to the JavaFX file format. Therefore, we will give each layer a descriptive name prefixed by `jfx:` to cause the plugin to use the name as provided.

4. Now, export the Photoshop artwork to the JavaFX FXZ file format. Select, menu item **File | Automate | Save for JavaFX** to start the JavaFX export plugin from within Photoshop. This will bring up the plugin's preview screen. Save the FXZ file to a location inside your JavaFX application's source path for easy access. For this recipe, the exported FXZ file is saved in the project's source directory at `ch08/source-code/src/fxzdemo/SymbolsPS.fxz`.

How it works...

In this recipe, we have discussed how to use the JavaFX Production Suite's plugin to export graphics objects from Adobe Photoshop to JavaFX. The plugin produces a single JavaFX FXZ file containing all graphical assets exported from the Photoshop PSD file. Let's see how this file format works.

▶ *The FXZ file*—when you export your graphics objects from Photoshop using the Production Suite plugin, the resulting FXZ file is a zip-compressed file that contains:

  ❑ Graphic assets exported from the original PSD file such as the images generated from each layer of the Photoshop file

  ❑ Any embeddable fonts that are used

  ❑ A data file with an FXD extension (see *There's more* ahead)

▶ *Generated PNG files*—each layer in your Photoshop file is rasterized down into a separate PNG image file. Photoshop layers with the `jfx:` prefix in their names will be exported using the the name provided. For instance, the Photoshop layer named `jfx:target` will be exported as an image named `target.png`.

▶ *Text objects*—text layers will be rasterized down to PNG files by default, or can optionally be exported as JavaFX `Text` nodes, which allows direct programmatic manipulation of the text content in JavaFX.

There's more...

Once the FXZ file is created, you can preview the exported file in NetBeans or using Production Suite's Viewer tool. Both NetBeans and Viewer give a device-dependent preview of the exported graphics objects embedded in the FXZ file.

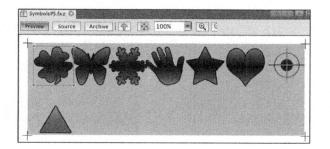

The FXD data file

The FXD file, embedded in the FXZ file, contains the object literal representation of a scene graph containing all of the images (and other assets) exported by the Photoshop plugin. Let's do a quick dissection of the file, shown below:

```
/*
 * Generated by JavaFX plugin for Adobe Photoshop.
 * ...
 */
Group {
  clip: Rectangle { x:0 y:0 width:600 height:200 }
  content: [
    ImageView {
      id: "triangle"
      x: 25
      y: 135
      image: Image {
        url: "{__DIR__}triangle.png"
      }
    },

    ...

    ImageView {
      id: "target"
      x: 520
      y: 5
      image: Image {
        url: "{__DIR__}target.png"
      }
    },
  ]
}
```

Photoshop layers are organized into a group by default. The group is exported as a JavaFX `Group` instance, where each layer within the group is mapped on to an `ImageView` node. The group node is clipped at the same dimension as the original Photoshop artwork through the `clip:Rectangle` property.

Each exported PNG file, embedded in the FXZ file, is represented by an instance of `ImageView` with several properties, such as:

▶ id—this is the node's unique identifier in the group. Notice that the value for the ID matches the name of the layer from the Photoshop file.

▶ x and y location—this is the coordinate of the `ImageView` object within the scene graph exported by the plugin.

▶ image—this is an instance of `Image` that points to the PNG file embedded in the FXZ file. Notice the image's name matches that of the layer from the Photoshop artwork.

What gets exported

Although the Production Suite plugin exports Photoshop layers as PNG files, the following outlines additional assets that are exported in the FXD file (as of version 1.2 of the SDK):

- *Layer effects*—the plugin will export the following effects as native JavaFX effect objects:

  - Drop Shadow / Inner Shadow—supports color, angle, size, and opacity. However, blending options are omitted.

  - Outer Glow / Inner Shadow—supports color, size, and opacity. However, bleeding and gradient options are omitted.

  - Other layer effects from Photoshop are rasterized as part of the PNG image.

- *Color modes*—the plugin will export only gray scale and RGB colors.

- *Layer masks* or *clipping mask*—layers are converted to PNG format, and receive a JavaFX blending effect with a `BlendMode.SRC_IN` value.

Exporting Adobe Illustrator graphics to JavaFX

In the recipe *Exporting Adobe Photoshop graphics to JavaFX*, we saw how JavaFX's Production Suite tools are used to integrate creative assets into the development workflow. In this recipe, we are going to see how to use JavaFX's Production Suite to export Adobe Illustrator graphics objects as JavaFX graphics objects.

Getting ready

To be able to convert graphics objects from Illustrator to JavaFX graphics objects, you must first download Production Suite from `http://javafx.com/downloads/`, and install it.

> **JavaFX 1.2 Production Suite**
>
> A suite of tools and plugins that enables a collaborative workflow between designers and developers. Designers use familiar tools to exchange visual assets with developers building JavaFX applications.
>
> Release Notes | Installation Instructions | System Requirements

Production Suite is a set of tools that are part of the JavaFX platform that includes a plugin for Adobe Photoshop CS3/CS4, a plugin for Illustrator CS3/CS4, an SVG converter, and a JavaFX viewing tool named Viewer (see *Introduction* for further details).

This recipe assumes that you have a working knowledge of Adobe Illustrator. The recipe does not show you how to use Illustrator to create graphical content, but rather how to export artwork to be integrated directly into JavaFX projects. This recipe uses a simple artwork to illustrate the power of the Production Suite. However, the techniques covered here will work for more complex creative work as well.

How to do it...

For this recipe, we are going to walk through the steps of exporting graphics objects from an Adobe Illustrator to JavaFX FXZ format.

1. First, you should ensure that you have installed Production Suite tools properly. From Illustrator, go to the **File** menu on the main menu bar and look for menu choice **Save for JavaFX...**, as shown in the following screenshot:

    Place...
    Save for JavaFX...
    Save for Microsoft Office...
    Export...

2. Create a new or open an existing Illustrator project. For this recipe, we will be using the project located in `ch08/source-code/resources/Symbols.ai`. The following figure shows the Illustrator file used in this recipe. It consists of two artboards containing a series of symbols, with each symbol assigned to a layer, as shown in the next screenshot:

3. Each object in the Illustrator artwork will be exported as JavaFX scene graph nodes. Therefore, we give each layer a descriptive name prefixed by `jfx:` to cause the plugin to use the name provided, as shown in the next screenshot:

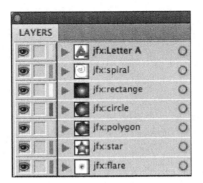

4. Now, export the artwork to the JavaFX FXZ file format. Select menu item **File | Save for JavaFX...** to start the Production Suite's plugin from within Adobe Illustrator. This will bring up the plugin's preview screen. Save the FXZ file to a location inside your JavaFX application's source path for easy access. For this recipe, the exported FXZ file is saved in the project's source directory at `ch08/source-code/src/fxzdemo/SymbolsAI.fxz`.

How it works...

The Production Suite's plugin for Adobe Illustrator produces a single JavaFX FXZ file containing all graphical assets exported from the Illustrator artwork. However, unlike Photoshop, Adobe Illustrator uses vector graphics to render its artwork (rather than bitmap). The plugin attempts to translates Illustrator's vector graphic objects directly into their JavaFX's vector counterparts wherever possible. Let's see how the exported file format works:

► *The FXZ file*—when you export your graphics objects from Adobe Illustrator using the Production Suite plugin, the resulting FXZ file is a zip-compressed file containing one or more data files (with FXD extensions). Additionally, the FXZ file will also contain other graphical assets exported from the original Illustrator file, such as embedded images and fonts.

► *The FXD data files*—this is a textual file format which contains JavaFX object literal declarations of a scene graph, where the nodes in the graph represent objects exported from the Illustrator artwork. (see *There's more...*, ahead).

► *Artworks with Artboards*—if artboards are used to group graphics objects in the Illustrator artwork, the plugin generates the data files as follows:

  ❑ An FXD file, with name pattern `content-n.fxd`, is generated for each artboard, where n represents the artboard's ordinal value. For this recipe, the artwork contains two artboards (have a look at the artboards' figure under the previous *How to do it* section); the generated FXZ file has two FXD data files named `content-1.fxd` and `content-2.fxd`.

- ❑ A FXD file named `content.fxd` serves as the entry point for the scene graph. It contains references to all other generated FXD when artboards are used to group artwork objects (see previous bullet). When there are no artboards grouping, the plugin only generates this file.

► *Generated PNG files*—when the original Illustrator artwork contains embedded bit-mapped images, they are rasterized down to PNG image files. These images are embedded in the FXZ files and are represented as `ImageView` nodes in the FXD scene graph data (see *There's more* next).

There's more...

The plugin converts the vector graphics from the Illustrator artwork to a scene graph of native JavaFX graphics nodes. Let's see how the graphics objects from Illustrator are exported in the JavaFX FXD file.

The code given next shows an abbreviated snippet of the FXD file generated for artboard 1 (refer to `ch08/source-code/src/fxzdemo/SymbolsAI.fxz` for a full listing):

```
/*
 * Generated by JavaFX plugin for Adobe Illustrator.
 */
Group {
  clip: Rectangle {x: 0.0 y: 0.0 width: 640.0 height: 480.0}
  content: [
    Group {
      id: "flare"
      content: [
...
      Group {
        id: "star"
        content: [
          Polygon {
            points:[194.69,43.67,210.08,74.85,244.50...]
            fill: RadialGradient{
              proportional: false
              centerX: 194.69 centerY: 91.03
              focusX: 194.69 focusY: 91.03
              radius: 48.60
              stops: [
                Stop {offset: 0.000 color: Color.WHITE},
                Stop {offset: 1.000 color: Color.BLACK},
              ]
            }
```

```
            stroke: Color.BLACK
            strokeWidth: 1.0
        },
         ]
        },
...

        // Embedded images
        Group {
        id: "Letter_A"
        content: [
            ImageView {
              fill: null
              stroke: null
              x: 439.33 y: 13.93
              image: Image{ url: "{__DIR__}G2LAew0.png"}
            }
            ]
        }
        ]
    ]
}
```

The Illustrator plugin organizes the JavaFX objects as a collection of nested instances of `Group` classes as follows:

- *Root Group*—there is a root `Group` instance that maps to the Adobe Illustrator artboard as a container for all other graphics objects.

- *Exported layers*—each layer exported from Illustrator is represented as an instance of `Group`, where the group's `id` property is set to the name of the exported layer. The graphics objects in the layer are then exported as native JavaFX graphic nodes inside the group's `content` property. Images embedded in the original artwork are exported as PNG images, and are represented by `ImageView` instances.

What gets exported

The following list outlines the objects supported by the Illustrator Plugin and how they are exported to JavaFX:

- *Primitive shapes*—basic Illustrator shapes (that is, line, polyline, rectangle, and polygon) map directly to the corresponding JavaFX shape objects.

- *Curves, paths, and complex shapes*—Illustrator curves are mapped to the appropriate JavaFX curve classes when possible. However, if there are no corresponding graphics classes for the shape being exported, the plugin will fall back to the JavaFX `Path` class. In some instances, the plugin will use SVG, via the `SVGPath` class, to export complex shapes.

- ▸ *Paint, Stroke, and Gradient*—the plugin supports the paint, fill, and shape stroke attributes from Illustrator to JavaFX using RGB colors. Gradients from Illustrator map to either the `LinearGradient` or the `RadialGradient` class.

- ▸ *Effects*—the plugin will export Gaussian Blur, Inner Glow, Outer Glow, and Drop Shadow and can be exported as native JavaFX effect classes. Other effects can optionally be exported as a rasterized images.

See also

- ▸ *Introduction*
- ▸ *Exporting Adobe Photoshop graphics to JavaFX*

Exporting Scalable Vector Graphics (SVG) to JavaFX

In previous recipes, we have seen how to use commercial designer tools as part of the JavaFX development workflow by integrating creative content from Adobe Photoshop and Illustrator CS3/CS4. If you are not using these Adobe tools, (or in some cases using a older version), or maybe you are a supporter of open source, is it possible to export creative content from other tools into JavaFX? The answer is an emphatic "yes!".

Continuing with the theme of designer integration with JavaFX in this recipe, we will look at how to integrate scalable vector graphics (SVG) into JavaFX projects using the Production Suite tools. This will allow you to integrate directly scalable vector graphics created in commercial or open source packages into JavaFX.

Getting ready

To be able to convert graphics objects from an SVG file to JavaFX graphics objects, you must first download Production Suite from `http://javafx.com/downloads/`, and install it properly. Production Suite is a set of tools that are part of the JavaFX platform, intended to let designers easily participate in the development workflow by integrating their work directly with JavaFX.

This recipe assumes that you have a working knowledge of scalable vector graphics and have used tools to create artistic content as SVG files. The recipe does not show how to generate graphical content from your designer tools, but rather how to use JavaFX's Production Suite tools to convert SVG files into the JavaFX's FXZ file format. The recipe will use an SVG file exported from Adobe Illustrator. However, any vector graphics package, commercial or open source, with a mature support for standard SVG rendering should work as well.

How to do it...

For this recipe, we are going to walk through the steps of exporting graphics objects from an SVG file to JavaFX's FXZ file format for creative content integration.

1. First, you should ensure that you have installed the Production Suite tools properly, and you can launch SVG Converter.

2. Next, create your artwork using your favorite vector graphics package, and save it as an SVG file. For this recipe, we wi l be using an SVG file that was created with Illustrator and is located `ch08/source-code/resources/Symbols.svg`. The following figure shows the SVG file used for this recipe:

3. Now, launch the SVG Converter utility tool that ships with the Production Suite. The converter has a simple interface (see next screenshot), where you only need to select the source SVG file being converted and a destination where the generated FXZ file will be stored.

Once you click on the **Convert** button, the ut lity will convert your SVG file to the FXZ file format at the location specified.

How it works...

Similar to the Adobe Illustrator Production Suite plugin, the SVG Converter utility corverts the vector graphics in the SVG file to produce a single JavaFX FXZ file containing all of the graphical assets exported from the SVG artwork. The plugin attempts to translate SVG objects directly into their JavaFX's vector counterpars wherever possible. Let's see how the exported file format works:

▶ *The FXZ file*—when you export your graphics objects from SVG using the Production Suite's SVG Converter, the resulting FXZ file is a zip-compressed file containing one data file, `content.fxd`. Additionally, the FXZ file will also contain other graphical assets exported from the original SVG artwork, such as linked or embedded images, and fonts.

- ▶ *The FXD data file*—the conversion step will generate a data file embedded in the FXZ compressed file named `content.fxd`. This is a textual file, which contains JavaFX object literal declarations of a scene graph that represents objects exported from the original SVG file.

- ▶ *Generated PNG files*—when the SVG file contains bit-mapped objects (embedded or linked), they are rasterized down to PNG or JPG image files. Similar to the Illustrator plugin, the SVG converter utility will rasterize complex visual effects that it cannot convert to native JavaFX objects. All generated images are embedded in the FXZ files and are accessed using an `ImageView` node in the FXD file.

- ▶ *Text*—the SVG Converter tool will automatically export `Text` objects from the SVG file as `Text` instances in the JavaFX FXD file. It will export the font's name, weight, and size. However, the SVG to JavaFX conversion does not support embeddable fonts; if the font is not there, it the `Text` object will default to a supported font.

There's more...

The current version of the Production Suite's SVG Converter supports several SVG standards, including SVG 1.1 and SVG Tiny 1.1. The exported FXD data file, `content.fxd`, contains a set of nested literal declarations of `Group` instances organized as follows:

- ▶ *Root group*—the FXD file contains a root `Group` instance that serves as a container for all other groups of objects exported from the SVG file.

- ▶ *Exported layers*—each `<g>` (or group) tag in the SVG document is mapped to a `Group` instance in the FXD document. The Group's `id:String` property is set to the value of the `<g>` tag's `id` attribute. The vector graphics objects in each `<g>` elements are then exported as either native JavaFX graphics nodes or as instances of `SVGPath`, with path values copied from the SVG file.

What gets exported

The following outlines the objects supported by the SVG Converter and how they are exported to JavaFX:

- ▶ *Primitive shapes*—basic shapes such as line, polyline, rectangle, polygon, and oval map directly to the corresponding JavaFX shape objects.

- ▶ *Curves, paths, and complex shapes*—SVG curves are mapped to the appropriate JavaFX curve classes whenever possible. However, if there are no corresponding graphics classes for the shape being exported, the converter will fall back to the JavaFX `SVGPath` class to export complex shapes.

- ▶ *Paint, stroke, and gradient*—the converter supports the paint and strokes, and stroke attributes from SVG to JavaFX using RGB colors. Gradients from the SVG artwork will map to either the `LinearGradient` or the `RadialGradient` class. If the gradient is part of a complex shape, the converter may choose to export it as a rasterized image.

▶ *Transformation*—the SVG Converter utility supports object transformation routines applied to objects in the SVG file. The utility will export transformation matrices using the `Transform.affine()` method.

Features not supported

As of version 1.2 of the SDK, the SVG Converter will ignore the following features when they are included in the SVG file:

Animations	Text Layout or Text on Path
Scripting or Interactivity	Color Profiles
Filter Effects	Element `<metadata/>`
Masking	Element `<use/>`
Embeddable Fonts	Element `<defs/>`

Inkscape and JavaFX

Inkscape is a widely used, open source alternative vector graphics editor. By default it uses SVG to save its graphics files. The format used in Inkscape uses non-standard SVG elements to save layer information. As of version 1.2 of the Production Suite, there's a bug in the SVG Converter that prevents it from properly exporting the layer ID values as the ID value of the `Group` object instance. Future release of the Production Suite should address this issue.

See also

▶ *Introduction*

▶ *Exporting Adobe Photoshop graphics to JavaFX*

▶ *Exporting Adobe Illustrator graphics to JavaFX*

Using objects loaded from FXZ files

In the previous recipes, we have seen how to integrate creative content from tools, such as Adobe Photoshop and Illustrator, into JavaFX projects using the Production Suite tools. In this recipe, we are going to see how to load graphics nodes from a FXZ file. You will learn how to use NetBeans to generate JavaFX UI stub classes that provide programmatic access to the objects inside the FXZ files.

Getting ready

Prior to continuing with the materials in this recipe, you must be familiar with the topic of generating FXZ files covered in the recipes *Exporting Adobe Photoshop graphics to JavaFX*, *Exporting Adobe Illustrator graphics to JavaFX*, and *Exporting Scalable Vector Graphics (SVG) to JavaFX*. You will need an FXZ file generated using the methods discussed in these recipes.

Another requirement for this recipe is the use of the NetBeans IDE. The techniques covered here use features available in that IDE. If you are not a NetBeans user, see the *There's more* section to see how to craft your own code in order to load and programmatically manipulate graphics objects from an FXZ file without NetBeans manually.

How to do it...

To use the embedded objects in the FXZ file, we are going to generate UI stubs using NetBeans. Follow these steps:

1. *FXZ file*—make sure that your FXZ file is in a location accessible by your code. The easiest location is to place the FXZ file in the same package (or sub-package) as the class that will be using its graphics objects. For this recipe, we are going to use the FXZ file `ch08/source-code/src/fxzdemo/SymbolsPS.fxz` to generate a UI stub class.

2. *Generate the UI stub class*—from NetBeans, right-click on the FZX file from which you want to generate the UI stub, and select **Generate UI stub**, as shown in the following screenshot:

This will bring up a dialog box for customization of the generated classes. Specify the package location and the name of the generated UI class, as shown in the next screenshot:

3. *The UI stub*—for this recipe, we generated class `ch08/source-code/src/fxzdemo/NbGeneratedSymbols.fx` from the FXZ file. The generated class extends class `FXDNode` as shown in the next snippet:

```
public class NbGeneratedSymbols extends FXDNode {
  override public var url = "{__DIR__}SymbolsPS.fxz";
  public-read protected var icon_1: Node;
  public-read protected var icon_0: Node;
  public-read protected var icon_2: Node;
  public-read protected var icon_3: Node;
  public-read protected var icon_4: Node;
  public-read protected var icon_5: Node;
  public-read protected var target: Node;
  public-read protected var triangle: Node;

  override protected function contentLoaded() : Void {
    icon_1=getNode("icon_1");
    icon_0=getNode("icon_0");
    icon_2=getNode("icon_2");
    icon_3=getNode("icon_3");
    icon_4=getNode("icon_4");
    icon_5=getNode("icon_5");
    target=getNode("target");
    triangle=getNode("triangle");
  }
}
```

4. *Using the generated stub*—as an instance of `Node`, the generated stub class can be added into a scene graph. The following abbreviated snippet shows class `NbGeneratedSymbols` used as the basis for a simple game. The full code for this is located at `ch08/source-code/src/fxzdemo/Targeting.fx`.

```
. . .
def symbols = NbGeneratedSymbols{};
def triangle = symbols.triangle as ImageView;
def target = symbols.target as ImageView;

target.x = triangle.x;
symbols.requestFocus();
symbols.onKeyPressed = function (e:KeyEvent) {
    if(e.code.equals(KeyCode.VK_RIGHT)){
        target.translateX = target.translateX + 15;
        triangle.translateX = triangle.translateX + 15;
    }
    if(e.code.equals(KeyCode.VK_LEFT)){
        target.translateX = target.translateX - 15;
        triangle.translateX = triangle.translateX - 15;
    }
    if(e.code.equals(KeyCode.VK_SPACE)){
        for(i in [0..5]){
            var icon = symbols.getObject("icon_{i}") as Node;
            if(icon.intersects(target.boundsInParent)){
                icon.visible = false;
                break;
            }
        }
    }
}
. . .
```

When the variable `symbols` is added to the scene, and the script is executed, it displays the game shown in the next screenshot. As the red triangle moves left or right using the arrow keys, it targets the icons lined up at the top portion of the window. When the Spacebar key is pressed to fire, the target icon goes off screen:

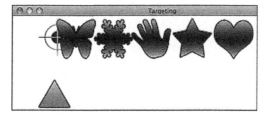

How it works...

In this recipe, we have loaded and programmatically manipulated graphics objects encapsulated in JavaFX's FXZ file. The recipe uses NetBeans to generate a UI stub class that exposes all of the objects inside the FXZ file. Let's see how the UI stub works:

- ▶ *UI stub class*—the UI stub extends `FXDNode`. In our recipe, the stub class is named `NbGeneratedSymbols`. It is a class designed to represent graphics objects from FXZ files. The UI stub class encapsulates all top-level group nodes (mapped to layers in original artwork) declared in the FXD file and exposes them as public properties in the generated class.

- ▶ `FXDNODE.contentLoaded()`—this method is called when the class has fully loaded all graphics objects. Here, it is overwritten to populate the public variables that expose the content of the FXD file as object properties. Notice the use of function `getNode(id:String)`, used here to retrieve a graphics node by its `id`.

  The other portion of this recipe deals with the usage of the generated UI stub. Let's analyze what is going on:

  - ❏ First, the code declares variable `symbols` as an instance of `NbGeneratedSymbols` class.

  - ❏ Next, the code pulls out the image for the `target` and the `triangle` as `ImageView` instances from the symbols object.

  - ❏ Then, `symbols` receives the window's focus; this will enable it to receive keyboard events.

  - ❏ Next, the code adds event-handler function `onKeypressed(e:KeyEvent)` to the `symbols` object to process keyboard input events. Here, *Left arrow*, *Right arrow*, and *Spacebar* key events are used to provide interactivity to the game. When the left or right arrow moves, it updates the position of both the triangle and the target icons. When the **Spacebar** key is pressed, the code hides the icon which intersects the target icon.

There's more...

Earlier in this recipe, we have seen how to generate UI stub classes from FXZ files using NetBeans to access graphics objects inside FXZ files. If you do not use NetBeans or want tighter control of how FXZ objects are loaded, you can use the FXD API directly, located in the `javafx.fxd` package, to customize how objects are loaded from the FXZ files. You can see listing of these techniques in files `ch08/source-code/src/fxzdemo/FxdNodeLoad1.fx`, `FxdNodeLoad2.fx`, `FxdNodeLoad3.fx`, and `FxdNodeLoad4.fx`.

Using FXDNode to load objects

You can use the FXNode class directly to load the top-most group encapsulated in the FXD file. This approach works well when you are interested in loading all objects in the scene graph as a group quickly, and place them on the scene or in another container node.

```
var artwork = FXDNode {
    url: "{__DIR__}SymbolsPS.fxz"
}
```

Variable artwork will be an instance of an orphaned Node. Therefore, you can nest artwork in a container node, such as Scene or another group as follows:

```
Scene{content: artwork}
```

Accessing Group nodes directly

If your artwork has several nested groups, as do vector graphics exported from SVG or Illustrator, you can use FXDNode to load them directly as shown below:

```
var artwork = FXDNode {
    url: "{__DIR__}SymbolsPS.fxz"
}

def flare = artwork.getGroup("flare");
```

This method returns a Group instance of the selected object.

Accessing objects directly

You can also use the FXDNode instance to access individual graphics objects nested inside the FXD file's scene graph by their IDs.

```
var artwork = FXDNode {
    url: "{__DIR__}SymbolsPS.fxz"
}
def triangle = artwork.getNode("triangle") as ImageView;
def target = artwork.getNode("target") as ImageView;
```

The code snippet demonstrates the use of FXDNode.getNode(id:String):Node to retrieve graphics objects using their id property value.

Placing non-orphaned nodes

When working with the FXD API to access objects directly, as shown previously, retrieving nested objects will return non-orphaned nodes that are part of the FXDNode scene graph (considered as a parent container). You will get an error if you attempt to move non-orphaned nodes into another parent container node. The scene graph engine in JavaFX only allows nodes to have one parent node and will not automatically re-assign parents. To get around this, the FXD API offers the Duplicator class which automatically returns a cloned, orphaned copy of the node:

```
def artwork = FXDNode{url:"{__DIR__}SymbolsAI.fxz"}
def flare = Duplicator.duplicate(artwork.getGroup("flare"));
Stage {
    title: "Targeting"
    scene: Scene {
        width: 200
        height: 200
        content:[flare]
    }
}
```

If you attempt to place flare directly on the stage without the duplicator step, it will generate an error.

Using FXDNode to load object asynchronously

FXDNode is designed to support asynchronous loading of your artwork from the FXZ file. This is helpful in cases when the FXZ file is either large or being loaded from a remote location (or both). Doing it asynchronously ensures that the UI stays responsive, even when the load operation takes a few seconds. The following loads artwork content from file SymbolsAI.fxz asynchronously:

```
def artwork = FXDNode {
    url: "{__DIR__}SymbolsAI.fxz"
    backgroundLoading: true
    placeholder: Text{ x:10 y: 10 content: "Loading..."}
}
```

Event notifications through FXDLoader

Your code can receive event notifications as the FXZ file loads using the FXDLoader class. The following code will be notified when the FXZ file starts to load and when it is done loading:

```
def artwork:FXDNode = FXDNode {
    url: "{__DIR__}SymbolsAI.fxz"
    backgroundLoading: true
    placeholder: Text{ x:10 y: 10 content: "Loading..."}
    loader:FXDLoader{
        onStart:function() {
            println ("Image loading started")
        }
        onDone:function() {
            println ("Image loading done");
            println ("Loaded "
            "{sizeof artwork.getRoot().content} objects");
        }
    }
}
```

See also

▶ *Introduction*

▶ *Exporting Adobe Photoshop graphics to JavaFX*

▶ *Exporting Adobe Illustrator graphics to JavaFX*

▶ *Exporting Scalable Vector graphics (SVG) to JavaFX*

A
Mobile JavaFX

As of the release of version 1.2 back in early 2009, JavaFX now includes support for both desktop and mobile development. The NetBeans IDE offers full support for mobile development, including mobile device emulator, packaging, and deployment. If you are not a NetBeans user, you can use the **javafxpackager** tool, along with the emulator tool, to emulate mobile content on your workstation.

 As of version 1.2 of the SDK, JavaFX Mobile development is only supported on the Windows platform.

JavaFX Mobile is a software layer that runs on top of the Java ME (specifically, the CDC profile) on smartphones capable of providing rich content and an engaging experience. Because Java ME is already supported on a large number of handset models, JavaFX has the potential to be widely available on mobile devices.

When writing your application, you need to select APIs carefully to maximize portability. If you know that your application will only run on the desktop, you are free to exploit the desktop APIs without portability worries. However, if you plan to push your application to both the desktop and the mobile environments, you will then be constrained to use APIs that satisfy both desktop and mobile runtimes. A good rule to follow is to program using common profiles as a common denominator to arrive at an application that can run on both profiles.

If, on the other hand, your application is strictly targeted for the mobile environment, then you will have more freedom to take advantage of the Java ME features for mobile devices, such as Bluetooth and GPS. Another interesting issue that arises with mobile development is the constraint created by physical characteristics of the device, including input mode, screen size, CPU, and memory. When targeting mobile environments, be aware of the limitations of the mobile profile. Use some of the following points as guidelines:

- *JME is not JS*—do not expect the standard Java libraries to be available on the mobile runtime. While some stripped down version of Java SE APIs are present in ME, others do not exist at all. For instance, avoid using Swing components in your application; instead, use the native JavaFX controls, and let the runtime module translate them to their Java ME component counterparts.

- *Screen reflow*—newer devices support screen orientation changes; you may have to create GUI layouts that let your components automatically resize or reflow based on the orientation of the screen. The layout of your controls should reflow gracefully to handle portrait or landscape screen modes.

- *Use vector graphics*—try to use vector graphics where possible, as they are easily portable between platforms and can resize with no degradation.

- *Apply affects ahead of time*—as of version 1.2 of the SDK , paint effects are not part of the common profile; therefore, if you need paint in your effects, create a bitmapped image with the paint effect already applied, then load the image.

JavaFX Composer

In late December 2009, **Sun Microsystems** (which eventually became part of Oracle) released the first preview version of **JavaFX Composer**—a **What You See Is What You Get** (WYSIWYG) tool for building rich, graphical GUIs. It borrows its visual metaphors from graphical design tools where developers drag components from a palette and arrange them on the **stage** during design. Composer generates the appropriate JavaFX code to keep both design-view and code-view synchronized. JavaFX Composer supports the following functionalities:

- *Drag-and-drop design*—Composer supports the ability to drag visual components and GUI controls directly on Stage. Composer provides a WYSIWYG designer environment with on-the-fly alignment guides, property editors, and round-trip code synchronization (these are the same characteristics found in **NetBeans Swing GUI Builder**). Besides visual components, developers can drag-and-drop other visual components, including paint, effects, and charts. Composer even provides a **Design Analyser** that dynamically detects design issues as they occur.

- *The Data source framework*—Composer introduces the DataSource API, designed to simplify and standardize access of data from different sources. Each source type comes with a corresponding DataSource, including HttpDataSource, DbDataSource, FileDataSource, StorageDataSource, and ClassPathDataSource. The DataSource API also offers a filtering mechanism to let users select data nodes, using an XPath-like expression. Composer provides configuration wizards as well, to help developers walk through the steps for setting up a data source.

- *States*—this is a mechanism that lets developers organize visual components based on a set of current property values (or **states**). This feature is synonymous to building a presentation, where the slide represents a state in which a component can appear. For each state (slide), the components may have different property values. When the user switches to a different state, the new property values are applied to the components. Users may switch between states by generating an event or through user actions. The action of switching between states can be controlled to include transition animations and effects that are automatically scripted by Composer.

▸ *Binding*—Composer builds on the data-binding functionality built in to JavaFX to facilitate binding of component properties to either simple values, data sources, or to other component properties. Within Composer, developers are able to specify arbitrary bound expressions with custom type conversion supported. Regardless of what the properties of a component are bound to, the mechanism is still the same: when the target expression is updated, the bound property is updated automatically.

JavaFX Products and Frameworks

Despite its infancy, JavaFX has commanded a tremendous following within a short period of time. Currently, there are a combination of commercial and open-source products and frameworks available for or in support of JavaFX:

▸ *WidgetFX*—this is a platform on which you can run desktop widgets built entirely in JavaFX. It is inherently cross-platform and will run on operating systems that support JavaFX. Other features of WidgetFX include a growing number of available widgets, a simple one-click installation, open source code, a robust security model based on Java's own setup, and a small footprint. See `http://widgetfx.org/` to find out how to create widgets.

▸ *On2 JavaFX Video Encoder*—JavaFX uses On2's technologies for its cross-platform and portable video codec called **FXM**. On2 provides two tools, Flix Pro and Flix Standard, to allow content creators to encode videos directly into the FXM format. See `https://flix.on2.com/` for details about On2's Flix product line.

▸ *Exadel JavaFX products*—Exadel, a company well-known for its enterprise view technologies, got in the JavaFX game early with two offerings for developers. Exadel offers **JavaFX Studio** as an alternative IDE for JavaFX development. JavaFX Studio is an Eclipse plug-in with features such as new project/class setup wizards, code editor with syntax completion/highlight, and deployment wizards. The other offering from Exadel is called **Flamingo**. It is a framework that provides client-side components for data connectivity so that JavaFX can be implemented as a view technology for server-side Spring, Seam, or Java EE components. Go to `http://www.exadel.com/` for more details on Exadel products.

- *JFXtras*—this is one of the earliest efforts to create a third-party, open-source extension to JavaFX. JFXtras boasts a sizeable collection of components, including layouts, borders, visual controls, persistence, and threading. From their website, JFXtras includes an entire community of users, complete with code samples, support, and other valuable resources. See `http://jfxtras.org/` to see all components available from JFXtras.

- *ReportMill's DataBox*—previously known as JFXBuilder, this an interesting tool. It allows its users to create fully functional and deployable JavaFX applications by simple point-and-click. As the name implies, `DataBox` has inherent support for data connectivity, including database, FTP, and the cloud. Applications created with `DataBox` can be deployed as applets and run on any browser that supports JavaFX. For details, visit `http://www.reportmill.com/dbox/`.

- *MemeFX*—this is another open-source component collection. It started out as an offering of multi-parameter analog gauges created in JavaFX. However, the project has evolved to offer other visual components including image controls, HTML text controls, menus, and stage extensions. See `http://code.google.com/p/memefx/` for details.

D

Best Practices for Development

Practitioners of JavaFX can easily abuse its ease of use to create applications that perform and scale poorly. This section provides a list of some practices that should help you avoid performance or usability penalties.

- ▸ *Declare your variables using the def keyword*—always use the def keyword to declare your variable, unless you know for certain that the variable will be updated later or is a bound variable.

- ▸ *Stay off the EDT*—JavaFX applications are inherently single-threaded running on one special thread called the **Event Dispatch Thread** (**EDT**). All GUI activities are handled on the EDT. If you execute long-running processes directly in your JavaFX code, they will degrade the responsiveness of the UI or make it outright unusable. JavaFX offers the Task API, which is designed to provide the mechanism to execute processes asynchronously.

- ▸ You can do this in three steps:

1. Create a Java class that implements javafx.async.RunnableFuture and overrides the run() method, which contains the asynchronous code that you want to run:

```
public class LongRunningRunnable implements RunnableFuture{
    private long limit = Long.MAX_VALUE;
    public LongRunningRunnable(long l){limit = l;} // constructor
    public void run() throws Exception {
        for(int i = 0; i < limit; i++){
            Thread.currentThread().sleep(200);
        }
    }
}
```

2. Next, create a JavaFX class that extends `javafx.aysync.JavaTaskBase` and overrides `function create():RunnableFuture`, which returns an instance of the newly-defined Java class above to be executed in its own thread:

```
public class LongRunningTask extends JavaTaskBase{
    public-init var limit = Long.MAX_VALUE;
    override protected function create () : RunnableFuture {
        new LongRunningRunnable(limit);
    }
}
```

3. Lastly, use the JavaFX class (defined above) to start your long-running process on its own thread:

```
var t = LongRunningTask{limit:Byte.MAX_VALUE}
t.start(); // start task on its own thread
```

▶ *Reuse image objects*—if you have an image that appears in multiple places, load the image once using the `Image` object, then reuse the `Image` instance in any image number of `ImageView` instances. That way, you don't have duplicated bytes wasting memory resources.

▶ *Scale media to size*—avoid using images or videos at larger resolutions than needed. When possible, encode your media to the size and resolution that you will actually need. This will avoid unnecessary scaling transformation penalties when scaled in JavaFX.

▶ *Turn off smooth*—when your scene graph contains a large number of shapes, you can gain performance by setting the `smooth` property to `false` in order to reduce the overhead required for anti-aliasing wherever possible.

▶ *Cache your visual nodes*—when the scene graph engine paints its node on the screen, you can avoid repaint penalties by caching complex non-rotated object graphs. Caching causes the engine to reuse previously rendered images, rather then repainting the scene every time.

▶ *Remove instead of hide*—to keep your node rendering time down, and increase performance, you should delete objects from the scene graph instead of setting property `visible` to `false` whenever possible.

▶ *Avoid Gratuitous Effects and Animations*—effects (paint, transformation, scale, and so on) and animations incur processing overhead, especially with large numbers of nodes. Avoid applying effects and animations unless absolutely necessary.

▶ *Ungroup paint effects*—when your nodes are encapsulated in a `Group` instance, apply your effects to individual nodes instead of the `Group` node. This provides granular control of where the effects are applied and helps avoid necessary rendition of effects.

- ▶ *Set timeline's frame rate*—when you are working with fairly complex animations, you can provide better directives for frames generated by specifying the `framerate` property. If not, the engine will attempt to determine the best frame rate value to achieve the animation, which can result in wasted frames being generated.

- ▶ *Use binding sparingly*—data binding is a useful and a killer feature in JavaFX. Just like anything else though, its unnecessary overuse can be troublesome. Improper or careless binding can lead to cascading triggers that causes unwanted performance degradation that are hard to find. Use data binding only when you understand the event path and values that are updated during binding update. In most cases, updating a variable directly by setting its value works better.

Best Practices for Deployment

The first impression of your application comes from the experience users have as they attempt to procure or launch the application for the first time. It is important to avoid the appearance of a broken application by giving your users the ability to find, download, or start your application easily. Here are some tips for application deployments:

- *Load JARs lazily*—JavaFX applications jars are downloaded eagerly by default using **Java Network Launching Protocol (JNLP)**. This is fine for smaller applications. However, when you have several large JARs that are part of your application's manifest, this can cause a delay in startup time. You can change this behavior and download JAR files lazily as needed. Update your JNLP file with:

```
<jnlp>
  ...
  <resources>
    <jar href="demo-util.jar" download="lazy"/>
    ...
  </resources>
</jnlp>
```

- *Index your classes*—one way to improve startup performance is through the use of JAR class indexing. Traditionally, the class loader will traverse each JAR to look for a classes to load. This can be a performance killer at startup to wait for JARs to download and classes to be loaded. Indexing is used to by the class loader to find classes quickly that are embedded in the JARs. To index your classes, use the `jar` command line tool with the `-i` option followed by a list of JAR files to be indexed (as shown next). The index information is saved as a text file embedded inside the first JAR file listed in the command.

```
jar -i main-app.jar \
        jar-module-1.jar \
        jar-module-2.jar \
        jar-module-3.jar \
        ...
        jar-module-N.jar
```

- *Compress JARs with Pack200*—it goes without saying that the size of your JAR files will impact startup time. You can further squeeze the size of your JAR files with the **pack200** option when packaging your application with the `javafxpacakger`, using the `-pack200` flag as follows:

```
javafxpackager -src src \
                -appClass draggable.demo.Main \
                -appName demo-app \
                -pack200
```

  - In addition to `demo-app.jar`, this command line also generates the file `demo-app.jar.pack.gz` that will be downloaded at runtime. The command also injects the property `jnlp.packEnabled` into the JNLP file as follows:

```
<jnlp>
  ...
  <resources>
    ...
    <property name="jnlp.packEnabled" value="true"/>
  </resources>
</jnlp>
```

- *Provide ample memory*—avoid application death caused by 'out of memory' exceptions. This is a nasty situation which can damage the reputation of your app as being broken. The good news is, it can be easily prevented by setting the heap size of your app in the JNLP file

```
<jnlp> ...
  <resources>
    <j2se version="1.6+" max-heap-size="256m" />
    ...
  </resources>
</jnlp>
```

▸ *Avoid excessive JAR update checks*—JavaFX applets and Web Start applications will automatically check for updates for the JAR files included in your application upon startup. You can either turn that off (if you don't plan on having updates), or do the update in the background by specifying it in your JNLP file as follows:

```
<jnlp>
    ...
    <update check="background"/>
</jnlp>
```

▸ *JAR versioning*—if you decide to have your JARs be updated automatically (see previous bullet point) you can use JNLP's JAR-versioning mechanism. It uses this mechanism to update JAR files when version number changes, instead of checking for updates for all JARs. To take advantage of this, name your JARs using this format *{jar-name}_V{version-number}.jar*, for example demo-util_V1.0.jar. Then, set the jnlp.versionEnabled attribute in the JNLP file as shown:

```
<jnlp>
    ...
    <resources>
        <jar href="demo-app.jar" main="true"/>
        <jar href="demo-util.jar" version="1.0"/>
        <property name="jnlp.versionEnabled" value="true"/>
    <resources>
</jnlp>
```

▸ *Avoid signing your application*—while a properly signed application can establish a certain level of trust, signing, however, can introduce new dialogue boxes that force users to confirm their trust in the application issuer. So, unless you absolutely need signing, avoid it. An unsigned application causes a security dialogue to appear only when the application attempts to execute privileged code. Furthermore, users can opt to trust the the unsigned application and no longer be presented with future security warnings.

Index

Symbols

@argfiles option 21
:Boolean type 27
.broad:hover{} selector 152
__DIR__ pseudo-variable
  about 159
  media assets, accessing 158
__DIR__ variable 158
.dmg file 10
-d option 21
:Duration type 27
.exe file 10
__FILE__ pseudo variable 159
:focused pseudo-class 152
:hover pseudo-class 152
:Integer type 27
.jar file 11
\n 63
:Number type 27
:pressed pseudo-class 152
:String type 27
:Void type 27

A

access modifiers, JavaFX
  about 73
  default 73
  package 73
  protected 73
  public 73
  public-init 73
  public-read 73
action:function() function 97
action:function() property 124, 223
action property 99

Adobe Illustrator plugin
  about 260
  graphics, exporting to JavaFX 269-273
Adobe Photoshop plugin
  about 260
  graphics, exporting to JavaFX 265-267
after clause 39
animate() function 138
animation
  building, KeyFrame API used 93-97
  composing, Transition API used 89-91
  creating, Transition API used 85-87
  custom interpolators, creating for 100, 101
AnimationPath class 87
animation types, JavaFX
  keyframe 82
  transition 82
API integration 37
AppletStageExtension Hooks
  appletDragSupport:Boolean 248
  onAppletRes-tored:function() 249
  onDragFinished:function() 249
  onDragStarted:function() 248
  useDefaultClose:Boolean 248
application organization 46
arcHeight property 52
Arc shape class 53, 54
Arc shape class, types
  ArcType.CHORD 54
  ArcType.OPEN 54
  ArcType.ROUND 54
ArcTo, path element 56
ArcType.CHORD type 54
ArcType.OPEN type 54
ArcType.ROUND type 54
arcWidth property 52

a:Shape[] property **57**
Atom
  about **186**
  creating, Feed API used **213-216**
  handling **218**
at() syntax 98
attraction:Number property 101
audio
  playing, with MediaPlayer **172-174**
autoReverse:Boolean property 87
autoReverse property 88, 91
azimuth property 113

B

backgroundLoading:Boolean property 162
BarChart class 223
BarChart.Data.barCreator property 223
before clause 39
binding
  variables, updating **28**
bin directory 11
bind keyword 28, 30
BlendedMode class 172
Blend effect 113
blending options, JavaFX
  BlendMode.ADD **172**
  BlendMode.COLOR_BURN **172**
  BlendMode.DARKEN **172**
  BlendMode.DIFFERENCE **172**
  BlendMode.LIGHTEN **172**
  BlendMode.MULTIPLY **172**
  BlendMode.OVERLAY **172**
  BlendMode.SCREEN **172**
BlendMode.ADD mode 172
blendMode:BlendMode property 171
BlendMode.COLOR_BURN mode 172
BlendMode.DARKEN mode 172
BlendMode.DIFFERENCE mode 172
BlendMode.LIGHTEN mode 172
BlendMode.MULTIPLY mode 172
BlendMode.OVERLAY mode 172
BlendMode.SCREEN mode 172
BlendMode.valueOf(:String) property 171
Bloom effect 113
boolean operations, CAG
  AND **57**

NOT **57**
OR **57**
bottomOpacity property 118
BoxBlur effect 113
b:Shape[] property 57
bSlide element 130
Button control 124, 141

C

CAG
  shapes, creating **58, 59**
  working **59**
Cascading Style Sheets. *See* **CSS**
Chart API
  charts, customizing **223, 224**
  data, visualizing **220-222**
CheckBox control 124, 141
Circle class 52
class definitions 71
classpath (-cp) option 21
clearAll():Boolean function 188
clear():Boolean function 188
ColorAdjust effect 113
Color class 107
color picker
  creating **130**
comparison operator 39
compositable:Boolean property 178
conditional binding 29
Constructive Area Geometry. *See* **CAG**
content:Node[] property 49
content property 49, 92
content:String property 61
Control class 120, 137
createFromPath(path:Path) 87
createJComponent() function 143
create() method 75
create():Node function 75
CSS
  applications, styling **143-145**
  paint properties, styling **147**
  text nodes, styling **146**
  CSSworking **145**
CSS files
  styles, applying **148-151**
CubicCurve class 54

custom class
controls 184
textual time progression 183
visual time progression 183
custom data model
using, with ListView control 127, 128
custom interpolators
creating, for animations 100, 101
custom JavaFX control
creating 134, 136
custom node
creating 73, 75
using 75
working 74
CustomNode class 75
CustomPaint class
creating 109, 111
custom parsing 212
custom Swing controls
wrapping, into JavaFX node 142

D

data
displaying, ListView control used 125, 126
data binding
animation sequences, driving 104, 106
working 106
Data class 223
data visualization 186
Deck.add() function 138
Deck.add(node:Node) function 137
Deck class
properties 137
using 138
working 137
Deck.frontToBack() method 138
default access modifier 73
def keyword 25, 26
DelegateShape class
shapes, morphing 102, 104
delete operation 39
deployment practices, JavaFX
about 295
ample memory, providing 296
classes, indexing 296
excessive JAR update checks, avoiding 297

JARs, compressing with Pack200 296
JARs, loading 295
JAR versioning 297
signing your application, avoiding 297
Design Analyser 287
directories, JavaFX
about 11
bin 11
docs 11
emulator 11
lib 11
profiles 11
samples 11
DisplacementMap effect 113
DistantLighting effect 111
docs directory 11
DOCUMENT_END pull event 212
Document Object Model. *See* **DOM**
DOCUMENT_START pull event 212
DOM
about 211
URL 213
DropShadow effect 111-116
Duration type 82

E

Eclipse
working 228
Eclipse IDE
JavaFX, setting up 16-19
Effect API 116
Effect class 112
effect:Effect property 111, 112
Ellipse class 52
emulator directory 11
encodeParameters(Pair[]):String function 199
END_ARRAY_ELEMENT pull event 212
END_ARRAY pull event 212
END_ELEMENT pull event 212
END_VALUE pull event 212
Event Dispatch Thread (EDT) 291
events, PullParser class
DOCUMENT_END 212
DOCUMENT_START 212
END_ARRAY 212
END_ARRAY_ELEMENT 212

END_ELEMENT 212
END_VALUE 212
START_ARRAY 212
START_ARRAY_ELEMENT 212
START_ELEMENT 212
START_VALUE 212
TEXT 212
Exadel
about 289
URL 289

F

FadeTransition class 85, 88
Feed API
Atom clients, creating 213-216
default parser, overriding 218, 219
RSS clients, creating 213-216
fill:Color property 49, 61, 130
fill property 107
fitHeight property 161, 178
fitWidth property 161, 178
Flamingo 289
Flickr
URL 159
Flood effect 113
Flow layout manager 69
Font class 61
Font.font() function 64
font:Font property 61
Font.getFontNames(familyName:Font.get
FontNames(familyNameString):Object[]
method 64
Font.getFontNames():String[] method 64
fonts
locating 64
FontWeight class 64
for-loop expression 126
form
creating, JavaFX controls used 120-124
forward(level:Integer) method 212
forward() method 212
fraction property 118
framerate:Number property 88
framerate property 293
framework integration 37

FSEM 80
Full-Screen Exclusive Mode. *See* **FSEM**
fullScreen property 79, 80
full-screen theater mode 79, 80
functionalities, JavaFX Composer
binding 288
data source framework 287
drag-and-drop design 287
states 287
function type 32, 33
FXD file 268
FXDLoader
event notifications 283
FXDNode
about 283
objects, loading asynchronously 283
FXDNODE.contentLoaded() method 281
FXM 289
FXZ file
about 267, 268
loaded objects, using 277-281
FZDNode
group nodes, accessing 282
non-orphaned nodes, placing 282
objects, accessing 282
objects, loading 282

G

Gartner
URL 222
GaussianBlur effect 113, 167
GET method 199
Glow effect 114, 167
Google API Key
URL 193
Google Static Map API 193
gradients
cool paint effects, applying 107, 108
Graphics Viewer 260
Group class
about 50, 75
working 171
gSlide element 130

H

HBox layout manager 69, 123, 141
height:Number property 49, 163
HLineTo, path element 56
HTML file 240
HTTP
    URL 192
HTTP methods 192
HttpRequest
    data, posting to remote servers 196-199
    files, uploading to servers 200-203
    images, downloading 192-195
    remote data, accessing 189-191
HttpRequest.headers property 203
HttpRequest object 186
HttpRequest.start() function 199

I

IDE
    working, with JavaFX application 228
id:String property 124, 141
Image class 160, 161, 163
image effects
    creating, with blending 167-171
ImageIO.read() function 111
Image object 292
images
    aspect ratio 163
    asynchronous loading issues 162
    automatic resizing 163
    displaying, with ImageView 159-162
    downloading, with HttpRequest 192-195
    effects 167
    effects, applying 163-167
    format support 162
    loading, in applications 260-264
    loading, with ImageView 159-162
    rotating 167
    scaling 166
    transformations, applying 163-167
ImageView
    images, displaying 159-162
    images, loading 159-261
ImageView class 160, 161
ImageView.fitHeight property 166

ImageView.fitWidth property 166
imgView.requestFocus() function 264
imgView.rotate property 167
impl_getPlatformPaint function 110
implicit coercion 26
init block 24, 25
initialization block. *See* init block
Inkscape
    and JavaFX 277
InnerShadow effect 114
Insert operation 37
installation, JavaFX SDK
    about 9
    Linux, requisites 9
    Mac OS X, requisites 9
    Open Solaris, requisites 9
    steps 9
    Windows, requisites 9
interpolation 98
Interpolator.DISCRETE, interpolator 99, 100
Interpolator.EASEBOTH, interpolator 98, 100
Interpolator.EASEIN, interpolator 98, 100
Interpolator.EASEOUT, interpolator 98, 100
Interpolator.LINEAR, interpolator 99, 100
InvertMask effect 114
items:Object[] property 126

J

Java
    interface, implementing in JavaFX 36
    JavaFX, calling 37
    JavaFX code, integrating 35, 36
    overview 8
Java Advanced Imaging (JAI) 162
Java applet
    about 237
    AppletStageExtension hooks 248
    controlling, JavaScript used 250-254
    drag-to-install 245
    drag-to-install, implementing 245-247
    drag-to-install, working 247
    post-installation behavior, controlling 249
    unintentional dragging, preventing 249
    working 240
java.awt.image.BufferedImage class 195

JavaFX
  about 8
  access modifiers 73
  Adobe Illustrator graphics, exporting to
    269-273
  Adobe Photoshop graphics, exporting to
    265-267
  and Inkscape 277
  animation framework 82
  application, building 46
  calling, from Java 37
  classes, creating 22
  classes, using 23
  code, integrating with Java 35, 36
  custom node, creating 73, 75
  deployment practices 295
  development practices 291-293
  directories 11
  functions, creating 32, 33
  functions, using 32, 33
  images, loading 260-264
  Java interface, implementing 36
  media assets, loading 158
  production suite 259
  resources, accessing ways 159
  Scalable Vector Graphics, exporting to
    274-276
  sequence loop query 40
  sequence operations 39
  sequence operators 39
  sequence slices 40
  setting up, for Eclipse IDE 16-19
  setting up, for NetBeans IDE 11-14
  string literal, marking as localized 42, 43
  string type 41, 42
  Swing components, embedding 139-141
  Swing control facade, creating 142, 143
  unified programming model 226
  variables, declaring 25
JavaFX animation framework 82
javafx.animation package 93
javafx.animation.transition package 85, 89
JavaFX APIs 226
JavaFX application
  arguments, accessing 244
  arguments, passing to 242, 243
  building 46

  building and packaging, with IDE 227, 228
  building and packaging, with javafxpackager
    229
  command-line arguments 244
  decomposing 48, 49
  JVM arguments 245
  packaging, as an applet 237, 239
  packaging, with Web Start 236
  requisites 46-48
  running, in full-screen 79, 80
  scene class 49
  skinning, with multiple CSS files 152, 154
  styling, CSS used 143-145
  window style, controlling 76, 77
JavaFX application, decomposing
  about 48
  nodes 49
  scene 49
  stage 49
JavaFX application framework 244
javafxc compiler
  JavaFX code, compiling 19-21
  options 21
javafxc compiler, options
  @argfiles 21
  classpath (-cp) 21
  -d 21
  sourcepath 21
JavaFX classes 36
  creating 22
  object literal declaration 24
  using 23
JavaFX code
  about 240
  compiling, javafxc compiler used 19-21
  integrating, with Java 35, 36
JavaFX Composer
  functionalities 287
JavaFX controls
  Button 124
  CheckBox 124
  form, creating 120-124
  Label 123
  RadioButton 123
  TextBox 123
JavaFX CSS 145
javafx.data.feed.rss package 213

javafx.data.pull package 204
javafx.ext.swing package 120, 139
javafx() function 254
JavaFX functions
  binding, to variable 34
  creating 32, 33
  using 32, 33
javafx.io.http package 190
javafx.io.http.URLConverter class 192
javafx.io package 186
JavaFX-JavaScript bridge mechanism
  JavaFX types 255
  JavaScript, accessing from JavaFX 256, 257
  scene graph, accessing 256
  using 254
JavaFX localization
  using 42, 43
JavaFX Mobile
  about 285
  guidelines 286
JavaFX NetBeans plugin
  downloading 15
JavaFX node
  custom Swing controls, wrapping 142
JavaFX packager tool
  about 230
  packaging flags 231
  tasks 230
javafx.scene.chart package 220
javafx.scene.control package 120-131
javafx.scene.effect package 111-116
javafx.scene.image package 160
javafx.scene.input package 65
javafx.scene.layout package 67
javafx.scene.media package 172-179
javafx.scene package 74
javafx.scene.paint.Color package 48
javafx.scene.paint package 107
javafx.scene.Scene package 48
javafx.scene.shape package 50-102
javafx.scene.shape.Rectangle package 48
javafx.scene.text.Font package 48
javafx.scene.text package 60
javafx.scene.text.Text package 48
javafx.scene.transform package 83
JavaFX SDK
  about 229

installing 9
installing, on Mac OS 10
installing, on Solaris 10
installing, on Ubuntu 10
installing, on Windows 10
JavaFX SDK, installing
  about 9
  Linux, requisites 9
  Mac OS X, requisites 9
  Open Solaris, requisites 9
  Windows, requisites 9
JavaFX SDK, transform operations
  Rotate 84
  Scale 84
  Shear 84
  Translate 84
JavaFX sequences
  creating 37, 38
  loop query 40
  operations 39
  operators 39
  slices 40
  using 37, 38
JavaFX software development kit. *See* **JavaFX SDK**
javafx.stage.Stage package 48
JavaFX, String type
  about 41
  capabilities 42
  working 42
JavaFX Studio 289
JavaFX types
  boolean 256
  integer 256
  number 256
  object 256
  sequence 256
  string 256
Java Image Tutorial
  URL 196
java.io.: classes 188
java.io.InputStream 188
java.io.OutputStream 188
Java IO Tutorial
  URL 189
JavaScript library services
  graceful degradation 241

HTML tags, generating 241
JRE detection 241
JavaScript Object Notation. *See* **JSON**
java.util.Formatter class 42
Java Virtual Machine. *See* **JVM**
Java Web Start
about 236
features 236
javax.imageio.ImageIO class 195
JComponent class 142
JFXtras 290
JNLP file
about 236, 241
configuration parameters 236
JNLP file name
overriding 241
jnlp.versionEnabled attribute 297
JSON 186, 204
JVM 35, 41

K

keyboard events
capturing 64-67
KeyEvent class 66
keyframe animation 82
KeyFrame API
animation, building 93-97
KeyFrame class 93
KeyFrame class, properties
time:Duration 97
values:KeyValue[] 97

L

Label control 123, 141
layout manager 69
length:Long property 188
letterSpacing:Number property 61
lib directory 11
Lighting effect 111-167
light:Light property 113
LinearGradient method 108
Line class 52
LineTo, path element 56
list():Object[] function 188

ListView control
custom data model, used 127, 128
data, displaying 125, 126
loadImage(url) method 195
loadImg() function 161-171
loadRssInfo(zip:String) function 216
local storage configuration
about 189
storage.enabled = [true | false] 189
storage.limit.domain 189
location property 192
location:String property 191

M

Mac OS
JavaFX SDK, installing 10
NetBeans, installing 12
MagneticInterpolator class 100, 101
maxLength:Long property 188
max:Number property 130
media assets
accessing 158, 159
Media class 172-175
MediaController class 182
media playback component
creating 179-184
media playback, JavaFX
platform-dependent implementations
    157, 158
platform-independent APIs 157
MediaPlayer
audio, playing 172-174
MediaPlayer class 172, 175
mediaPlayer.currentTime property 183
mediaPlayer.media.duration property 183
MediaView
video, playing 175-178
MediaView class, properties
compositable:Boolean 178
preserveRatio:Boolean 178
rotatable:Boolean 178
transformable:Boolean 178
MemeFX 290
min:Number property 130
mod operator 183

module
  about 71
  class definitions 71
  function members 71
    rules 72
  script-level members 71
  variables 72
  versus script 72
MotionBlur effect 113
mouse events
  capturing 64-67
MoveTo, path element 56
muffin 188
multiple CSS files
  applications, skinning 152, 154

N

name:String property 188
NetBeans
  installing, on Mac OS 12
  installing, on Open Solaris 13
  installing, on Ubuntu 13
  installing, on Windows 12
  working 227
NetBeans IDE
  JavaFX, setting up 11-14
NetBeans Swing GUI Builder 287
new line character. *See* **\n**
new operator 36
Node class 76, 163, 223
nodes
  about 49
  arranging 67, 68
nodes, Atom
  entry 218
  extension nodes 218
  feed 218
nodes, RSS
  channel 217
  extension nodes 217
  item 217
node tree. *See* **nodes**

O

object literal declaration
  about 24
  example 24
oblique:Boolean property 61
offset property 108
On2 289
onChannel: function(:Channel):Void event
    handler 217
onChannel: function(:Feed):Void event handler
  218
onForeignEvent:function(:javafx.data.pull.
    Event) event handler 217
OnForeignEvent: function(:javafx.data.pull.
    Event) event handler 218
onInput:function(:InputStream) property 195
onItem: function(:Entry):Void event handler
  218
onItem: function(:tem):Void event handler 217
onKeyPressed:function(:KeyEvent) property
  66
onMouseClicked event handler 128
onMousePressed:function(:MouseEvent)
    property 66
onOutput:function(:OutputStream) function
  199
opacity property 78
OpenSolaris
  NetBeans, installing 13
operations, JavaFX sequences
  delete 39
  union 39
operators, JavaFX sequences
  comparison 39
  reverse 39
  size of 39

P

package access modifier 73
packages
  about 72
  javafx.scene.Scene 48
  javafx.scene.shape 57

paint properties
   styling, CSS used 147
panel variable 123, 130
ParallelTransition class 89, 91
parse() method 213
Path API
   complex shapes, creating 55, 56
Path class 56
Path class, elements
   ArcTo 56
   HLineTo 56
   LineTo 56
   MoveTo 56
   VLineTo 56
PathTransition class 85, 87
pause() function 88
PauseTransition class 92
PerspectiveTransform effect 114
PieChart class 223
placeholder:Image property 162
**platform-dependent implementations 157,
   158**
platform-independent APIs 157
player.mediaPlayer.pause() function 178
player.mediaPlayer.play() function 178
player.mediaPlayer property 178
player.mediaPlayer.stop() function 178
player.play() function 175
player.stop() function 175
playFromStart() function 88
play() function 87, 88, 91
Polygon class 53
Polyline class 53
postData() function 199
POST method 197, 199
preserveRatio:Boolean property 178
preserveRation:Boolean property 163
preserveRatio property 161
primitive types, JavaFX
   Boolean 27
   Duration 27
   Integer 27
   Number 27
   String 27
production suite
   about 259, 265
   Adobe Illustrator plugin 260

   Adobe Photoshop plugin 260
   Graphics Viewer 260
   SVG File Converter 260
products, JavaFX
   Exadel 289
   JFXtras 290
   MemeFX 290
   On2 289
   ReportMill's DataBox 290
   WidgetFX 289
profiles directory 11
progress
   showing, progress controls used 131-133
ProgressBar control 131
progress controls
   progress, showing 131-133
ProgressIndicator control 131, 133
progress:Number property 133
proportional:Boolean property 108
protected access modifier 73
pseudo-class 152
public access modifier 73
public-init access modifier 73
public-read access modifier 73
**public static void main(String[] args) method
   34**
PullParser API
   RESTful clients, building 204-211
PullParser class 211
   custom parsing 212

Q

QuadCurve class 54

R

RadialGradient method 108
RadioButton control 123, 141
radius property 52
rate:Number property 88
readable:Boolean property 188
Rectangle.broad{} selector 152
Rectangle class 52
Rectangle class, properties
   arcHeight 52
   arcWidth 52
rectangle node 50

Reflection class **117, 118**
Reflection class, properties
  bottomOpacity 118
  fraction 118
  topOffset 118
  topOpacity 118
Reflection effect 167
  visual appeal, adding 116, 117
  working 117
repeatCount:Number property 87
repeatCount property 88, 91
ReportMill's DataBox 290
requestFocus() method 66
Resource class 188
Resource class, properties
  length:Long 188
  maxLength:Long 188
  name:String 188
resource object 187
resource.openInputStream() function 188
resource.openOutputStream() function 188
RESTful clients
  building, with PullParser API 204-211
REST-style development 186
reverse operator 39
rotatable:Boolean property 178
Rotate transformation 83, 84
RotateTransition class 85, 88
rSlide element 130
RSS
  about 186
  creating, Feed API used 213-216
  handling 217
run() function 34, 72, 229, 291

S

samples directory 11
Scalable Vector Graphics (SVG)
  exporting, to JavaFX 274-276
Scale transformation 84
ScaleTransition class 85, 87
scaleX transformation 84
scaleY transformation 84
Scene class 48, 49
Scene class, properties
  content:Node[] 49

  fill:Color 49
  height:Number 49
  width:Number 49
scene graph 49
Scene.lookup(id:String) function 141
Scene.lookup(id:String) function 162
Scene.lookup(id:String):Node function 124
scene:Scene property 49
Scene.stylesheets property 155
script
  modularization 70, 71
  organizing, into packages 72
  rules 72
  versus module 72
script-level members 71
seek(element:Object, level:Integer) method 212
seek(element:Object) method 212
seek() method 212
selectedIndex property 126
selectedItem property 126
selectors, JavaFX CSS
  .broad:hover{} 152
  Rectangle.broad{} 152
  Text#titleText{} 152
SepiaTone effect 114, 167
sequence loop query, JavaFX 40
sequence operations, JavaFX
  delete 39
  insert 39
  union 39
sequence operators, JavaFX
  comparison 39
  reverse 39
  sizeof 39
sequence projection 40
sequence slices, JavaFX
  sequence projection 40
SequentialTransition class 91, 92
Series class 222
Shadow effect 114
Shape API
  circle, drawing 52
  ellipse, drawing 52
  line, drawing 52
  rectangle, drawing 52

shapes, creating 50-52
  working 52
Shape API, classes
  CubicCurve 54
  QuadCurve 54
ShapeDelegate.shape property 104
ShapeIntersect class 57
ShapeIntersect operation 60
shape:Shape property 104
ShapeSubtract class 57
ShapeSubtract operation 60
Shear transformation 84
shiftBackToFront() function 138
shiftFrontToBack() function 138
SimpleInterceptor class 100
SimpleInterpolator class 102
sizeof operator 39
slices, JavaFX sequences
  sequence projection 40
Slider control 166
  color picker, creating 130
  numeric values, inputting 128-130
  Slider controlworking 130
smooth property 292
Solaris
  JavaFX SDK, installing 10
sourcepath option 21
spacing property 69
Stack layout manager 69
Stage class 48
Stage class, properties
  height:Number 49
  scene:Scene 49
  title:String 49
  visible:Boolean 49
  width:Number 49
  x:Number 49
  y:Number 49
StageStyle.DECORATED style 78
StageStyle.UNDECORATED style 78
START_ARRAY_ELEMENT pull event 212
START_ARRAY pull event 212
START_ELEMENT pull event 212
START_VALUE pull event 212
stop() function 88
stops:Stop[] property 108

Storage API
  about 185
  data, storing on user's device 187, 188
  working 187
Storage API, classes
  Resource class 188
  Storage class 187
Storage class 187, 188
Storage class, functions
  clearAll():Boolean 188
  clear():Boolean 188
  list():Object[] 188
storage.enabled = [true | false] configuration 189
storage.limit.domain configuration 189
storage organization 188
storage.properties file 189
Storage.source property 187
Stroke:Color property 61
strokeWidth:Number property 61
styleClass property 151, 152
style property 76, 77, 145
style:String property 145
surfaceScale property 113
SVG File Converter 260
SwingButton class 141
SwingCheckBox class 141
Swing components
  embedding, in JavaFX 139-141
SwingComponent.wrap() function 142
Swing control facade
  creating, JavaFX used 142, 143
SwingLabel class 141
SwingRadioButton class 141
SwingTextField class 141

T

textAlignment property 63
TextBox control 123, 141
Text class
  letter shapes, drawing 60, 61
Text class, properties
  content:String 61
  fill:Color 61
  font:Font 61
  letterSpacing:Number 61

\n 63
oblique:Boolean 61
Stroke:Color 61
wrappingWidth:Number 63
Text component 48
Text effect
creating 114
working 115
text node
styling, CSS used 146
TextOrigin.BASELINE option 62
TextOrigin.BOTTOM option 63
TextOrigin class 62
TextOrigin class, options
TextOrigin.BASELINE 62
TextOrigin.BOTTOM 63
TextOrigin.TOP 62
textOrigin:TextOrigin property 62
TextOrigin.TOP option 62
TEXT pull event 212
Text#titleText{} selector 152
textual time progression 183
Tile layout manager 69
Timeclass class, functions
pause() 88
play() 88
playFromStart() 88
stop() 88
Timeclass class, properties
autoReverse 88
framerate:Number 88
rate:Number 88
repeatCount 88
time:Duration 88
time:Duration property 88, 97
Timeline class
using, as timer 99
time property 99
title:String property 49
ToggleGroup instance 123
toggleGroup:ToggleGroup property 123
topOffset property 118
topOpacity property 118
toString() function 127
transformable:Boolean property 178
Transform.affine() method 277

ransformation API
shapes, modifying 82, 83
working 84
Transform.rotate() function 84
Transform.scale() function 84
Transform.shear() function 84
transforms:Transform[] property 84, 178
Transform.translate() function 84
transition animation 82
Transition API
animation, composing 89-91
simple animation, creating 85-87
Translate transformation 83, 84
TranslateTransition class 85-138
translateX transformation 84
translateY transformation 84
transparent style 77
trigger
about 31
example 32
using 32
tween keyword 98
type:ArcType property 54
type integration 37

U

Ubuntu
JavaFX SDK, installing 10
NetBeans, installing 13
unified programming model 226
union operation 39
update() function 252, 255
ur:String property 110
user input events 46

V

value:Number property 130
values:KeyValue[] property 97
variable scope, JavaFX
about 27
instance level 28
local level 28
script level 27
variables, JavaFX
binding, to code block 30
binding, to condition 29

binding, to function 30, 34
binding, to object literal 31
binding, to variables 29
declaring 25
declaring, ways 26
explicit type declaration 26
implicit coercion 26
instance variables 28
local variables 28
script variables 27
triggers 31
updating, binding used 28
var keyword 25, 26
VBox layout manager 69, 123, 141
video
playing, with MediaView 175-178
visible:Boolean property 49
visual time progression 183
VLineTo, path element 56

W

What You See Is What You Get tool. *See* **WYSI-WYG tool**
where clause 40
WidgetFX
about 289
URL 289

width:Number property 49, 163
Windows
JavaFX SDK, installing 10
NetBeans, installing 12
window style, JavaFX application
controlling 76, 77
opacity, controlling 78
wrappingWidth:Number property 63
writeable:Boolean property 188
WYSIWYG tool 287

X

XmlHttpRequest object 186
x:Number property 49

Y

Yahoo ' s weather services
URL 213
y:Number property 49

Z

Zillow Real Estate engine
URL 204

Thank you for buying
JavaFX 1.2 Application Development Cookbook

About Packt Publishing

Packt, pronounced 'packed', published its first book "*Mastering phpMyAdmin for Effective MySQL Management*" in April 2004 and subsequently continued to specialize in publishing highly focused books on specific technologies and solutions.

Our books and publications share the experiences of your fellow IT professionals in adapting and customizing today's systems, applications, and frameworks. Our solution based books give you the knowledge and power to customize the software and technologies you're using to get the job done. Packt books are more specific and less general than the IT books you have seen in the past. Our unique business model allows us to bring you more focused information, giving you more of what you need to know, and less of what you don't.

Packt is a modern, yet unique publishing company, which focuses on producing quality, cutting-edge books for communities of developers, administrators, and newbies alike. For more information, please visit our website: www.packtpub.com.

Writing for Packt

We welcome all inquiries from people who are interested in authoring. Book proposals should be sent to author@packtpub.com. If your book idea is still at an early stage and you would like to discuss it first before writing a formal book proposal, contact us; one of our commissioning editors will get in touch with you.

We're not just looking for published authors; if you have strong technical skills but no writing experience, our experienced editors can help you develop a writing career, or simply get some additional reward for your expertise.

Apache MyFaces 1.2 Web Application Development

ISBN: 978-1-847193-25-4   Paperback: 408 pages

Building next-generation web applications with JSF and Facelets

1. Build powerful and robust web applications with Apache MyFaces

2. Reduce coding by using sub-projects of MyFaces like Trinidad, Tobago, and Tomahawk

3. Update the content of your site daily with ease by using Facelets

4. Step-by-step and practical tutorial with lots of examples

BlackBerry Java Application Development

ISBN: 978-1-849690-20-1   Paperback: 368 pages

Build and deploy powerful, useful, and professional Java mobile applications for BlackBerry smartphones, the fast and easy way.

1. Develop professional, rich, and smart Java applications using BlackBerry SDK

2. Discover the powerful components provided by the SDK to build a powerful user interface with a common look and feel

3. Explore the complex, but important, topic of network communications

Please check **www.PacktPub.com** for information on our titles

Google Web Toolkit GWT
Java AJAX Programming

ISBN: 978-1-847191-00-7   Paperback: 248 pages

A practical guide to Google Web Toolkit for creating AJAX applications with Java, fast.

1. Create rich Ajax applications in the style of Gmail, Google Maps, and Google Calendar

2. Interface with Web APIs create GWT applications that consume web services

3. Completely practical with hands-on examples and complete tutorials right from the first chapter

Flex 3 with Java

ISBN: 978-1-847195-34-0   Paperback: 304 pages

Develop rich internet applications quickly and easily using Adobe Flex 3, ActionScript 3.0 and integrate with a Java backend using BlazeDS 3.2

1. A step-by-step tutorial for developing web applications using Flex 3, ActionScript 3 0, BlazeDS 3.2, and Java

2. Build efficient and seamless data-rich interactive applications in Flex using a combination of MXML and ActionScript 3.0

3. Create custom UIs, Components, Events, and Item Renders to develop user friendly applications

4. Build an end-to-end Flex e-commerce application using all major features of Flex covered throughout the book

Please check **www.PacktPub.com** for information on our titles

CPSIA information can be obtained
at www.ICGtesting.com
Printed in the USA
BVOW09s1646070517
483405BV00004B/63/P